W9-AFA-344

SOCIOLOGY OF EDUCATION SERIES
Aaron M. Pallas, Series Editor

Advisory Board: Sanford Dornbusch, Adam Gamoran,
Annette Lareau, Mary Metz, Gary Natriello

School Kids/Street Kids:
Identity Development in Latino Students
NILDA FLORES-GONZÁLEZ

Manufacturing Hope and Despair:
The School and Kin Support Networks of U.S.-Mexican Youth
RICARDO D. STANTON-SALAZAR

Restructuring High Schools for Equity and Excellence:
What Works
VALERIE LEE with JULIA SMITH

Finding One's Place:
Teaching Styles and Peer Relations in Diverse Classrooms
STEPHEN PLANK

PreMed: Who Makes It and Why
MARY ANN MAGUIRE

Tracking Inequality:
Stratification and Mobility in American High Schools
SAMUEL ROUNDFIELD LUCAS

Working for Equity in Heterogeneous Classrooms:
Sociological Theory in Practice
Edited by ELIZABETH G. COHEN and RACHEL A. LOTAN

Who Chooses? Who Loses?
Culture, Institutions, and the Unequal Effects of School Choice
Edited by BRUCE FULLER and RICHARD F. ELMORE
with GARY ORFIELD

Hosting Newcomers:
Structuring Educational Opportunities for Immigrant Children
ROBERT A. DENTLER and ANNE L. HAFNER

Mandating Academic Excellence:
High School Responses to State Curriculum Reform
BRUCE WILSON and GRETCHEN ROSSMAN

From the Series Editor

The United States has long struggled with how best to incorporate immigrants into American society. The simple hope that the passage of time will suffice has been proved unfounded. In fact, second-generation immigrant children can be less engaged with American social institutions than first-generation children. This lack of engagement presages a life-course trajectory marked more by constraints than opportunities. School failure is a particularly powerful marker for limited adult social and economic success.

In *School Kids/Street Kids*, Nilda Flores-González challenges conventional explanations of the scholastic problems of Latino youth. Immigrant family life is not an adequate explanation of the problem: immigrant parents, like other parents, want their children to succeed in school. Nor is the lack of English-language proficiency a suitable rationale, for even Latino students who are English-dominant are at risk of dropping out of school. Flores-González reconfigures the terms of the debate, drawing attention to the role of the school in constructing the problem.

Shifting the blame from the family and community to the school is not a new strategy in the literature addressing the etiology of school failure. But Flores-González finds a new angle from which to analyze the phenomenon. Drawing on role-identity theory, she argues that our schools shape the social identities of young people, positioning them either as "street kids" or "school kids." By default, nearly all youth develop street identities, but some find a niche in the social structure of their school through extracurricular activities or relationships with teachers and develop an academic identity that can inoculate Latino youth against some of the threats to their academic achievement. Schools can, she claims, purposefully design their social organization to maximize the likelihood that students will find such a niche.

School Kids/Street Kids is a heady mixture of sociological theory and an impassioned commitment to social action. The balance is nearly perfect: The lives of the students at Hernández High School are illuminated by the application of role-identity theory, and Flores-González's deep concern for these students and others like them propels the reader to develop a new vision for urban schooling. This book has the capacity to change lives.

Aaron M. Pallas

School Kids/Street Kids

Identity Development in Latino Students

Nilda Flores-González

FOREWORD BY
SONIA NIETO

Teachers College, Columbia University
New York and London

Published by Teachers College Press, 1234 Amsterdam Avenue, New York, NY 10027

Library of Congress Cataloging-in-Publication Data

Flores-González, Nilda.
    School kids/street kids : identity development in Latino students / Nilda
Flores-González ; foreword by Sonia Nieto.
       p. cm. — (Sociology of education series)
    Includes bibliographical references and index.
    ISBN-8077-4224-4 (cloth : alk. paper)—ISBN 0-8077-4223-6 (pbk. : alk. paper)
      1. Hispanic American students—Psychology. 2. School dropouts—Psychology. 3.
Identity (Psychology) I. Title: School kids/street kids. II. Title. III. Sociology of
education series (New York, N.Y.)

    LC2670 .F56 2002
    371.829′68073—dc21   2001058537

ISBN 0-8077-4223-6 (paper)
ISBN 0-8077-4224-4 (cloth)

Printed on acid-free paper

Manufactured in the United States of America

09 08 07 06 05 04 03 02   8 7 6 5 4 3 2 1

To Joel and Elena

&

To the young men and women
Who shared their stories with me

Contents

Foreword

The challenge of educating Puerto Rican, Mexican-American, and other Latino students in U.S. schools has never been greater. Despite numerous commissions, reports, research studies, and books written on the topic in the past several decades, Latino students continue to drop out in exceptionally high numbers. Only a relative few go on to college and an even a smaller number earn college degrees—this at a time when a high school education is indispensable as a gateway to higher learning. In spite of small steps forward, improvements on the whole have been few and far between, leaving educators, policy makers, families, and community members with the conundrum of what to do to help reverse the fortunes of Latino students in our schools.

The book you are about to read provides significant insights on both the problem and the solutions to address it. *School Kids/Street Kids* makes the unequivocal claim that despite the myriad problems facing Latino students we have it within our power to reach them all. This is a startling claim in a time of despair and skepticism about public education, especially as experienced in the dilapidated and poorly resourced urban schools that most Latino students attend. But Nilda Flores-González's thesis is as revolutionary as was the promise of public education made over a century ago: as a society, we have the responsibility of educating all children of all families. The research reported in this book serves both as a wake-up call and a reminder of the common belief we share in public education as a way to improve the life chances of young people who might not otherwise have such opportunities.

School Kids/Street Kids presents the moving stories of 33 Latino students attending a Chicago high school. With keen understanding and sensitivity, Nilda Flores-González describes how young people shape their identities in relation to school, becoming either "school kids" or "street kids." Moreover, she demonstrates that it is not necessarily intelligence that determines success (some are extremely bright, capable of high-level college work, but end up dropping out), nor is it simply that they do not speak English (most of the students in her study, in fact, are English-dominant). In the end, she shows that the academic success of Latino students is above all attributable to the environment in the schools they attend and the nature of the relationships they have with their teachers.

This book is full of hope. Nilda Flores-González's conclusions imply that the solutions to the problems facing Latinos in U.S. schools are not "out there" somewhere; they are within our grasp. No longer can we view the culprits for students' lack of school success in a simplistic way, as too often has been the case. It is not simply the conditions in which students live, or the structure of their families, or the fact that they don't speak English that is to blame. Schools must also understand their complicity in creating conditions that allow students to succeed or fail. For the students in this book, it was the "niches"— those curricular and extracurricular spaces where they found a place to belong—that made the difference between developing an academic identity or a street identity. If this is the case, then surely there is hope for the future of other Latino students: Showing that schools are capable of developing environments where students can become "school kids" obligates them to do so.

Although it instills hope, this book is also unsettling. It tests our collective resolve, and it questions our avowed commitment to social justice. It dares us to imagine new futures for Latino students, futures in which they are capable of joining the ranks of the thinkers and doers and leaders of our society. This is a formidable challenge, but one we must meet if we are serious about giving all students the chance to imagine all their possibilities.

Sonia Nieto

Preface

In the spring of 1990, I taught at an alternative high school that mostly served drop-outs from Hernandez High School, the pseudonym for the school on which this study is based (see Flores-González, 1990). I was puzzled because these students did not fit the "profile" of the drop-out. They were as different as Carmen, the homely "good" girl; Sara, the single mother of two girls; Rosie, the tough girl who boasted of kicking a pregnant girl in the stomach, causing her to miscarry; Edwin, a rather quiet, shy, and respectful student; Samuel, a graffiti tagger; and Jose, who offered to find me a bicycle "real cheap." Although the majority of the students I taught were Latinos, mostly Puerto Rican, with the exception of a Native American and a few African Americans, the group was as diverse in other ways as were their reasons for dropping out of school. Some, like Samuel, read at the college level; others, like Mabel, were reading at the fifth-grade level. Most were English-dominant. They also had varied family backgrounds: Samuel's parents were college-educated and held white-collar jobs, while Carmen's parents worked in factories. Some came from two-parent families, others from single-mother households. Some had siblings who had dropped out of school, while others had siblings who had graduated or were still in school. Some completed the program, while others dropped out from this alternative school. It became impossible for me to come up with a "drop-out profile." Neither could I make sense of why this diverse group of youths had dropped out but returned to school, unlike those who did not.

The incongruities I found between my experiences at the alternative school and the research literature stirred my curiosity. I immersed myself in the literature on school achievement, attainment, and school completion, and I still could not find a satisfactory explanation as to why students graduate, drop out, or return to school. I decided then to focus my research on unraveling the processes of high school completion and dropping out, not at this alternative school but at a nearby neighborhood high school—Hernandez High.

ORGANIZATION OF THE BOOK

In this book, I describe the process whereby kids develop identities in relation to school. Chapter 1 places my study within the literature on high school drop-outs, and offers new insights on Latino high school drop-outs. Chapter 2 sets the theoretical context of this study by discussing how role identity provides a viable explanation for explaining high school graduation or dropping out. In Chapter 3, I lay out the elementary school experiences that form the basis for the development of school kid and street kid identities. In Chapters 4, 5, and 6, I describe the situational context of the study. Chapter 4 discusses how school stigma makes identification with school problematic and shows how students cope with the stigma of attending an academically and socially devalued school. Chapter 5 describes the school-oriented and street-oriented peer cultures, elaborating on the effect that each culture has on the academic trajectories of students. In Chapter 6, I discuss how the structuring of extracurricular opportunities at the school affects the development of school identities.

The latter part of the book—Chapters 7, 8, and 9—discloses the process of high school graduation, dropping out, and returning to school. Chapter 7 shows how students solidify their school-kid identity, making high school graduation possible. By contrast, Chapter 8 exposes the increasing disappointment with school that leads students to take on street identities that clash with school, and ultimately to drop out of school. Chapter 9 describes the process whereby some drop-outs adopt an "in-between" identity, a mixture of street-kid and school-kid identities, and then return to school. The concluding chapter—Chapter 10—blends theory with reality and offers specific recommendations on how schools can facilitate the development of school-kid identities among Latinos. It concludes with a discussion of school reform that can lead to Latino students' success.

Acknowledgments

I want to thank the young men and women who participated in this study for sharing their stories with me. I am grateful and touched by their honesty and candid depictions of their lives. I also admire their courage and determination to overcome tremendous obstacles and adversity, even when their attempts led to troublesome paths. I have sought to portray them realistically and to show their humanity. I wish to thank the students, faculty, and staff of Hernández High School for letting me share a school year with them.

Many people contributed to different aspects of this book, and I truly appreciate their help. I am most indebted to Gerald Suttles, who believed in this project and has given me his unwavering support since the first day I walked into his office as a graduate student. Charles Bidwell and George Steinmetz also provided invaluable input. I want to thank Peggy Thoits for introducing me to role-identity theory and providing critical feedback for the theoretical development of this project. I appreciate the encouragement and guidance from Steve Warner, and the thoughtful comments by John Johnstone and Richard Campbell on earlier drafts of this book. I also want to thank Sandy Dornbusch for presenting my work to Teachers College Press, and Aaron Pallas, Susan Liddicoat, Aureliano Vázquez, and two anonymous reviewers for their editorial contributions at the last stages of this book. I am also touched by Sonia Nieto's interest in my work.

I am blessed with the support of an incredible group of women: Aixa Alfonso, Mina Andújar, Frances Aparicio, María Teresa Fernández-Aceves, Irma Olmedo, Amalia Pallares, and Pamela Quiroz. I am also grateful for the friendship and support of Natalie Henry and Laura López, and for the research assistance provided by Geraldine Franco, Rosa Silva, and especially Sonia Oliva, who kept another research project going while I worked on revisions to this book. I want to express my gratitude to the friends who made my graduate school years endurable: *mis compadres* Aníbal Aponte and Reina Andújar, Héctor Cordero-Guzmán, Sylvia López, Mara Pérez, Rosa Rodríguez, and Luis Zayas. This book was inspired by many people who in different ways are seeking to improve the lives of Puerto Ricans in Chicago (Marixsa Alicea, Maura Toro-Morn, Gina Pérez, and Ana Yolanda Ramos-Zayas whose research documents the life of Puerto Ricans in Chicago), and by the members of the Puerto Rican community who continue to struggle to improve life in the community. I am also indebted to Toni Brucato for sharing with me her thoughtful insights and experiences with Latino youths.

I am indebted to the institutions that provided support for this research: the University of Chicago, the Inter-University Program, the Social Science Research Council, the Danforth-Compton Dissertation Award, Sigma Xi Foundation, the Institute for Research on Race and Public Policy at the University of Illinois at Chicago, and the Great Cities Institute at the University of Illinois at Chicago.

Finally, I want to thank my family for their support: my parents, Erving and Eva; my siblings, Angie, Evi, Naydi, Machin and Diani; and my in-laws, Stan and Maureen Palka. I could not have finished this project without my husband's support. Joel, thanks for reading the many drafts of this book, for respecting my need for time and space to write, and for being there unconditionally. I owe the motivation to finish this project to my daughter Elena, who, like the young men and women whose lives I write about, gives me a new perspective on life.

CHAPTER 1

Perspectives on Latino High School Drop-out

I dropped out because I wasn't going to any of my classes. I wasn't motivated. It was like I was bored in school so I dropped out. I got sick of it so I just stayed home. My grades were bad 'cause I wasn't coming to classes. I knew I wasn't gonna graduate on time so . . . it made my hopes go down so I just didn't bother even going . . . I had started taking care of my brother's baby. I just got really involved with it. It was just a newborn. I just stayed taking care of her. That's why I didn't do nothing. I had quit my job too because it was the same with school. 'Cause I would work till late so that was also the reason why I couldn't get to school. I was working in downtown and I was working till like 10:30 [P.M.]. I would get home about 11:00 [P.M.] and wouldn't have time to do my [school] work or anything. I was working every day from 4:00 to 10:00 [P.M.] . . . When I was gonna drop out, they [school staff] had told me that . . . my attendance was so poor [that] . . . I couldn't stay in school no more. So then, they had told me they were going to transfer me into night school . . . but they didn't find out first that the night school program was already closed and it was too late for me to go into night school . . . Well, it was about two or three weeks [later], and the school called my house telling me why I wasn't going to day school and I was like, "Well, you guys had kicked me out. You guys had told me that I could not attend day school no more." They told me [that] the lady that had told me [that] didn't process the paper . . . they hadn't transferred me out, really. So then they let me come back [to school] . . . but it was about four months till June and there was no way that I could catch up. So then, I just decided not to come back [to school] . . . Then I just stopped coming [to school].

—Jenny, a returner

While Jenny's initial explanation for dropping out of school focuses on her lack of motivation, her subsequent narrative paints a more complicated picture. Although she lacked motivation, Jenny's story also speaks about family responsibilities thrust on teenagers—her father is an alcoholic who had recently left the family, making it necessary for Jenny to go to work—and the incompetence of school bureaucrats who push kids out of school without offering them tangible alternatives. Although the details of the stories told in this book vary, the narratives given by Jenny and the other 32 young men and women I talked to show the difficulties that inner-city kids face in becoming school kids. This book focuses on how Latino inner-city kids construct identities in relation to school, and discusses the implications these identities have for school completion.

Statistics show that the road to school completion is filled with obstacles, particularly for Latino kids like the ones in this study. According to the National Center for Educational Statistics (2000), 28.6% of all 16- to 24-year-old Hispanics are drop-outs, compared with 7.3% of Whites, 12.6% of Blacks, and 4.3% of Asians. Also, only 62.8% of Hispanics (25–29 years old) have completed high school, while 94% of Whites and 86.8% of Blacks have done so. Fligstein and Fernández (1985) found that among Latinos, Cuban Americans have the highest high school completion rate (89%), followed by Mexican Americans (57%) and Puerto Ricans (49%). Some studies place the drop-out rates of Puerto Ricans between 65% to 85% (Barreto et al., 1986; Calitri, 1983; Kyle & Kantowicz, 1991). In Chicago, the Puerto Rican dropout rate is over 70% (Kyle, 1984; Kyle & Kantowicz, 1991; Lucas, 1971), but no studies have investigated these rates among other Latino groups. The Chicago Public Schools provides a racial/ethnic breakdown of the student population in each school but does not track graduation or drop out rates by group. However, the two high schools with the largest Mexican population (85% or more) have graduation rates of 47.7% and 59.5%. Although graduation rates have reportedly improved since I conducted my study in 1993, the eight Chicago public high schools with the highest Latino populations (70% or more)—Mexican, Puerto Rican, or a combination of Latino students—still have low graduation rates, 47.7% to 71.1% (Illinois State Board of Education, 2000). Hernández High School, where my study took place, currently has the third lowest graduation rate among predominantly Latino high schools—54.6% (Illinois State Board of Education, 2000).

I selected Hernández High School in Chicago for my investigation because it has a large Latino population and scores low on almost every measure of school success. According to the 1992 School Report Card (Illinois State Board of Education, 1992), the student body at Hernández High was 83% Hispanic, 12.5% Black, 2.6% Asian, and 1.8% White. The Racial/Ethnic Survey of 1991 (Hernández High School, 1991), which breaks down the Hispanic category further, found that 57.6% of all students were Puerto Rican, 23% Mexican, 2.2% other Hispanic, and 0.3% Cuban.

Since Hernández High is located in the inner city, it suffers from the ravages of urban poverty. The 1992 School Report Card states that 70.5% of

Hernández High students are low-income. Low-income students are those "from families receiving public aid, living in institutions for neglected or delinquent children, being supported in foster homes with public funds or eligible to receive free or reduced-priced lunches" (Illinois State Board of Education, 1992). According to the report card, 21.8% of the students had limited English proficiency, and thus were eligible for bilingual education. The attendance rate of students at Hernández High was 77.3%; thus the average student attended 77% of school days. The student mobility rate was high, with 32.5% of the students transferring in or out of the school during the school year. It also had a very low graduation rate in 1992, with only 37.1% of the students graduating (Illinois State Board of Education, 1992). My calculations of the graduation and dropout rate confirm the report. For the class of 1993, I calculated that 39% graduated in June 1993, 47% had dropped out, and 14% were still in school. These rates exclude the students who transferred in and out of the school.

In this study, I focused on 33 youths: 23 students and 10 former students of Hernández High. The criteria for participation in the study were that (1) the student must be a Puerto Rican (or half Puerto Rican) (2) who had enrolled as a freshmen at Hernández High at least 3 years earlier. I decided to focus on Puerto Rican students—although some of the participants were half Mexican—to avoid lumping Latinos into one category regardless of their national, ethnic, racial, and class status, and because I thought that as a Puerto Rican, I would have an easier time gaining the trust and rapport I needed to develop with the participants of the study. However, as the study unfolded, the emphasis moved from being a study about Puerto Rican kids to being a study about inner-city students.

I gathered the life histories of these students to find out what has made them take different educational paths, that is, how and why they either graduated or dropped out of high school. I believe that the ethnographic approach I followed allowed me to get much information that would have been impossible to gather otherwise. I was at the school virtually every day for a whole academic year. This permitted me to become part of the school and participate in daily life there. Undoubtedly, my presence there had an effect on the participants and the staff. They could see me every day, attending school events, walking in the hallways, and even at the graduation ceremony. I was surprised by the trust that the students, and some of the staff, had in me. They shared their lives with me, even things that nobody else knew. Our unstructured conversations made it possible for them to articulate their feelings and direct the conversation to what they thought was important. A more structured research approach would have denied them this opportunity, which incidentally enriched this study. (See Appendix A for further information on the methodology of my study.)

I divided the students in my study into three categories, according to their educational status: stayers, leavers, and returners. A stayer is someone who enrolled in Hernández High as a freshman, never dropped out of school, and was a senior in 1992–93. A leaver is someone who enrolled as a freshman at the school but left and, as of 1992–93, had not enrolled in any educational program nor obtained a General Equivalency Diploma (GED). A returner is someone who enrolled as a freshman at Hernández High, dropped out at some point, but re-entered the school by 1992–93.

The three categories I use (stayers, leavers, and returners) are inclusive of all students and represent the "typical" student at Hernández High. Dropping out is a serious possibility for all students at Hernández High because life in this low-income community is unpredictable, and events that would have minor or no effect on middle-class students are often devastating for Hernández High students. Thus, in a school where at least half of the students drop out, it is impossible to come up with a single definition of the "typical" student. Instead, by using the three categories (stayers, leavers, and returners), I challenge the notion of "typicality" in a school with such diverse educational outcomes, and present a more complex picture of what it is to be a student in an inner-city high school.

There is a vast literature on high school completion that can be grouped into four general theoretical orientations: deficit, structural, reproduction, and resistance/oppositional theories. While all contribute to our understanding of high school completion and dropout, I find that they are insufficient to explain what happens to the students in this study. Trying to make sense of my data, I found that role-identity theory, which I discuss in Chapter 2, is useful in explaining my findings. In general, I argue that the kinds of identities students take on has much to do with their staying in or dropping out of school. Students whose home, school, and community identities are school-oriented develop a school-kid identity and graduate from school. By contrast, students whose home, school, and community identities are discrepant—some of their identities are not school-oriented—experience more difficulty in developing and maintaining a school-kid identity and may eventually drop out of school. Although family and community life matter, I argue that school is the crucial element in the development of school-kid identities. Although there were variations in family and community experiences, there were drastic differences in the way school kids and street kids experienced school. My study shows how school produces both school-kids and street-kids.

THEORETICAL EXPLANATIONS FOR DROPPING OUT

Informed by role-identity theory, I find lacking the deficit, structural, reproduction, and resistance/oppositional explanations for high school completion and dropping out. These four perspectives offer partial explanations, but they cannot account for the "exceptions to the rule," nor do they explain the experiences of all kids I interviewed. They do not explain how kids with similar backgrounds—such as siblings—have different educational outcomes. In this section, I review each theoretical perspective and explain its limitations.

Deficit Explanations

I question the "deficit" explanations that argue that low achievers, including underachievers and drop-outs, lack the characteristics that lead to school success. These studies place the cause of the problem on the individual, family, or culture. Low achievers are said to lack motivation and involvement in school activities, be frequently absent and suspended from school, have friends who are also low achievers, be fatalistic, and come from unstable families where parents are indifferent to education (Barrington & Hendricks, 1989; Beck & Muia, 1980; Kronick et al., 1989). For instance, Delgado-Gaitan (1988) found that Chicano students whose parents were involved in their education were more likely to stay in school. Proponents of the cultural mismatch theory argue that students fail because of competing value systems—their cultural values are incompatible with middle-class American values, and their cultures do not provide them with the skills required for good school performance (Caplan, Choy, & Whitmore, 1991; Labov, 1982; Villegas, 1988).

While individual, family, and culture undeniably play a role in school achievement, these deficit explanations tend to focus on identifying initial conditions and turning points without spelling out the process by which students become low or high achievers. They attach outcomes to demographic data so that specific characteristics seem to "cause" low or high achievement in school. Often the data are faulty in predicting, for instance, who is going to drop out, since many students who do not fit into the at-risk profile still drop out of school (Fernandez & Shu, 1983). For instance, Streeter and Franklin (1991) found that middle-class dropouts do not fit into the at-risk profile. Some of the participants in my study did not fit the at-risk profile, and no one could have predicted, using the deficit model, that they would eventually drop out.

Deficit explanations also obscure the different effects that individual, family, and cultural factors have across racial, ethnic, class, or gender groups. For example, authoritarian or non-democratic parenting style is generally associated with low achievement, yet among Latino and African Americans it often produces high achievers (Clark, 1983; Gándara, 1995; Steinberg, Dornbusch, & Brown, 1992). I also found that high achievers at Hernández High had authoritarian parents. Lydia was one of the many high achievers who told me that her parents kept a tight grip on her. Her parents insisted on meeting her friends and knowing where she was at all times. She was not allowed to "hang out" or even sit on her front steps, but was free to go to her girlfriends' homes, to the library, and to the movies (see Chapter 7).

Another problem with deficit explanations is that they cannot tell us why people with similar attributes, such as siblings, have different educational outcomes. Many of the students I interviewed were the first persons in their immediate and extended family to finish high school. They, like Roberto, had older siblings who dropped out of school (see Chapter 7). Finally, deficit explanations cannot account for the dropouts who eventually return to school or obtain their general equivalency diplomas. Most striking is the story of Diana, a teenage mother and "troublemaker" whose siblings were involved in gangs and had all dropped out of school. Although Diana dropped out of school, and based on demographics the odds were against her, she returned to school and graduated at age 21 (see Chapter 9).

Structural Explanations

The structural characteristics of schools and schooling practices have been linked to student achievement by some researchers. In general, these studies argue that certain school traits and practices cause low achievement, particularly among racial/ethnic minorities and low-income students. For example, researchers have shown that the size of large high schools has a negative effect on school achievement because in larger schools disciplinary concerns supersede stress on academic achievement, and students have less opportunities for involvement in school programs (Barker & Gump, 1964; Fowler & Walberg, 1991; Garbarino, 1980; Gregory & Smith, 1987; Metz, 1978; Ornstein, 1990; Pittman & Haughwout, 1987). Hernández High, with 2,600 students, poses the typical challenges of large inner-city schools, and its staff spent much time and effort in planning disciplinary and security measures. While they came up with fairly innovative and less dehumanizing techniques, searches of bags—without x-ray machines—were conducted frequently, and students still complained about the treatment they received from security staff. The large size of the school also had a profound effect on the opportunities for extracurricular participation. At Hernández High, slightly over 20% of the students (about 500 students) participated in extracurricular activities, leaving the remaining 2,000 students with no ties to extracurricular programs (see Chapter 6).

Other research focuses on the effect of teacher expectations on student achievement, particularly their unfavorable bias toward racial/ethnic minorities and lower-SES students. These studies show that teachers tend to hold lower expectations and perceive more problematic behavior (disciplinary as well as academic) among lower-income students and racial/ethnic minorities (Finn, 1972; Laosa, 1979; Rist, 1970). Valenzuela (1999) argues that many Mexican American students were frustrated by classes that were boring and unchallenging, and teachers who seemed not to care about them. She found that successful teachers recognize and acknowledge students' problems in school, family, and community and challenge individualistic notions that blame the students by placing these problems in the larger context of the life of minority students in this country. By contrast, unsuccessful teachers, lacking an awareness of students' lives, interpret students' lack of engagement in school as a signal that "they do not care," and refuse to waste their time and energy on what they perceive to be "lost causes." Because most schools are staffed with the latter, Valenzuela argues that schools end up "subtracting" resources from Mexican American youths. At Hernández High, most students expressed similar feelings, with the exception of the honors program students, who reported that their honor classes were interesting and challenging, and the honor program teachers more enthusiastic and dedicated to the students. Yet even they were critical about some of their teachers and were aware that teachers and classes in the regular program were far different, in content and quality, from those offered in the honors program (see Chapter 7).

Other structural theorists challenge the assumption that schools are equalizing institutions, arguing instead that students are sorted out by race, class, and/or gender into tracks that offer a different quality and quantity of education. The lower achievement of racial/ethnic minorities, women, and low-income students is due to their disproportionate assignment into the nonacademic tracks—vocational, general, and special education (Brantlinger, 1993; Mickelson, 1981; Oakes, 1985). Overall, the quality of education at Hernández High ranked low, but students in the honors program received a better, but not much better, education than their peers. I found that how students were selected for the honors program, and extracurricular activities, was not necessarily by chance or merit. There were numerous formal and informal constraints that limited student recruitment and participation in these activities. Furthermore, these constraints ensured that only a small and selective group of students had access to these programs (see Chapter 6).

Reproduction Theory

Much of the research on schooling inequities is tied to reproduction theory, which argues that schools are instruments of the dominant group designed to foster low achievement among racial/ethnic minority and low-income students and in this way replicate and re-create social relations (Bourdieu, 1973; Bowles & Gintis, 1976). Schools replicate the structure of class relations in two ways: by rewarding knowledge of the dominant culture and by providing different kinds of education based on class, race, and gender. Bourdieu (1973) argues that under the guise of meritocracy, schools hide the advantage of upper-class students, who due to their class position possess the cultural capital valued at school, that is, the general cultural background, knowledge, dispositions, and skills that are passed through generations. He adds that schools transform cultural capital into economic capital because knowledge of dominant culture leads to better performance, which results in access to better schools and more prestigious universities. Upper-class children end up in high-status and high-paying jobs because of the market value of their superior academic credentials. Similarly, Bowles and Gintis (1976) argue that a meritocratic ideology is used to legitimize unequal schooling along class lines. They contend that there are vast differences in the amount and content of education, expenditure, resources, and socialization of students of different social classes. While upper-class students are usually in the academic track, attend well-funded schools, and are socialized for leadership roles, their lower-class counterparts are found disproportionately in the vocational track, attend underfunded schools, and are socialized for subservient roles.

While structural and reproduction theories clearly show the existence of inequities in schooling that result in low achievement among racial/ethnic minorities and low-income students, they cannot account for individual or group challenges to the "system," nor can they explain high achievement among members of subordinate groups. These theories assume that students do not realize or react to inequality, yet the history of schooling in the United States attests to the struggles of minority groups for inclusion and equal education. Individual court suits as well as massive student demonstrations during the Civil Rights era have resulted in drastic changes in the educational system. These theories also assume the homogeneity of subordinate groups, overlooking differences within groups. Consequently, they cannot explain why there were high and low achievers at Hernández High, or why or how some of the students there became high achievers in spite of the strategies aimed at pushing them to underachieve.

Resistance or Oppositional Theory

I found more promise in resistance or oppositional theory, an extension of reproduction theory that poses that low achievement is behavior intended to challenge some aspect of schooling (Felice, 1981; Fine, 1991; Fordham, 1988; Fordham & Ogbu, 1986; MacLeod, 1987; McLaren, 1994; Richardson & Gerlach, 1980; Willis, 1977). Proponents of this view argue that students develop identities in opposition to school culture when they believe that high school graduation will not improve their socioeconomic status, and/or the behaviors required for academic achievement are deemed incompatible with their racial/ethnic or class identity. Low achievers are said to have developed a critical consciousness that rejects the false promises of the educational system. These students may have high regard for education, but they do not believe that it is a means for social mobility. For them, hard work in school does not necessarily translate into success later in life because structural forces such as gender, class, race, and ethnicity circumscribe one's opportunities.

These studies also show that for racial/ethnic minorities and low-income students, high achievement in school has class and/or racial/ethnic connotations. Racial and ethnic minorities (and lower-income students) tend to experience difficulty maintaining a racial/ethnic (or class) identity and academic success simultaneously because academic success is perceived by them as a characteristically "White" (or "middle-class") behavior (Fordham, 1988; Fordham & Ogbu, 1986; Labov, 1982, Villegas, 1988). For racial and ethnic minorities to succeed academically implies the adoption of "Whiteness," while forsaking their ethnicity. McLaren (1994) refers to an ethnic minority's success in school as cultural or racial suicide because in order to succeed, these students must reject their culture in favor of "White" culture. Other studies add that high-achieving minorities pay a high price because they are accused of "trying to join the enemy," or "acting white," and tend to be more depressed, less politically aware, less assertive, and more conformist than low achievers (Fine, 1991; Fordham, 1988; Fordham and Ogbu, 1986). Fordham adds that fear of censure and physical harm from their peers leads African American students to underachieve, mask their accomplishments by portraying themselves as low achievers, or assume a raceless persona by not identifying themselves with African American culture.

EXPLANATIONS FOR MINORITY ACHIEVEMENT

Recent research, however, finds that academic success does not necessarily come at the expense of ethnic identity for all groups (Flores-González, 1999; Foley, 1991; Hemmings, 1996; Matute-Bianchi, 1986; Mehan, Hubbard, & Villanueva, 1994). Focusing on students of varied ethnic and class backgrounds, these studies—including my study at Hernández High—show that racial/ethnic minorities do not have to choose between performing well in school or maintaining their ethnic identity; they can be "ethnic" and "model" students simultaneously. These studies also show that racial/ethnic minorities do not necessarily associate school success with "Whiteness," nor are they subjected to peer pressure that leads to not doing well in school. Rather, they suggest that many racial/ethnic minorities view school success as a middle-class trait, and since they are, or aspire to be, middle class, achieving in school is appropriate behavior for them. While some, especially males, were initially harassed by their peers, high achievers at Hernández High went on to occupy their own social space in school and were not pressured to underachieve (Flores-González, 1999). For them, high achievement was necessary to become middle class, and it did not question their ethnicity.

The key to school success, some argue, lies in the students' ability to manage their multiple "worlds": home, school, and neighborhood (Davidson, 1996; Gibson, 1988; Mehan, Hubbard, & Villanueva, 1994; Phelan, Davidson, & Yu, 1998; Valdés, 1996). Phelan, Davidson, and Yu (1998) conclude that successful students are those who effectively manage transitions between these worlds, and particularly those whose worlds are compatible. Valdés (1996) argues that for poor immigrant children to succeed in school, differences between home and school must be reconciled, and not at the expense of family values. Valdés adds that "ideals about success are perhaps not incompatible with other values. I believe that it should be possible to move into a new world without completely giving up the old" (p. 205). Vigil (1982) found that Mexican American students who adopted a nativist acculturation performed better in school than their more acculturated peers. Vigil defines the term *nativist acculturation* as a dual process of learning a new culture while retaining the old one. This goes along with the phenomenon that Gibson's (1988) calls "accommodation without assimilation," whereby immigrants and minority students "choose in certain situations to subordinate their ways [culture] to those of the dominant group" (p. 25), yet continue to maintain their separate culture and identity. Mehan, Hubbard, and Villanueva (1994) found that high-achieving Latinos and African Americans engage in accommodation without assimilation, taking on a new culture while maintaining the old one. They contend that this strategy allows minority students to effectively manage and maintain dual identities, one at school and one in the neighborhood. Their study implies that students change identities as the setting changes (one identity at school and one identity at home). This may be plausible for students, such as those in Mehan, Hubbard, and Villanueva's study, who attend school away from their neighborhood. When students attend neighborhood schools— that is, when they all live in the same neighborhood and attend the same school—it is much more difficult to shift identities in different contexts. In my study, I found that for most students at Hernández High, identities were stable regardless of context because they lived in the same area and attended school together. A Hernández High School graduate who did not participate in this study told me recently that he lived in fear of being exposed for assuming different identities at school and in the neighborhood. While at school he behaved as a school kid, but outside he often faked being mute or walked dragging one leg when confronted with potentially dangerous situations. He thought that neighborhood bullies and gang members would not bother a person with a disability. However, he feared that someone from school might see him acting this way and expose him.

Nevertheless, all these studies show that minorities can and do find ways to achieve on their own terms without jeopardizing cultural or family affiliation. Yet I question the implicit assumption made by these studies that minorities either oppose or accommodate to schooling practices. As Davidson (1996) so aptly concludes: "Opposition is not necessarily synonymous with academic failure, accommodation is not the sole route to academic success. Rather, opposition can be communicated in many and multiple ways" (p. 213). At Hernández High, many students expressed opposition through what is commonly interpreted as "oppositional behavior" (underachievement, disciplinary problems, truancy), but others did so in unexpected ways (parenthood, care-giver for family member, church involvement) that did not necessarily lead to school failure.

CONSTRUCTION OF IDENTITIES

The theoretical basis of this study departs from resistance theory. Unlike previous studies that focus on the effects of schooling on oppositional behavior and the consequences of oppositional behavior on achievement, I examine why and how some students develop oppositional, or non-school-oriented, identities while others do not. Similarly to Phelan, Davidson, and Yu (1998), I followed an ecological approach with the intent of uncovering the students' worlds and how they individually and jointly affect the students' educational trajectories. While Phelan, Davidson, and Yu argue that these students are successful because their worlds are congruent, I take my analysis a step further by utilizing role-identity theory to argue that because their worlds are congruent, they have adopted an all-encompassing school-kid identity that is expressed in their different worlds. I show how this school-kid identity is constructed.

More than an identity bounded to school, this school-kid identity represents an image of how these youths view themselves and how they want to be viewed by others—as good kids. Although I could have used the "good kid" label for this all-encompassing identity, I chose to call it the school-kid identity because it more appropriately conveys the social role assigned to adolescents in American society—that of being a student—even though the participants of this study did not use that term. Images of the good kid, in the media as well as in everyday life, are primarily constructed from their status as students. The school-kid identity is crafted from the different identities they have. Thus it is a cumulative (additive/aggregate) identity, the sum of other identities that conform to a view of the self. As a cumulative identity, it is composed of family, school, and community identities, such as the obedient and dutiful daughter, the all-American school athlete, and the church-boys and -girls. School-oriented behavior need not be interpreted so much as conformity or lack of a critical view of schooling, but rather as an affirmation and display of their all-encompassing image as school kids. Because students want to maintain this image, identities that have the potential to conflict, disrupt, or negate their claims to being school kids are quickly discarded. As a result, students are successful in school to the extent that they are able to adopt and sustain a school-kid identity.

Students who do not become school kids and who behave contrary to school norms are usually labeled "bad kids." Because images of the bad kid invariably evoke images of the street and street culture—gangs, rowdy boys, teenage mothers—I chose to use the term "street kids" (also street boys and girls) to identify youths who take on non-school-oriented identities and who engage in behaviors contrary to accepted norms. It is not that these students are intrinsically street-oriented, or want to have—and maintain—a street-kid identity, but rather that circumstances often beyond their control force them to take on an all-encompassing street-kid identity. Once they have adopted this identity, it is very difficult and very unlikely that they will or can become school kids.

In this book, I show how school can make or break the school-kid identity by offering different educational experiences to students (access to extracurricular programs, close relationships with teachers, challenging classes). My work points to the ways in which school produces school kids and street kids by giving or denying them certain conditions needed to become engaged in school. Developing and maintaining this identity is contingent on the presence and configuration of seven factors I identified (see Chapter 2):

1. Social appropriateness of the role
2. Social support
3. Prestige and rewards
4. Extensive and intensive relationships
5. Role performance
6. The presence of identity-enhancing or identity-threatening events
7. Possible selves

Newmann, Wehlage, and Lamborn (1992) point to some of these issues when they identify the factors that affect students' engagement in school. According to them, students become engaged in school when they feel competence; that is, when they acquire the intellectual and social skills that lead to adequate performance in school. To achieve competence, they must develop a sense of membership or belonging to school through meaningful interactions with teachers and peers. They must also find academic work to be meaningful, connected to the real world, engaging, fun, and rewarding.

Although my book examines family and community life to some extent, it focuses on how school facilitates the development of the school-kid identity among some students, while it fosters the development of street-kid identities among others by denying them opportunities to become engaged in school. My study shows that indeed schooling is a "subtractive process," as Valenzuela (1999) so clearly demonstrates. While Valenzuela focuses on how schools "are organized formally and informally in ways that fracture students' cultural and ethnic identities," my work pays less attention to ethnicity and focuses on deciphering how schools—in formal and informal ways—hinder the development of academic identities among inner-city Latino kids. Along with Nieto (1999), Romo and Falbo (1996), and Valenzuela (1999), I contend that to increase Latino graduation rates, we must challenge the basic tenets of education and transform schooling into a truly enriching experience for Latino kids (see Chapter 10).

While not denying that family and community play a role in the students' conversion into street kids, I believe that schools can provide students with a safeguard that can prevent that development or pull them out of street culture. The problem is that for too many kids, schools are not conducive to the development of socially appropriate roles. Instead, schools deprive many students of the social support, prestige, rewards, meaningful relationships, and alternative routes to achievement they need. At the same time, schools expose them to, and further drive them toward, street identities. That is, school directly contributes to the development of street kids. After all, it is the students who lack connections to school who take on street identities and end up dropping out. The next chapter lays a theoretical framework to explicate how kids construct identities in relation to school and how these identities impact school completion.

CHAPTER 2

Patterns of Identity Differentiation

Although I grouped the young people I studied at Hernández High School into three categories according to their educational status—stayer, leaver, or returner—as the research unfolded I realized that these categories were more than objective status groupings. They revealed patterns of identity differentiation among the participants. That is, members of a category shared more than status: They had undergone a similar process of student-identity formation. For the stayers, becoming school kids proceeds smoothly, and their experiences in school, family, and community help them build a solid student identity. Returners and leavers encounter more difficulties in becoming school kids because of conflicting school, home, and community identities. Role-identity theory helps us understand their identity formation, maintenance, and exit, and it is the focus of this chapter. For simplicity, I use the terms *identity* and *role-identity* interchangeably.

INTRODUCING ROLE-IDENTITY THEORY

According to the role-identity model of the self, people have many role identities, each one corresponding to a social position they hold, and each having a particular value to them. A role-identity is a self-definition or an understanding of who one is as a result of occupying a particular role or social category (Hogg, Terry, & White, 1995). Role-identities are organized hierarchically according to the value they have for the individual, with those that are highly valued and frequently enacted occupying the top of the hierarchy, while those that are not valued highly and are seldom enacted being near the bottom of the hierarchy (Callero, 1985; McCall & Simmons, 1978; Stryker, 1968). Although terms such as *salience* and *prominence* are used to describe the value and place of role-identities in the hierarchy, for simplicity I classify role-identities as either dominant or subordinate. Dominant identities are those that are high in the hierarchy level, while subordinate identities rank low. Role-identities are also organized into clusters of interrelated identities. That is, some role-identities tend to go together, such as being a spouse and parent, while other identities are the result of having a particular role-identity, such as being a student and a student-athlete. Identities that are interrelated tend to be dominant, since they are directly or indirectly enacted more frequently, and also because exiting one usually entails exiting its interrelated identities.

The value of a role-identity is not fixed, but varies over time; it may increase or decrease as situations change. Factors that may affect the ranking of a role-identity include the role-identity's social appropriateness, social support, prestige and rewards, commitment, role performance, the presence of identity-enhancing or identity-threatening events, and possible selves (Marcus & Nurius, 1987; McCall & Simmons, 1978; Stryker, 1968; Thoits, 1991). Role-identities become dominant when they are perceived as being socioculturally appropriate according to the person's characteristics such as gender, occupation, or age. A subordinate identity may become dominant when the person masters a skill level, or reaches a certain age or educational level required for its successful performance (McCall & Simmons, 1978). A dominant identity may become subordinate or abandoned when it stops being relevant or socioculturally appropriate, or is outgrown (McCall & Simmons, 1978). Evaluations from others, level of prestige, and the rewards engendered by a role-identity also affect its status in the hierarchy. Positive evaluations from others, high prestige, and gaining of rewards motivate people to value the role-identity more. These factors are closely linked to the level of competency in performing the role. When people perform a role appropriately, they receive social recognition from others, higher status, and rewards, all of which make people feel good about themselves.

Another factor determining the status of role-identities in the hierarchy is the level of commitment to it. Dominant identities are those to which the individual is highly committed. The degree of commitment is displayed in the person's immersion in social relations that support the identity (Stryker, 1968). According to Stryker (1968), commitment can be measured by the number of relationships, and the depth of involvement with others that share the identity. As Burke and Reitzes (1981) put it: "High levels of commitment (strong forces toward congruity) will result in involvement in activities, in organizations, and with role partners, all of which support the person's identity" (p. 245). Someone who participates in identity-related activities, interacts with others as a result of the identity, and forms emotional ties to others can be said to be highly committed to that identity. An individual with a high level of commitment to an identity will not only work hard to maintain it, but he or she will go to great lengths to maintain it (Kielcolt, 1994).

The presence of identity-enhancing events or identity-threats can affect the standing of a role-identity. Identity-enhancing events are those that make the performance of dominant identities easier or add positive dimensions to a role-identity (Thoits, 1991). Role-identities are strengthened when the conditions conducive to competent role performance are present. They are also strengthened when the role-identity expands to include other roles. The clustering of identities results in overlapping of role identities that may become so intertwined that boundaries are blurred, making these role-identities insep- arable and dependent on each other. To devalue one identity would mean devaluing the other, engendering drastic changes in the hierarchy. By contrast, when identity-threats are present, the status of the dominant identity is in peril. Thoits (1991) defines identity-threats as events that disrupt or can po- tentially disrupt a highly valued role-identity. Identity-threats can take differ- ent forms, ranging from factors that make difficult or impede the performance of a role-identity to the coexistence of incompatible role-identities that are impossible to sustain because they require the performance of conflicting be- haviors or must be performed simultaneously. Thus, the coexistence of multi- ple roles can enhance or disrupt role-performance.

Finally, the identities people aspire to or seek to avoid also affect the value of role-identities within the hierarchy. Possible selves are conceptualiza- tions of the self in the future or what we envision our selves to become (Mar- kus & Nurius, 1987). They have positive and negative dimensions: What we hope to become, and what we fear becoming. Although possible selves are future identities, they serve as the basis for action in the present. Positive possible selves can foster the maintenance of identities that are related or relevant to what we hope to become in the future, while negative possible identities can avert the development of identities associated with what we fear becoming.

Multiple Roles and Role Strain

Role accumulation or the coexistence of multiple roles has repercussions on the value of role-identities and ultimately bears on the psychological well- being of individuals. There are two divergent views on the effect of role accu- mulation. One argues that role accumulation is enhancing to the self-concept because it increases the number of rewards gained by individuals (Sieber, 1974). The other view emphasizes the deleterious effects of having multiple roles and its result in role strain or the inability to perform multiple roles (Goode, 1960). While these views may seem contradictory, they can be recon- ciled by arguing that role accumulation has positive effects on individuals as long as the multiple roles can coexist together in relative harmony without disrupting and/or infringing on their performance or becoming too numerous for the individual to meet role demands.

According to Sieber (1974), role accumulation can yield more benefits than stress and can even compensate for role strain because it brings about rewards for individuals. Sieber identified four kinds of rewards: privileges, resources for status enhancement and role performance, status security, and personality enrichment and ego gratification. According to Sieber, people de- rive exclusive privileges or rights for role occupancy that are out of reach to others who are not in that role. These privileges are formal benefits granted as a result of occupying that role. He adds that the more roles they hold, the more privileges they enjoy. In addition, roles offer informal resources and perks that enhance the individual's status. These grow out of the relationships that are cultivated in the role. Having multiple roles also adds to status security because if the performance of one role fails, individuals can fall back on other roles and continue to maintain their status in spite of the role depreciation or loss. Lastly, Sieber argues that role accumulation results in personality enrichment and ego gratification because people with an elaborate role system not only feel more fulfilled but also give the impression of superior status to others, bolstering their status in this way. Because of its benefits, Sieber believes that role accumulation can be more gratifying than stressful.

Although not preaching the positive consequences of role accumulation, Marks (1977) argues that the assumption that multiple roles leads to role strain may be exaggerated. He posits that people control how and when they will use their time and resources and thus have flexibility to shift their attention to different roles as they see fit. Marks suggests that people devote more time and energy to roles to which they are highly committed and less attention or even neglect those to which they are undercommitted, and in this way attain role balance and avoid role strain. Marks and MacDermid's (1996) later work, elaborates on the concept of role balance, suggesting that people who do not organize their roles hierarchically but instead maintain balance across roles experience less role strain than those who organize them hierarchically.

While most researchers do not deny that role accumulation can have some positive effects on people, they warn about the negative and unhealthy consequences of having multiple roles. Role accumulation is associated with role strain (Goode, 1960; Merton, 1957) because presumably the more roles a person has, the more difficult it is to meet role expectations and role demands. As roles accumulate, individuals may experience incompatible expectations and an overload of demands from the different roles pulling them in different directions. On the one hand, fulfilling the role requirements of one identity may conflict with meeting the role demands of other identities. On the other hand, there may be too many demands placed by the numerous roles, and not enough time, resources, or energy to fulfill them.

Role strain is common because the total role obligations people have as a result of their multiple roles are often overwhelming and interfere with adequate role performance (Goode, 1960). Role strain can take the form of role conflict or role overload. Role conflict occurs when two or more role-identities conflict or become incompatible because conflicting role obligations require contradictory performances. Role overload occurs when the multiple roles' demands cannot be met due to conflicts in time, place, or resources. Because people have limited time and resources and can be in only one place at a time, meeting the conflicting demands of their multiple roles is impossible.

The inability to perform a role or roles adequately brings about psychological distress because individuals are motivated to perform in ways that reinforce, display, and confirm their role-identities. To claim an identity, they must act or behave in ways consistent with that role-identity, or their claim to that identity can be questioned by themselves and others. How psychological distress is experienced and dealt with varies among people according to their social status and the status of the role-identity in the hierarchy. Lower social status makes people prone to psychological distress. Thoits (1991) posits that lower-status individuals experience more identity-threatening stressors and fewer identity-enhancing experiences than their higher-status counterparts. She argues that "social characteristics (gender, age, minority status, and SES) influence not only the number, types and organizations of role-identities that one holds, but also the financial and psychological resources that are available" (p. 108). The identity hierarchy of low-status individuals is smaller not only because they hold fewer roles and less prestigious roles, but also because they have less money and smaller social networks to help them negotiate multiple role demands effectively (Thoits, 1987). For example, middle- and upper-class individuals can pay for services that free them of certain role obligations, while lower-status individuals cannot afford these services. As a result, the latter are likely to encounter more identity-threatening stressors than identity-enhancing experiences. Because they are exposed to more identity-threatening stressors, they tend to experience more psychological distress than do higher-status individuals.

The status of the threatened role-identity in the identity hierarchy also contributes to psychological distress. This is more severe when role strain disrupts or threatens to disrupt dominant role-identities, and less critical among less important identities (Thoits, 1991). When the questioning involves a dominant identity, a threat to the self ensues because the identity is central to the individual's self-concept. Usually people will try hard to maintain or restore the status of highly valued role-identities that have been affected, often at the expense of less valued role-identities. When role-identities of different value conflict, the most valued identity, or the one the individual is more committed to, will be preserved (McCall & Simmons, 1978), while the subordinate identity is neglected or abandoned altogether. Because the subordinate identity is not central to the self-concept, abandoning it does not pose as much psychological distress as would a dominant identity (Thoits, 1991), nor is the status of the dominant identity within the hierarchy affected.

By contrast, when the role strain involves two or more dominant role-identities, the psychological distress is much higher because these role-identities are central to the self-concept (Thoits, 1991). If altering role performance does not resolve the role strain, individuals must make changes in the identity hierarchy, lowering the status of one of the role-identities or even giving one up. This happens when people see themselves as incapable of performing both roles competently enough. Which of the role-identities is devalued or abandoned depends on the presence of factors, such as increasing social approval, rewards, prestige, and positive evaluations from others, that favor one role-identity over the other.

Changes in the status of dominant identities within the hierarchy are often temporary. As Schmid and Jones (1991) note, some identities are suspended because the present conditions make their enactment impossible. Suspended identities are not abandoned but rather lay dormant until they can be enacted once more. These often involve circumstances out of people's control, such as a prison sentence, that over time may come to be resolved, enabling the suspended identity to be reactivated. However, the conflict between two or more dominant identities sometimes causes so much psychological distress that people are unable or unwilling to put them on hold or even lower their value. Instead, they opt to abandon one or more of the conflicting role-identities.

Role Exit

Abandoning a dominant role-identity, or role-exit, is often a long and emotionally painful process in which people come to reformulate a new self-concept that excludes a once highly valued role-identity. This process entails the progressive disengagement from the dominant role while contemplating, learning, and ultimately taking on an alternative role. That is, the role-identity is left behind and replaced by another role-identity, sometimes a lower-valued identity. This process is twofold, involving disengagement from a previously highly valued role-identity and socialization into a new role-identity. Ebaugh (1988) described the process of role-exit as "the process of disengagement from a role that is central to one's self-identity and the reestablishment of an identity in a new role that takes into account one's ex-role" (p. 1).

Role-exit is triggered by the increasing uneasiness and unhappiness experienced while being in a specific role. While at first the source of discontent or stress may be undefined, over time people identify a particular role as the source of their distress. According to Ebaugh (1988), this realization initiates the four-stage process of role exit: experiencing first doubts, seeking alternatives, reaching a turning point, and creating an ex-role. The following four subsections provide a summary and explanation of Ebaugh's four-stage process of role-exit.

Experiencing First Doubts. According to Ebaugh (1988), the role exit process begins with the first doubts, when individuals come to recognize the source of their dissatisfaction as emanating from a specific role, and begin to question their commitment to that role. Questioning can be prompted by organizational changes, burnout, changes in relationships, and events, all of which make the source of dissatisfaction clear. As people discern the root of their disappointment, they begin to reinterpret past experiences and construe everything that happens from then on according to their new reinterpretation.

People also begin to exhibit cuing behaviors, "those signs, conscious or unconscious, that an individual is dissatisfied in his or her current role . . . these symbolic behaviors are early warning signs of erosion in commitment" (Ebaugh, 1988, p. 70). Cuing behaviors alert others to the increasing dissatisfaction and decreasing commitment to the role. How others react to these signs accelerates, retards, or may even stop the role-exit process. When others are supportive of a role change, individuals continue the process rapidly. However, when others oppose a role change, individuals either reconsider and may even halt the role-exit process, or shift reference groups in search of others who are supportive of the role exit.

Seeking Alternative Roles. After the initial doubts, Ebaugh (1988) found that individuals progress to a second stage where they begin seeking alternative roles to replace their current role. As they become convinced that their dissatisfaction is due to a particular role, they begin to consider alternatives, weigh the costs and rewards of role change, compare and narrow down their options, exhibit cuing behavior more overtly, shift reference groups, and engage in role rehearsal.

While people may have been vaguely thinking of possible options, it is at this point that they seriously and deliberately search for alternative role-identities. In this search, they compare different role options and evaluate the costs and rewards of changing roles. Some people scrupulously compare their options, going as far as making lists of pros and cons, while others are much less meticulous. Some are so avid to exit the role because they are unhappy that they pay little or no attention to the costs and rewards of role change. The side perks accrued in the current role, such as status or prestige, and the translatability of skills or a realistic assessment of personal qualities and qualifications in a new role play major parts in the evaluation of cost and rewards. When people have too much vested in the current role, the deliberation is more difficult and lengthy because they have much to lose. People must also consider their skills, interests, and present situation and their chances for a successful transition into another role. Through this process they compare different possibilities and narrow their options to a realistically achievable alternative role.

By this time, most people are overtly exhibiting cuing behaviors that prompt reactions from others. The reactions from others can validate or discredit their feelings about their current role, accelerating or slowing down the search for alternatives. Social support not only confirms what people already feel about their current role, but others can also substantiate their claims and provide ideas and approval about alternative roles. Lack of social support, especially when the current role is socially desirable, may lead to social disapproval and stigmatization, add to the costs of role change, and steer individuals to shift to a reference group that will approve of the role exit.

Regardless of the presence or lack of social support, there is a definite shift of reference groups and a process of socialization into the role. As the search narrows and an alternative role is recognized as the most feasible, people begin to identify with it, to learn and internalize its values and norms, and to conform to its behavioral expectations. Contact with others already in that role facilitates the learning of the role, and provides a more realistic perspective of what the role entails, serving as a role model. While the learning of the role involves mostly observation of others, most people also engage in role rehearsal by imagining or actually trying out the role. Role rehearsal provides a more realistic assessment of the fit between the role and the individual, giving people a clearer idea of what it would be like in the role before they complete the role change.

Reaching a Turning Point. While people have been preparing themselves for a role change, Ebaugh (1988) argues that it is not until they reach a turning point that they make a definite decision to exit. This third stage of the role-exit process is characterized by the occurrence of an event that provides an opportunity to exit. Turning points are precipitating factors that push individuals to make a decision about exiting. They can be reached gradually, but often turning points are marked by abrupt and dramatic events that follow a long time of doubting and searching for alternatives. Unable to make a decision, individuals are eventually confronted with an event, or a turning point, that tips the scale in favor of exiting a role.

Ebaugh identified five types of turning points: specific events, excuses, "the straw that broke the camel's back," either/or alternatives, and time-related factors. Specific events are incidents that confirm the doubting and frame exiting as the only solution. These can be significant events, such as a death, or seemingly insignificant events, such as a dream, that take on a symbolic meaning. Events can also serve as an excuse or justification to exit a role. They provide a legitimate explanation that enables a graceful exit, especially when the exit may not be socially acceptable. Insignificant events can also function as "the straw that broke the camel's back." The last straw refers to the gradual accumulation of events that reaches a saturation point when people can no longer tolerate remaining in a role. An event can also trigger an either/or situation in which individuals are forced or pushed to make a decision. Not making the decision to exit will bring about consequences that individuals want to avoid, such as being forced to leave school. Timing is another factor leading to the decision to exit a role. When time-limited opportunities arise, people who have been doubting and searching for alternatives are moved to make a decision before the window of opportunity closes.

Reaching a turning point is crucial because it moves individuals from deliberation to action. It communicates the impending role change clearly to others, relieves stress by liberating individuals from a dissatisfying role, and allows them time and energy to focus on seeking and mobilizing the emotional and social resources needed for the role change. Once the decision is made, people feel liberated and relieved, but at the same time fearful of what awaits them. They often experience a "vacuum" or period of feeling "in between," brought on by their dual feelings of relief and anxiety about the future. After some time, people readjust to their new situation by building "bridges" that facilitate their transition to a new role and help them break with the past role. These bridges can take the form of social support that initiates them into the new role.

Creating an Ex-Role. After exiting a role, Ebaugh (1988) found that people create an *ex-role*, an identity that derives from a previous role. Shaking off a previous identity is difficult and often takes a long time, even when the role change is socially desirable. Only very infrequently can people leave a role behind and not look back. They usually continue to identify with the previous role, and to face some of the expectations and norms associated with it, for at least some time after exiting. There are a number of adjustments that individuals must make if they are to successfully create an ex-role. These include drastic changes in the presentation of self and in social relations.

As individuals exit a role and enter into a new one, they must change their behavior not only to conform to the new role but to make it obvious to others that there has been a role change, and that they should be treated accordingly. Cuing behaviors, such as drastic physical or behavioral changes, convey the role change to others and prompt varied social reactions. When the role-exit is socially desirable, others tend to readily accept and treat the exiter accordingly. However, it is more difficult for others to accept role change when the role left behind is stigmatized. For example, people continue to be apprehensive and suspicious of ex-convicts. When the role-exit is socially undesirable, there is a decrease in social status and a possibility of social stigma being attached to the role change, such as when a mother relinquishes custody of her children.

Role changes also involve changes in relationships. Most role changes require shifts in friendship networks, and on how to relate to previous and new role partners. It is also challenging to form new relationships and to disclose the past role, especially when the role change was undesirable or the previous role was stigmatized.

How successful people are in stopping identification with a past role varies not only according to the desirability and social approval of the role change, but also to the role residual that lingers after people have exited it. After exiting a role, most people still continue to identify with the previous role and to retain some of its behaviors and values, therefore impeding complete disconnection from the previous role, and in this way maintaining the ex-role.

USING ROLE-IDENTITY THEORY TO EXPLAIN HIGH SCHOOL GRADUATION AND DROP-OUT

Role-identity theory provides a viable way to explain high school graduation and drop-out. This section provides an overview, developed in more detail in the rest of the book, of how the student identity becomes dominant, enabling students to become school kids and graduate from high school, or so subordinate that it leads to the adoption of street identities and eventually to dropping out. I depart from the assumption that the configuration of multiple identities affects students differently, boosting the self-concept in some while producing role strain in others even under similar structural conditions, such as socioeconomic status and ethnicity. What kinds of multiple identities each status groupings (stayers, leavers, and returners) dealt with were markedly different. While the stayers flourished in the presence of multiple but non-conflicting identities, the leavers and returners experienced role strain brought about by the irreconcilable conflicts that emerged among their multiple, and conflicting, identities.

I found that the configuration of identities varied by student category in number, value, and interconnection of identities. The stayers have more identities, most of which are school-related, than do the other groups. Because their multiple identities are connected to school, they invariably support and add value to the student identity. It is better to cluster these multiple identities under the *school-kid* label, a term that incorporates school, family, and community identities, rather than refer to them as dominant student identities. Having a school-kid identity makes leaving school all the more difficult and costly because it would entail exiting other identities as well. By contrast, the leavers and returners tend to have fewer school-related and more nonschool, or street-related, identities. These multiple identities then fall under the *street-kid* label, which includes identities that clash with the student identity, eventually leading these students to drop out of school.

I also found that opportunities to engage in the school kid identity differ for the three status groups. Those who become school kids (stayers) have drastically different experiences in school than the street kids (leavers and returners). The difference in experiences has to do with the presence or absence of the factors needed for the development of identities described at the beginning of the chapter (social appropriateness of role, social support, prestige and rewards, commitment, role performance, presence of identity-enhancing or identity-threatening events, and possible selves). Essentially, the stayers become school-kids because they have access to the conditions conducive to the development of their socially appropriate role as students. They are competent in the performance of the student role, engendering positive evaluations from others, rewards such as good grades and social perks, and social prestige in school. Doing well in school not only boosts the self-concept, but it also provides privileges, such as participation in extracurricular programs and increased popularity in school. Stayers are also deeply immersed in social relationships brought about by the identity. Not only is much of their day spent in school-related activities, they also form deep emotional ties with others in the school. Finally, identity-enhancing events, in the home and community, facilitate the performance of the student role and foster interconnections with other school-oriented or school-supportive identities. As a result, stayers experience less role conflict among their multiple identities, and less role strain. Although their identities are connected with school, they are not totally immune to the conflictive demands and obligations of these multiple identities. When confronted with conflicting demands, they consistently choose to fulfill the demands of the student role at the expense of less valued identities.

However, establishing a school-kid identity is not easy, particularly among ethnic and racial minorities in the inner-cities, such as the students in this study. Many of the factors needed to become school kids are not present or simply are unavailable to these students. First, inner-city schools are low-status institutions stigmatized as academically and socially inferior. Students must contend with the lack of prestige of the school and what being a student there says about them. Second, the overwhelming presence of street culture in and out of school, and its appeal to many youths, makes street identities socially acceptable alternatives to the conventionally prescribed student role for adolescents. Third, alternative cultures are more appealing to students who do not fit the student role. Those who do not excel socially, academically, or athletically are denied rewards, perks, and social prestige in the opportunity structure at school. Instead, they may seek rewards and social recognition through other means such as the street culture. Fourth, the prevailing street culture and the limited access to the school's opportunity structure translate into more chances to spend time and create closer relationships with non-school-oriented peers. Finally, as inner-city minorities, these students are exposed to many identity-threatening stressors that impede their attachment to school.

APPLYING ROLE-IDENTITY THEORY TO STUDENT CASES

The following cases illustrate the patterns of identity differentiation among the three status categories: stayer, leaver, and returner. In choosing these cases, I searched for people who were in the middle of the pack, that is, people who did not fall into the extreme ends of each category. These are not typical cases, since each category has a wide range of cases. I selected them because they most clearly illustrate how and why students become school kids or street kids and the implications that these identities have for school completion.

Ana: A Stayer

Ana is 17 years old and a senior at Hernández High. She embodies the school-kid image because her student identity is central to her self-concept, so much that she says, "I don't want to leave [graduate]. I like it a lot. If it was 8 years [of being here, that] is different but 4 is too little [time]. Time goes too fast, very fast." The centrality of her student identity comes from the overlapping identities she has assumed in connection to school. Her student identity has expanded to include being a student, musician, athlete, friend, student aide, leader, and girlfriend. Ana is committed to her role as a school kid because she has developed extensive and intensive relationships with peers and teachers. Although she has not excelled academically, she has done so socially, reaping the prestige and the many rewards that come with popularity. Ana has strong social support and social approval for her school-kid identity. She also manages her multiple, but interconnected, identities and rarely runs into conflict because they all are part of her school-kid identity. That she has so many identities connected to school and that she gets so many perks for being a school kid make it too costly for her to give up that identity because it would wipe out many other identities as well.

Ana developed and established her school-kid identity early in elementary school. She describes her elementary school as good days when she got along well with teachers and peers, and started to shine among her peers for her skills playing the clarinet. While in elementary school, she became part of the school orchestra, and was immediately recruited into Hernández High's orchestra as a freshman. Although she gets frustrated by the low musical skill of her peers, she has remained in the orchestra for the whole 4 years.

Ana has never excelled academically and her grades are average, yet she maintains friendships with people who do. Because of her connections with the academic elite of the school, she is aware of, and is sharply critical of, the two-tier system that provides the scholars, or honors group, and other students enrolled in honors courses with extraordinary academic experiences while denying these same opportunities to the "regular" students. She knows that first-rate teachers concentrate in the scholars program and that the scholars have access to information about college programs and scholarships that are not accessible to other students. Ana believes she is among the few non-scholars who find out about opportunities, but that this is just because of her friendship with some scholars.

Ana may not belong to the academic elite, but she is definitely part of the social elite. Eckert (1989) and Coleman (1961) found that the athletes, or jocks, dominate the social scene at school, and are often the most recognized and popular members of the student population. Although she does not describe herself as "popular," Ana was selected as the "Most Athletic Female" and "Most Musically Talented" in the yearbook. Ana and her boyfriend, Alberto, were voted Homecoming Queen and King and appear in the yearbook as the "Most Cute Couple." In addition, Ana appears in numerous photos in the yearbook, as does her boyfriend. She was also voted class representative in the senior council. Because of her involvement in sports and her school spirit, Ana was given a small scholarship for college expenses at the Athletes' Banquet.

It is through sports that Ana has carved a niche for herself in the school. Sports have made her visible, and among all female athletes, she stands out for being a member of the volleyball, basketball, and softball teams. Her participation in sports reinforces her school-kid identity because it keeps her busy all year long, shifting between practices and competitions. Even during the summer, she maintains her connection to school sports while participating in a volleyball team with the other girls from the school. Ana's athletic identity is intertwined with her school-kid identity to the point that she cannot separate one from the other.

> I come to school to learn and play sports. ¿Si no hay sports, que voy a hacer? [If there are no sports what am I gonna do?] Ay no, estoy acostumbrada a jugar. [Oh, no, I am used to playing sports.] Si no juego me ensorro. [If I don't play sports I get bored.]

As a result, Ana does not have time to "hang around," but must manage her time and activities around her family life and school sports.

Ana lives with her father, whom she describes as supportive and affectionate but strict. Ana worries about her father, who suffers from diabetes, and she rushes home when she can to prepare dinner for him before going to her sports practices and meets. While her father does not require that Ana fix his meals, she prefers to do so to ensure that he will eat well after coming home tired from his factory job. All this shuffling around has made Ana develop good time management skills and keeps her busy with school and home activities.

Participation in school sports has led to the development of other school-related identities. Because she is an athlete, Ana has close relationships with coaches, especially with the softball coach. Ana felt that Ms. Morgan cared about her, and they often talk about Ana's problems. For the past 2 years, Ana has been Ms. Morgan's "student aide," running errands or being in charge of supervising the students who come for their study hall in Ms. Morgan's room. Ana is also close to her volleyball coach, who watches over her and pushes her to pursue a college degree.

In addition, Ana is part of a closely knit group of athletes that share friendship. She is usually seen around the school wearing a sports jersey, in the company of other athletes. Her social life outside of school includes these same athletes, with whom she goes out to eat or to the movies. Her boyfriend is part of this group. Alberto plays on the football and baseball teams. Often, when Ana's practices are over, she watches Alberto's practices and games.

Practically, everything Ana does revolves around school and her family. Because so many of her identities are connected to school, she has too much vested in the school-kid identity to even consider other identities. When discussing involvement in street-like behaviors, Ana confessed to cutting classes once in a while, mostly to go home and prepare dinner for her father before going to her sports practices at school. She has never participated in a fight; is never disrespectful to her teachers; is neither involved with gangs nor maintains friendship with gang members; does not use drugs, smoke, or drink; and is not sexually active. Because Ana is so much into school and so far from street life, she is a clear example of a school kid.

Lisa: A Leaver

Lisa is a 19-year-old who has dropped out of school twice. The first time she dropped out was at the end of the spring semester of 1991, during her sophomore year. She stayed out of school for a year, returning in the fall of 1992. Lisa stayed in school for 2 months before dropping out again. Since then she has not returned to school. Lisa is an example of a student who gradually becomes a street kid as her identities become less connected to school over time. The lack of school-related identities is manifested in her inability to build a school-kid identity. Lisa was an average to mediocre student who did not have any particular talents that could set her apart and give her recognition at school. Nor did she develop any extensive or intensive relationship with teachers or school-oriented peers. Instead, Lisa went on to forge her own niche in the street peer culture, where she became known as a "smartass" who could fool the staff. Already disengaged from school, Lisa used the injuries sustained in a car accident as justification to drop out of school a second time. Along with her reasonable excuse, Lisa talks about returning to school, but these plans never materialize. School just does not engender the rewards that she finds in other aspects of her life, and thus she is unlikely to gather the determination needed to complete high school.

Lisa was not always disconnected from school. In elementary school, she got along with teachers and received good grades. It was not until she entered Hernández High School that her attitudes toward school changed. This change was prompted by problems at home when her mother became physically abusive. Her mother demanded that Lisa and her sister return home right after school and punished them if they delayed. They were expected to do house chores and prohibited from being outside. Lisa recalls watching other kids playing outside while they scurried around cleaning the house and preparing dinner. Feeling like prisoners at home and scared of their mother's beatings, Lisa's sister became pregnant and married to escape, while Lisa turned school into her vehicle to freedom. According to Lisa, "Since I wouldn't get freedom when I was at home, I figured I take it while I'm out there [in school]."

Lisa's newfound freedom was in the school's street peer culture. Lacking academic, athletic, or musical talent, Lisa did not find a niche in school-sanctioned activities, but she found it among her peers. With her friends, who were as disconnected from school as she was, Lisa found a home in the street peer culture at school. Soon she began to cut classes and sneak out of school. What started as a game of outsmarting the staff became a habit. She also began to fight in school, mostly to establish her reputation. She was labeled a "troublemaker," known by the school staff because of her transgression of norms and her defiant attitude when confronted. Lisa acknowledges that she "would have an attitude. I would rule myself. I wouldn't let nobody tell me what to do. And then teachers would kick me out of my classes and everything."

Lisa is particularly proud of her "escapades" at school, boasting on her skills to outsmart the staff. As she says, "I would always get caught in the hallways or cutting a class or something, but I would always find a way to slide through and they wouldn't give me a hard time." She also knew what she needed to do to pass her classes in spite of her heavy cutting and lack of studying.

> My teachers would report me, "Oh, she hasn't been in class." I would always be my smartass and I would tell them, "Oh, if I'm not going to your class, how [come], am I passing your class?" I would find my way. Even though I wasn't in the class, I would still hit the books at home once in a while, and I would know when to take the test.

After a while, it became increasingly difficult for Lisa to keep up this game. In addition to her strained relationship with her mother, Lisa's sister got married young to get out of the house, leaving Lisa without emotional support to deal with their mother. Lisa began to move back and forth between her mother, godmother, and sister's homes. This only made her school attendance more erratic and pushed her to drop out when she could no longer sustain these roles. After a year, Lisa returned to school, but injuries sustained in a car accident 2 months later gave her the final push to leave school for good. She later went to live with her father and stepmother and takes care of their children. While Lisa acknowledged that a high school diploma is very important and talks about returning to school, her plans have not materialized. Lisa's story shows how school kids turn into street kids and spiral down a road that makes it more and more difficult for them to return to school. Although she no longer is a street kid, her new role caring for her siblings serves as another justification not to return to school.

Diana: A Returner

Diana is 20 years old and is a senior at Hernández High. She has adopted a street-kid identity that is interspersed with school-kid qualities. The centrality of her street-kid identity in the elementary school years is apparent from Diana's participation in fights. As she approached high school, the influence of her street-savvy siblings and friends gave Diana a reputation for trouble that she often lives up to. Her reputation is aggrandized by her family connections to a local gang, and by her boyfriend's gang activities. Diana broached her street-kid identity by cutting classes, obtaining poor grades, and engaging in fights. Because of her poor academic record, she transferred to an alternative program but dropped out because "the distance was too much for me." She enrolled at Hernández High, but her frail connection to school became weaker after becoming pregnant. Diana left school to care for her son but returned when she realized that to offer him a better life she needed to get a good job. While it is not easy for Diana to suppress her street manners at school, she devotes much effort to control and contain them in school. She is determined not to let anything or anybody jeopardize graduation from high school.

   Diana grew up in poverty exacerbated by her father's death in a house fire when she was 6 years old. The fire was set by members of her brothers' rival gang. Diana's mother struggled to feed and raise her six children, but was not able to prevent Diana's brothers and sisters from joining gangs. Although Diana did not join a gang, her life revolves around them because of her siblings' involvement in them. Her family's reputation, and Diana's propensity to fight, have earned her a reputation as a street kid. During elementary school, Diana was on her way to cementing a street-kid identity of her own. She fought with other students in and out of school. She began to become disillusioned with school, especially when she realized that she was being singled out by the teachers. She says that she received harsher punishments for her infractions than other students. For example, she was not allowed to go on a field trip because of fighting, while the other girl who was involved was allowed to go. Diana says that she also refused to do things for teachers just to win their favors. For instance, she could not understand why she was expected to remove lint from her teacher's coat using masking tape like the teacher's pets in her classroom did.

Initially, Diana was reluctant to attend Hernández High because her brothers belong to a gang considered mortal enemies of the largest gang there. She enrolled in another high school, but the commute was so long that her boyfriend persuaded her to transfer to Hernández High after just one semester. Diana's boyfriend, Cheo, attended Hernández High and belonged to the largest gang there. Upon entering the school, Diana automatically began associating with gang members. Her association with gang members, her family's street reputation, and her own street-like behaviors at school kept Diana from finding a niche within school other than in her peer group. Although Diana says she would like to participate in some extracurricular activities, she has never been approached by a teacher to encourage her to join such programs. She adds that even if she was, her academic record would disqualify her, because good academic standing is required for participation in extracurricular programs at Hernández High.

Finding no niche in school, Diana turned more and more to her peer group. She started cutting classes, sneaking out of school, coming in late, or not coming to school at all. She also fought in school. Diana's street behavior only got her into additional trouble at school. She was suspended from school several times for fighting. As a result, Diana's progress in school was so slow that she began to lag behind her cohort. Trying to catch up, she transferred to an alternative school but soon dropped out at the same time that her friends and her boyfriend were dropping out.

Diana returned to Hernández High, only to drop out after giving birth to her son because she wanted to be a full-time mother. Since she could not be a full-time mom and a student at the same time, she gave up on school and stayed home to raise her child. However, after several months she realized that in order to support her son she needed to get a good-paying job, and her chances were slim without a high school diploma. She recognized that her boyfriend, who supplements her governmental assistance, is unreliable because being a gang member and drug dealer, he can go to prison or get shot by rival gang members any day. Besides, she does not want that kind of life for her son and says that she only tolerates her boyfriend, with whom she is still "going out," for the financial support he provides for them. As soon as she is on her feet, Diana plans to leave him. In the meantime, Diana has moved in with her brother and his family, and talked her boyfriend into taking care of their child during school hours.

Upon returning to school, Diana joined the Teen Parents program, which provided her with support and assistance. She also became a student aide at the library, working there during her study periods. Diana tries hard to curtail her street-like behaviors at school and has succeeded to some degree. Although she does not cut classes, she is absent whenever her son gets sick or has a doctor's appointment. However, she is often challenged by street kids who know of her street reputation. She was involved in a school fight the first week of classes and was suspended for 10 days. Since then, Diana has been extremely cautious about her school behaviors. She now hangs around with school kids and avoids getting in trouble. She knows that the next fight or serious transgression will result in expulsion from school, especially now that she is 21 years old. With one foot in the street and the other in school, Diana works hard to balance an identity that lies somewhere between the street-kid and the school-kid identities.

CONCLUSION

The three stories presented above show the contrasting experiences that lead kids to develop school or street identities and how these identities impinge on school completion. Although these processes are discussed at length in Chapters 7, 8, and 9, these stories give a glimpse of how role-identity theory becomes translated into everyday life. In Ana's story, we learn that she became a school kid because her multiple identities did not conflict but were all intricately connected and related to school. By contrast, Lisa's world became increasingly disjointed as she sought emancipation from an abusive and restrictive home life in the street-oriented peer group at school. Trying to mediate both worlds, Diana learned the hard way to keep these two worlds as separate as she can and to avoid clashes. The following chapter shows how elementary school experiences shape the kind of identity taken on by kids and shows that by eighth grade these identities are usually firmly established.

CHAPTER 3

Foundations of School and Street Identities: The Elementary School Years

The elementary school years are a crucial time in the development of school or street identities, since the experiences that students have there determine to a large extent how they conceive of and express their student identity. Although these early identities may be drastically changed during the high school years, for most students they are stable and are a reflection of what they will later become (stayer, leaver, or returner). That is, which identity students assume in elementary school has repercussions on their staying in school or dropping out.

During elementary school, which in Chicago extends through eighth grade, children are expected to learn to be school kids. Many become school kids within the first few years and maintain this identity throughout high school. Others form a more marginal school-kid identity that is later replaced by the street-kid identity. The degree to which they form a strong or weak school-kid identity is related to how well the factors conducive to the development of the school-kid identity are met (see Chapter 2). Learning to be school kids is affected by the amount of social support, prestige, and rewards they accrue as students. It is also related to the number and depth of relationships they develop with others and the adequacy of their performance as students. And it is a response to the kind of identities—supportive or conflictive—they develop in relation to school. What students become is intricately connected to the kind of school experiences they have. In the next section, I describe how school experiences mold the way the school-kid identity is formed in elementary school.

LEARNING TO BE SCHOOL KIDS

The stayers' recollections of elementary school have an almost nostalgic twist to them. They long for their elementary school days, mainly because they are marked with academic and social accomplishments. There they found the conditions necessary to build a strong student identity. They had the chance to engage in a socially appropriate role because they received social support, recognition, and rewards, developed warm relationships with teachers, found different opportunities for achievement—social and academic—and were exposed to school-related identities. Elementary school was a safe place where they were sheltered from trouble, fights, or being bullied or victimized. These students also regarded elementary school as less laborious than high school. As Isabel put it, "you have to study hard in high school to graduate," but less so in elementary school. Although many stayers point to elementary school as being "easy" and "safe," it was really their relationships with teachers that they mostly remembered. As Miguel recollects: "I loved it. I miss it. Sometimes I want to go back and visit the teachers. They really taught and they really help us a lot. A lot of activities they did. There were a lot of things."

Most stayers had close and often personal relationships with a favorite teacher. Indeed, many recall having a favorite teacher, and some being a "teacher's pet." As teacher's pets, they enjoyed a special status among classmates. Yet even those who were not teacher's pets say that their teachers were nice to them. Luis explains: "They treated me the way I was supposed to be treated . . . I had no foul teachers. I did my work, I did everything. All the teachers in grammar school helped me out to get into high school . . . They helped me out with schoolwork. They talked realistic. They'll tell me how the real world is . . . " These close and intense relationships with teachers fostered commitment to school.

Even stayers who attended several schools reported positive experiences and a growing attachment to school that was not interrupted by school changes. Marta is among the few stayers who attended several elementary schools, so many that she cannot recall their names, yet she holds fond memories of a magnet school she attended.

> In seventh, I went to another school. It was a bus school [students were bused in]. That was a good school. I learned so much in that school. There were hardly any minorities, but there was no racism either. It was so much fun. I mean, they used to do fiestas every Friday 'cause they liked the Spanish stuff. They used to do fiestas with piñatas and everything. When I went there, I learned all my 50 states. I learned everything about history. I learned art. It was more advanced, a lot more advanced. Then I went back to eighth grade, it was like a snap for me. I went to Washington because of busing problems. I mean at 7:40 you had to be waiting for the bus outside freezing, and I was like, "No, I can't do this anymore."

Elizabeth, who started elementary school in Boston, moved to Puerto Rico when she was 8 years old, and then moved back to Boston when she was 11 years old, has mixed feelings about her early schooling. Although she initially experienced language difficulties when she moved to Puerto Rico, she quickly overcame them and excelled academically.

> It was hard because they separated [students] smart from slow and since I didn't know that much Spanish, they put me in [the] slow [group]. They didn't under-level me from the grade but they separated me. It was like an A-group and a B-group, so I had to be stuck with the B-group. But then in fifth grade, they changed me into the A-group.

When she returned to Boston, however, Elizabeth "didn't find the fun of it," but did well enough in school.

Despite some stumbling blocks, the stayers' elementary school performance shows that they had become school kids and learned the student role expectations early. Most had no difficulties and sailed smoothly through elementary school, often excelling socially and academically among their peers. Yet it was not smooth sailing for all. Learning to be a student in elementary school proved to be a challenge to some stayers, not because they were intellectually incapable or had disciplinary problems, but because they seem to have been emotionally immature and needed more time to adapt to their new role. Miguel explains:

> Well, I failed first grade. Messed up. Take it over. 'Cause I was bad, real bad. Starting trouble, starting a lot of trouble. 'Cause it was like when I came out of nursery home, I was doing real good in nursery home, but when I came out of there, I went to [elementary school]; it was like it was a totally different thing, different for me. I was used to playing a lot like in kindergarten you play a lot. I was used to playing a lot so I was like I can play here too.

Some say that they could have avoided repeating a grade by attending summer school. However, because of family vacations to Puerto Rico, students such as Iván were not able to make up the work during the summer.

> I failed in the fourth grade. I wasn't doing the work or passing the tests. I really don't know. I can't remember that far or that year. Nothing happened at home. I just didn't do my work or passed any of the tests. I could have gone to summer school but I didn't. I wanted to go to Puerto Rico instead.

Something similar happened to Vanessa, who had to repeat third grade because her family would not cancel a summer trip to Puerto Rico so that she could attend summer school. Repeating a grade gave these students more time to figure out the student role expectations, and does not seem to have adversely affected their attitude toward school or marked them as problematic students. Grade repetition was the result of emotional immaturity and their inexperience in the student role. Since it was not the result of mischievous behavior, they were not labeled as problem students, or at least they do not recall being so labeled. Once they matured and learned what was required of them, their academic and social performance improved, and they went on to excel academically and socially in high school. Miguel went on to take honors classes and became a talented baseball player in high school, while Vanessa and Iván became scholars and were involved in diverse extracurricular programs.

Regardless of initial academic and social difficulties, by the end of elementary school, the stayers had definitely become school kids. As school kids, they never ran into trouble with teachers and school staff. Because of this, they were not labeled as problematic students, as the street kids were early on. However, some street kids initially developed marginal school kid identities that were put to the test later on, prompting them to become street kids.

LEARNING TO BE STREET KIDS

Some leavers and returners also became school kids in elementary school, but this identity seemed more fragile than the one developed by the stayers. The narratives of the leavers and the returners are somewhat negative, and at the very least not as enthusiastic as those of the stayers. Most of their stories lack accounts of social support, prestige, or rewards received as students, nor do they convey the formation of meaningful ties with peers and teachers. As a result, they form a more marginal school-kid identity that leaves them susceptible to the development of a street-kid identity at the end of elementary school or during high school. However, some of them recall elementary school as a pleasant time marked with social and academic accomplishments. They enjoyed school, liked their teachers, got along with their peers, and did well academically. For example, Ernesto, a leaver, had good grades in elementary school:

> Because like I said in elementary school, I used to get, I mean, I can show you, my mother still has those things. I could show you my report card and all my report cards they would have A's and B's. And I would never miss a day of school or nothing.

In addition to liking school and obtaining good grades, some leavers and returners were involved in school activities. For instance, Lisa liked elementary school and did well there. She always got "A's and B's, I would never bring home a F, never." She had good relationships with her teachers and peers, and participated in many extracurricular activities. Lisa was a member of the girls' football team, the pompom squad, and the flag squad. Her school life was exciting until she reached high school, where she began experiencing school trouble:

> It was okay . . . I didn't have no problems . . . I didn't have no gang problems. I would always get along with my teachers. I would make friends with my other teachers. It was like I didn't have no problems. You know, I would like going to school until I got here [Hernández High].

Other returners and leavers were not as happy in elementary school. They described their experiences as just "okay," even in comparison to their negative high school years. For some, the lack of enthusiasm may be due to the frequent school changes they experienced. While most changed schools once or twice, others transferred between schools often. Marisol changed schools nine times, attending seven different elementary schools from kindergarten to eighth grade. As a result, her elementary school memories are clouded by the fact that she "never stayed in the other schools too long" to be able to make friends and enjoy school. Although changing schools entails adjustment to a new environment, it is not always a negative change. Some students, like Jenny, a returner, welcomed the change of schools because they ended up attending a better school, or a school they liked more.

> I went to Snyder for about 6 years and then I transferred to Colón. At first I didn't [like elementary school], but when I transferred to the new school it was okay. I liked it. Snyder, it was like, I don't know. It was like you go to school, you just go to school. It's like they really didn't care. I really didn't like it out there. And the kids were different, they were like, I don't know, more streetwise . . . [I transferred to Colón] because I moved out . . . 'Cause we sold the house from where we used to live. And we rented an apartment and was closer [to Colón]. But I stayed a year after we moved out at Snyder so I could finish six grade. Then I transferred out when the new school year began. I did like Colón better. It was a high school before. I don't know . . . I liked it much better. It was more fun there. I didn't know anybody but I made friends real fast. That's why I got so that I liked it.

For others, it was the presence of identity-threatening events that affected their attachment to school. Elementary school is expected to be a safe haven, a place devoid of dangers, where children can thrive and learn social and academic skills. However, some students challenge this notion, arguing that their elementary schools were far from being a safe haven. They became acutely aware that street culture reigned in school and that the school could not, or would not, protect them. These kids came to the early realization that in school they had to fend for themselves. Angel describes being intimidated and fearful in a tough environment where nobody is safe and one must fend for oneself to survive:

> Grammar school was not that good. I had bullies [picking on me], and I was fighting all the time. I wasn't fighting [I didn't start the fights]. I didn't grow up like that. But basically it was . . . I don't know, I had pretty much a hard time . . . Insecure . . . I was a quiet person. I didn't grow up like all these kids around here, messing around while young. I was pretty much quiet. . . . I was so quiet and that attracted people to come mess with me 'cause I was so quiet, you know. So that was it.

Regardless of their experiences with street culture in school, it is the lack of meaningful relationships that has the most negative repercussions. The students denounce the foul treatment they received from teachers. These students say that unprofessional and uncaring elementary school teachers hurt them deeply. Although they may describe some of their elementary school teachers as friendly, they do not recall developing close attachments to them. More often, they offer detailed descriptions of elementary school teachers who trespassed the limits of their authority, engaging in what the street kids believe are unprofessional behaviors. Diana, a returner introduced in Chapter 2, explains:

> Teachers are like, they put us to do things. I had a teacher that if you wanted to be her pet you had to sit there and get this masking tape and take the hairs off her coat. Do this for her, do that for her. I mean doing all her personal things. And if you weren't like that, she'll be like, if you wouldn't do what she want you to do, she's like always tried to yell at you.

Some unprofessional teachers engaged in actions that emotionally hurt the leavers and returners. These identity-threats, such as perceptions of unfairness, became an issue for the street kids and impacted their perceptions of school. They describe incidents in which they believe an injustice was done, and this usually involved a humiliating experience, where they felt defeated and shamed in front of others. For example, Diana recalls:

> . . . just that one time, a misunderstanding when I got into a fight with another girl and then the girl is from another classroom. So the

teacher was like, "Oh, she still fought." And she got to go to the Springfield trip and I didn't get to go. And it wasn't fair. We both fought. We both should not have went.

The stories of street kids include times when they felt bad about themselves because they were judged harshly and cruelly by teachers, not given a second chance, held up as a bad example, or exposed to public humiliation. César, a leaver, tells about an incident that made a strong negative impression on him:

And there's a lot of things that I just remember that I always hated. I don't know. It's kind of stupid but in my first grade, you know, this probably was a big thing. 'Cause it always bothered me when you're little. A little problem you're always gonna remember and always stays in your mind. When I was little, this little girl, she said that I called her a 4-eyes. And in [front of] all the school, my teacher got mad at me, yelled at me 'cause she had glasses on. "Don't make fun of that." Took me to the principal. And I never called the girl nothing. You know, and it always got on my nerves . . . And either way, if I was to call her that, they don't have to go to the extremes. Just say, "Don't call her 4-eyes." Why you gotta make it a big issue whether I call her 4-eyes or not.

Street kids' disconnection from school is marked by drastic changes in their behavior that express their discontent with the student role. Many students show "cuing behaviors," or early signals of increasing disengagement, by skipping school or cutting classes. Although not typical, César began to skip school in first grade, and thereafter his truant behavior continued to escalate.

I started cutting school like in first grade. 'Cause I failed my first grade . . . I don't know, I just got tired of going to school, you know. And then after that, I got caught a few times and then I started going back. But I had failed, but I went back to school and I passed. I started passing again. So I didn't cut no more until I got [to] fourth grade. I stopped going altogether, and I ended up missing a lot of school there. I had a little argument with my teacher 'cause I'd come late. I was making it a big habit. She was getting, started getting mad at me, wanting to see my mother and stuff, and I just ended up arguing with her. Really arguing. Walking out of the school. I walked out like three times on my sixth grade, but they had a police looking up [for me].

Julio, a returner who attended elementary school in Puerto Rico, was absent from school for prolonged periods of time. Since Julio left the house every morning, his mother had no clue that he was not going to school, and the school never called the house to report his absences. Afraid that he would fail eighth grade because of his absences, Julio made up an elaborate story about being injured in a car accident. He even wore a neck brace to school to drama-tize his injury: "I wore it [neck brace] to school. I would leave the house like nothing, with the neck brace in my bag. When I was close to school, I would look around to make sure nobody was seeing me and [put on] the neck brace."

Some street kids display aggressive and violent behavior in elementary school. Many recall being mixed up in frequent school fights they often initi-ated. These schoolyard fights seldom brought them major consequences, usually no more than one-day suspensions, or a suspension of particular privi-leges. Although fighting with peers is most common, two say that they hit a teacher. Physically assaulting a teacher occurred when these students felt that they were treated unfairly, humiliated, or misinterpreted by the teacher. In-variably, this brought about their expulsion from school, as Manuel explains:

> I got kicked out of grammar school. Well, I have a temper, and I was real nervous and for anything I got mad. So I grabbed the chair and I threw it at her [teacher] and I broke her arm in three places. And they kicked me out . . . It was worse. All I used to do is fight, just fight. I used to be a bad kid . . . I had some cookies, and she [teacher] took them away. That's when I threw the chair. For any lit-tle thing I used to get mad and I used to mess up.

Julio, a returner, told me that he was expelled from military school after assaulting an instructor. He had just moved from Puerto Rico to New York, and his mother enrolled him in a military boarding school, even though he did not understand or speak English. When the bell rang in the morning, Julio was supposed to get up, get dressed, make his bed, and be ready for inspec-tion, but nobody had bothered to tell him—at least in Spanish. The first morn-ing, Julio was still in bed when the instructor came for inspection. After the instructor yelled at him, Julio got up but had no idea what was going on. When the instructor pushed him to the floor (presumably to do push-ups as a punishment), Julio began hitting him. After being restrained, he was placed in solitary confinement until his mother came to get him the next day.

Problematic behavior during elementary school, ranging from class cutting to fighting to striking a teacher, is a manifestation of the students' discontent with schooling and can signal the early stages of formation of the street-kid identity. Early on, some students begin to find in street culture a supportive network that is the source of prestige, reward, and positive evalua-tions not found at school. They soon realize that while not being good in school matters, they excel in street ways. "Being good at being bad" furthers their exploration of street culture at the expense of schooling.

TRANSITION TO HIGH SCHOOL

Eighth grade and the summer before entering ninth grade mark the transition for some school kids into street culture. Aware of stories that circulate about gang activity and violence at Hernández High, some rush to join gangs or to build stronger reputations (see Chapter 5). Although some students adopt street identities early on, incursions into street culture are more pronounced in the last years of elementary school. This is when the gangs begin to recruit students into their rank and file. Much pressure is exerted by gangs at the school for youths, especially boys, to join them. Vitín's story illustrates clearly the fast deterioration of school performance during eighth grade. According to Vitín, he was a good student until he transferred to another school in eighth grade. Being the new kid in school, Vitín was befriended by members of a gang. Soon his personality began to change, his grades dropped, and he started to come home late. He also changed his physical appearance, getting a haircut and his ear pierced, and began to smoke marijuana.

> That's when everything changed because I used to bring her [his mother] B's in grammar school. But I was never home. I was coming at three o'clock in the morning, four o'clock in the morning. I was coming late. I got my ears pierced there. I had my long hair. I mean, at that school, that's something I never did when I was smaller, in seventh grade. 'Cause in seventh grade, ask the majority, you don't know about gangs. Before eighth grade I never had problems. I had my temper. But I never did the things I did in eighth grade.

He joined the gang, with his initiation ceremony taking place in the school's bathroom.

> They were in a gang, and I wanted to follow their footsteps because everybody had respect toward them and I've seen that. And they told me, "What's up? When are you gonna be one of us," and this and that. I said, "I don't know." And then one time we got high, and I said, "You know what? Turn me in 'cause I'm always with you guys. I might as well get it over with and turn in." So they gave me that V-in ["violation-in" or initiation] inside a washroom [in school]. And one of the big pres came from the neighborhood and went inside the school, and there was no security guard or nothing like that. Inside the bathroom in the school and they told him, "Oh, this is the guy that wants to be violated-in." And he came and he said what he had to do and then he went. And we went to our class like if nothing happened. They hit me a lot, but I didn't feel it until the next day.

Not surprisingly, soon Vitín ran into problems at the school. The behaviors required by his gang conflicted with the behavior required at school. He was often in fights, and as a result, he was suspended many times. Still, Vitín was able to keep good enough grades to pass eighth grade.

The summer prior to high school entrance is itself a trying time for many leavers because this is the time to "prepare" for high school. Worried about their impending entry into high school, many scurry around to adopt street-boy and -girl identities, such as joining gangs, hoping that these identities will provide them with protection and a "don't mess with me" attitude in high school (see Chapter 5). As they adopt street identities, they inevitably change peer groups. Ernesto describes how after graduating from eighth grade, he moved into a different social circle that drove him further from school.

> Actually, it was everybody, it was everybody that I hung around. The influence, let's put it that way. *La amistad* [the friends]. Because in elementary school I used to get A's and B's. I used to go home with A's and B's. I don't know. Everything happened after graduation. After eighth grade. But see, I wasn't interested interested [his emphasis], into it [school], you know what I mean. I started finding *diferentes amistades* [different friends]. Then I started to hang out with these people. Then I hung out with those people.

The pressure to become "somebody" and to prove oneself in the street culture leads some leavers to take extreme actions or to do "crazy things," as Vitín explains:

> 'Cause in the summer when I graduated from grammar school, I used to use, we used to fight with the opposite gang and shoot at the opposite gang and do some crazy things. I never got caught. The only time, the only three times I got caught is only in school. Out there when the cops used to come we used to break. [Find] places to hide or we would hide under a car. One time I was under a car, this is when I wanted to be a cop, "This ain't for me." And then from that, "Well, forget it. I'm gonna have fun." So I did it [gang banging].

Vitín refers to that summer as "two whole months in the streets," reflecting the drastic changes that happen after eighth grade.

While some school kids make incursions into gang life during this period, these are often short-lived, and they tend to leave the gang after a few months. Yet some become committed to gangs, initiating a no-return journey into street culture that profoundly affects different aspects of their lives. Gang activities consume their time and create strife between them and their families, as was the case for Ernesto:

> After graduation [from eighth grade] everything wasn't as good be-
> cause it was like, *yo venía como a las 2 o las 3 de la mañana* [I
> would come at around 2 or 3 in the morning] and my father would
> always be *peleando* [arguing] with, you know, fighting with me."

Like Vitín and Ernesto, many students who eventually become street kids begin elementary school as school kids, but their school experiences along the way change their orientation. For most of them, it may be the fear of what awaits them in high school, and their exposure and familiarity with street culture in elementary school, that tilt the scale in favor of adopting a street-kid identity.

FACTORS HINDERING THE DEVELOPMENT
OF A SCHOOL-KID IDENTITY

Although elementary school experiences shape students' identities, they cannot fully account for how and why students take on a particular identity. I do not want to downplay the fact that some teachers are unfair and unprofessional and that many schools are not the safe havens they paint themselves to be. The stratification of students begins early, resulting in the differential treatment of students, the unequal distribution of rewards, and the arbitrary labeling of children who do not conform to the school-kid ideal type (see Rist, 1970). The formation of a street-kid identity in the early grades can be a response to their marginal status at school due to the lack of social support, prestige, and rewards; their inadequate performance of the student role; and the absence of meaningful relationships. It can also be due to the presence of identity-threatening events, such as the presence of street culture, affording them chances to explore alternatives. Other aspects of their lives also affect their experiences at school by making them more distant from the school-kid ideal and also by making them more likely to interpret schools' actions as attacks on them. Students who do not fit the mold because of personal and family characteristics and/or those who are experiencing difficulties at home are more vulnerable to interpreting ordinary events at school as attacks. Thus, it may be that school kids and street kids give different meaning to similar events. For example, having cookies taken away by a teacher does not generally lead to assaulting the teacher and breaking her arm, as Manuel did. Most kids would interpret it as a consequence of not following rules about eating in the classroom, and accept the punishment, and its accompanying humiliation, for breaking rules. Generally, they would not see it as a personal attack on the part of the teacher. However, the street kids perceive such events as attacks on their selves because they have been treated unfairly before and/or because their experiences inside and outside of school (within the family) make them more vulnerable to such interpretations.

What is different about the street kids and sets them apart from the school kids is that their narratives about family and community life suggest the presence of identity-threatening events in their lives. Their stories convey troubled childhoods that sometimes are manifested in elementary school but other times are not expressed until high school. Street kids, then, are not only responding to conditions in school but also to a generalized feeling of being constantly under attack that is aggravated at school. These students are already vulnerable because of circumstances in their lives, and the school drives them further away.

A recurring theme in their narratives is their feeling of being unloved by their parents. These stories take on different forms, but the underlying theme is feelings of rejection that are often conflated by other family issues. To further complicate matters, they also feel unloved by uncaring teachers at school. For instance, César's truancy may have much to do with his status as the "odd one" or the "black sheep" of his family, and his certainty that his mother did not love him as she loved his brothers.

> My brother, he has heart problems. I was like 9 years old . . . and I punched him in the stomach a few times and then he was getting sick. And she said I tried to kill him. She always tells me that I tried to kill him. When we start arguing, she brings it up. And I hate that. It makes me mad. So I get mad at her 'cause when she was younger and she was gonna have me, she tried to take some pills to kill me because she didn't want a kid. And then, it didn't happen. I still was born. And she hates when I remind her of that.

Evidence of the tensions at home came to light when César's school troubles disappeared after he went to live with an uncle in a suburb. Besides having a "real good year there," he joined the soccer team and a theater group. Yet his school troubles resumed the next year when he went back to live with his mother.

> And I had the 7th grade year there [the suburb], and I had a real good year there. I passed [classes] and everything. I only missed like a few days of the school year. And then I moved back with my mom, and when I went to 8th grade, I don't know, the environment . . . but the environment and all that made me cut a lot . . . but they passed me anyway. I ended up only going to school for one semester, but since I took the Constitution test in 7th grade while I was out in

[the suburbs], you know, and my report card was good there, they
passed me.

For Manuel, it was the mixture of family violence and his status as the darkest
child that seem to have profoundly affected him. Manuel always felt different
from his siblings because of his darker skin.

> Every time I talk to my mom and dad they look at me like, "Man,
> odd one." 'Cause they're all white. The darkest is me from my family.
> Different father, same mother. Like their father is almost dark, I don't
> know how they came out [white]. Well, my mom is light skin. If you
> look at my mom and you look at me you'll be like "That's your
> mom?" But of all my brothers and sisters, I'm the darkest one. And
> people thought, "Oh, he's the darkest one. He's gonna be the odd
> one. He's gonna be the bad one."

Manuel's childhood is marred by his father's alcoholism and physical abuse of
his mother and siblings.

> When I was 3 years old, that's when they [parents] broke up. I wish I
> was older in those days because my mom really left my father 'cause
> he used to beat on her. When we were young, he used to hit her,
> beat her for no reason. He used to come home drunk, he's an alco-
> holic. He used to always beat on her and everything so she left him
> then. I wish I was older in those days. I would've beat him up. He
> started hitting me and everything.

Growing up amidst violence, it is not that surprising that Manuel ended up
striking a teacher. Yet, to further complicate his feelings of rejection from
being dark-skinned, and from the general physical abuse his family was subjected to at the hands of his father, Manuel was kicked out of the house by
his mother. "And then, when I got kicked out of there [school for striking a
teacher], my mom threw me out. I was nine. I went to live with my dad and
that's when he started whipping me." Perhaps Manuel's anger and feelings of
injustice at home made him more likely to perceive injustices in school.

Other children do not experience physical abuse but are subjected to
other problems that leave profound scars on them. For instance, Angel's earli-
est childhood recollections are related to his father's drug addiction.

> At night he [father] would leave. [He would] come back and he
> would leave [again]. My mother would wake me up and tell me to
> stay awake with her 'cause she was afraid [when he was acting like
> that]. And I'd stay awake all night and always watch him. Sit down,

just watch him. We'd just sit there. Just wait until he fell asleep or left again. I wasn't [afraid]. My mother was afraid he was gonna OD [drug overdose] or something, you know what I mean. She'd tell me to stay awake, and I'd just stay awake. It's just the way he used to act. He's too crazy. Walking around the house and searching for I don't know what the hell. Look in the garbage. You know, it was crazy . . . I've been living with this all my life. Since I can remember.

While Angel's mother relied on him, she is "the type of person that she shows no affection. She's always putting me down. She never has anything positive to say about me, never, ever, ever. So I have to deal with her always, I got to block that away." Angel's reaction to his father's drug problem and his mother's rejection was to close himself up from others. He describes himself as a child as "insecure" and "a quiet person" who kept to himself but was harassed by bullies.

Perhaps the most extreme case of a troubled childhood was experienced by Angie, who was first abandoned by her mother, sexually molested by a cousin, and then subjected to cleansing rituals by her mother, who was an *espiritista* [spiritist].

My mom had me when she was 15 and she couldn't handle it . . . then, they forced her to marry my father . . . and he gave me my last name. But they hated each other . . . so they got divorced here in Chicago and my mom left me in Puerto Rico 'cause she didn't want me. My grandmother raised me. I stayed there until I was six. And then, I came here. She [mother] made a big fuss that she wanted me back . . . I came to live with them [mother and stepfather] . . . and I stayed here for a while and then she sent me back with my grandmother. So I was like back and forth. I stayed here [Chicago] again when I was like 10.

Angie talked about a cousin who sexually molested her.

He [cousin] molested me when I was little. He came here to visit. I saw him out the corner of my eye, and I was trembling. When I was in Puerto Rico and then when I came here, he followed and came to live with us. I was about 10. I was always afraid of him . . .

She was subjected to ritual cleansing because her mother was "one of the most powerful" *espiritistas* and "every time they [other *espiritistas*] would throw something [spell] at her, I would catch it." Angie explains that the witchcraft made her sick, causing her asthma. She says that she almost died, and her mother sent her back to Puerto Rico to protect her. When she returned, her mother started to perform rituals to protect her.

> And she used to kill chickens . . . and she would cut the head off and pour the blood in front of the door and then pluck the feathers and put the feathers on top of the blood in front of the door. 'Cause she said that she was cleaning me . . . So she would take the chicken and she would hold it by the legs. She would put it in front of my head and in back of my head. And then she would spin me around and sing a song, and she would go like this with the chicken, like cleaning, all around my body. And then she would kill the chicken . . . Once she told me that the devil told her to clean me. So me and her went to the forest preserve, and she had that scented water . . . and she had a bucket of water from the river and she told me to take my clothes off . . . So I took my clothes off, and she took some branches off the tree and she dipped it in the water and she started hitting me with it. And I had red marks all over me. And I'm wondering, "What did I do to deserve this?" And then she picked me up, and she scraped my back against the bark of a tree, and I didn't have no clothes on. I had blood dripping all over me . . . I had to be cleaned and that's the way they clean people . . . after she cut me and everything, she put the [scented] water on me and that burned . . . after she told me to get dressed, she hugged me . . . And then after that she was all nice to me and everything. Took me out to eat. 'Cause I think that she felt guilty . . . she would say that I would have to be cleaned because I wasn't in it.

When she was 14, her mother sent her away to live with an aunt in the middle of the night.

> Then they told her that she had to slice one of her wrists, and if she survived she would have the power. Or that she had to sacrifice me, 'cause I was the oldest daughter . . . So that night she came into my room and she told me to leave . . . It was two in the morning, and I'm walking to my aunt's house and luckily she lived just 2 blocks away . . . And then my mom came into the house like 3 weeks later and told me that everything was okay.

Although her mother ultimately left this cult and joined a Pentecostal church, Angie still suffers the vestiges of her mother's past "because they think my mom one day is gonna go back to that stuff and she will still be as powerful as she was before, so they're like after me." While Angie's story is an exception, it clearly conveys the difficult and complex childhoods that some children have.

Other kids experience troubled childhoods that have less to do with family issues than with exposure to community violence. For example, Ernesto told me of the violence in the community.

> I was still young, but I was still seeing the violence. One time I was by Maple and Elm [streets], and some man from the roof shot another guy with a machine gun and just killed him. That was years ago . . . [I was] like about 12 [years old]. And then I moved to Main Street [another area of the community] . . . and it's the same violence over there. Drug dealings, gangs, shootings, auto theft, police chasing people, people getting robbed.

Up to this point, Ernesto had done well in school, but all this changed after he joined a gang upon graduating from elementary school. These troubled childhoods make kids more apprehensive and prone to interpret events as attacks on themselves.

CONCLUSION

The stories I present here are not representative of most children in the community, nor of most students at Hernández High, but they are nevertheless the lives of some children. Their stories are important because they give a name and a face to the ravages of poverty. And while drastic societal changes are needed to change these realities, their suffering is further exacerbated by uncaring schools that reject them as much as they feel their families reject them. The stories presented in this chapter suggest that schools, and teachers, are generally unsympathetic to students' needs and penalize those who are already feeling low. What I want to emphasize is that kids who act out in school or who have trouble becoming school kids are not just naughty. They may be acting out in school from the frustrations they carry from other aspects of their lives, and the treatment they receive at school does not ameliorate their pain. Instead, negative school experiences tilt the scale toward street-oriented identities among students who are already vulnerable in other aspects of their lives. They may have to put up with their families and neighborhoods, but they are simply not willing to take it from school, too. School is the only aspect of their lives that they can walk out of, or tune out.

The remainder of this book describes in much detail the contrasting experiences of the stayers, leavers, and returners during high school. These chapters show how Hernández High further splits their paths, driving street kids away from school while reinforcing the connections school kids have with school. In this way, Hernández High exacerbates what was already put in motion at the elementary schools—the segmentation of the student body into two opposite cultures.

CHAPTER 4

Dealing with School Stigma: "I Guess One Reason Why I Stayed in This School Is to Show People"

Everybody thinks that this is a school of criminals. That everyone here is bad.

—Roberto, a stayer

Well, I was scared because they have a lot of rumors in the streets [about Hernández High]. "Oh, it's a lot of gangs." "They kill people in there." "There's always fights." I was always scared.

—Lisa, a leaver

The allusion to Hernández High School as a reject or low-life school conveys an image of its students as social misfits and none too smart. While only a minority of its students fall within these categories, the continuing perception of Hernández High as a school for social and academic rejects has become a stigma that marks individual students. It is seen as a last-resort high school where students go when they lack other alternatives; that is, as a dumping ground where they go if they do not get admitted or are expelled from other high schools. The troubled history and continuous controversies in the school and the "high drama" media coverage contribute to the labeling of the school as a "social problem."

This chapter describes the factors that contribute to the academic and social stigma attached to Hernández High School and the effects of the low prestige it bestows on students. I also discuss how fear of the school initially drives some students to street culture, how school kids and street kids cope with the stigmatization that comes from attending such a low-ranking school with such a pervasive reputation, and why they "choose" to attend Hernández High.

THE REPUTATION OF HERNÁNDEZ HIGH SCHOOL

Of the many high schools in the city, Hernández High is one of the most known and among those that get the most publicity. It is not infrequent that Hernández High makes the evening news, especially in the local Spanish language stations, as Iván reports:

> The news, what they hear in the news. My parents, they tell me that they'll be watching the news in the Spanish channel, 'cause they show Hernández a lot I guess. My parents watch it all the time. They'll be telling what they see on TV.

Much of the press coverage focuses on problems at the school, and it is rare for something positive to be reported. The school has had its share of controversy since the 1960s, and this has contributed to this image. It has been at the center of community struggles, student protests, and student walkouts, which have been amply reported by the media. Yet more stigmatizing than its history of community and student activism are the stories of academic mediocrity and daily violence and struggle that frequently appear on the news. It seems as if every other school horror story in the evening news is about Hernández High. In the collective imagination, Hernández High stands out as the prototype, the exemplary case, of what is wrong with the school system.

Being aware of the school's reputation, my first visit to Hernández High was filled with a mix of curiosity and apprehension. From a sociologist's perspective, Hernández High appears to have all the features that made it a great research site. At the same time, I was wary about doing research there because, in addition to the media's coverage of the school, I knew of the rumors that circulated in the neighborhood. A few years before, I had heard many stories about how dangerous the school was while teaching and doing research at a nearby alternative school; most of the students were former Hernández High students who enjoyed telling hair-raising stories about their days there. I was also advised by a well-meaning friend and lifetime resident of the area to do the study in another school that has "fewer problems." Other people also wondered why I wanted to spend time at Hernández High when there were nicer, and safer, schools in the area. It was this same reasoning, and my uninformed perception of Hernández High as a chaotic school, that drew me to it. Until I visited Hernández High, almost everything I had heard about the school was negative. It was not long before I realized that the media and the community grossly misrepresented the school.

Before entering Hernández High, most students had also formed preconceived ideas about what to expect, based on news reports and rumors that circulated around the neighborhood. Elizabeth, for example, could effortlessly recite a long litany of rumors about Hernández High and its students.

> You hear rumors like the school is not good and . . . like the school
> wasn't worth a thing. The school has a lot of drop-outs, the school
> has a lot of pregnant girls. That the teachers don't teach you as well
> as in other schools. That's the kind of rumors I heard. They kill at the
> school and the students hit the teachers and stuff like that.

These rumors are usually vague but convey a chaotic image of a school where
fights, weapons, and lack of control by the staff are the rule.

Most students have heard many stories, at times very detailed, of incidents that have supposedly happened at Hernández High. One particular
story that I heard several times involved the throwing of a student through a
window. According to Miguel, a stayer, "That [rumor] is all out there. 'Hernández High is no good. Oh, I hear they throw people out windows,' they [people]
say. A lot of rumors." At other times, the same incident was told in more
detail, such as by Ernesto, a leaver: "A long time ago, if you haven't heard,
there was a black guy, he got thrown out a window in Hernández. It wasn't
too high 'cause he's alive. There's so many things [that have] happened in that
school. It's crazy." I was unable to confirm that any student has ever been
thrown through a window. According to the staff, nothing like that has ever
happened at the school.

Another popular story that circulates in the community is about shootings
inside the school building. Outsiders believe that shots have been fired inside
the school, but I could not find anyone who could verify that this has ever
happened. Students are often questioned about shooting incidents that have
supposedly taken place at Hernández High. Iván, a stayer, said to me, "It's
exaggerated a lot. The other day, some girls that go to Thomas [another high
school, asked] 'Are they still shooting inside Hernández?' That has never
happened. They exaggerate Hernández' reputation a lot." Although these
claims could not be substantiated, the stories continue. Regardless of their
veracity, they are part of the sustaining myth surrounding Hernández High
that makes an archetype that can be tossed around by both sides in the controversy over schools and any number of other local or political issues that need
a social disaster to make a case. The students know that outsiders are quick
to accept the rumors about Hernández High as real because they fit into the
collective perception of the school and its students. It is the students who are
left to pick up the fragments and make some meaning out of the school's
dismal reputation.

COPING WITH STIGMA

None of Hernández High's students is exempt from the intimidation that results from school tales or immune from the reputation that the school bestows

on them. What differs is how they deal with it and what happens to their identities as a result. As discussed in Chapter 3, most students develop well-defined identities as school kids or street kids in elementary school, but these are put to the test as high school entrance approaches. School kids may start to doubt their commitment to the student identity because they are afraid of being left unprotected and thus vulnerable when they enter Hernández High. In their desperation, they may join gangs just so they have a group to fall upon. For example, Ernesto joined a gang the summer before ninth grade because he was afraid of what would happen to him at the high school if he did not. Even kids who were already street-oriented told me about becoming "wilder" the summer preceding ninth grade. Vitín, who was involved in a gang while still in elementary school, became "crazy" the summer before entering ninth grade. Both Ernesto and Vitín, like many of their peers, were driven to street culture because they believed the stories about Hernández High and were convinced that to make it out "alive," they needed protection (in the form of a gang) or to build their own reputation as street kids. While street kids become more and more involved in street life, incursions into street culture do not last long among the school kids. They quickly realize that street culture is not for them and retreat from it. Iván, one of the stayers, joined a gang but soon realized that gang life was not for him. Because his brother was a gang member, Iván was allowed to simply walk out without being subjected to a V-out (a beating inflicted on those leaving a gang).

Once students enter Hernández High, the stigma attached to the school is transferred to them. A stigma is a deeply discrediting characteristic that casts the individual in an inferior light (Goffman, 1963). It signals a gap between what "should be" and what "is." Stigma is then conferred on those who deviate from the norm or the ideal. It affects not only how people are evaluated by others, but also how they view and evaluate themselves. People must learn to deal with a stigma by either succumbing to it and fulfilling expectations or overcoming it and succeeding in spite of the obstacles. At Hernández High, I found that most students cope with stigma in one of two ways: living up to the myth, or countering the myth. Street kids' commitment to street culture leads them to engage in behaviors that only confirm other people's stigmatized perception of the school and its students. Not only do they "live up to the myth" of Hernández High, but they often reinforce it and contribute to its growth. By contrast, school kids react by fighting the negative image of the school. They "counter the myth" by engaging in behaviors and role performances that contradict the stigma attached to the school and its students.

Street kids believe that they have much to gain from the stigma of the school. Because they subscribe to street culture, they welcome any opportunity to boost their street images. Attending Hernández High automatically inflates their street reputations, prompts positive evaluations, and increases their prestige among their street-oriented peers. Being a student there is enough to elicit suspicion among outsiders who view Hernández High as problematic. That the street kids are always ready to live up to the stereotype only fosters the perpetuation of these views. The reputation of the school is partly due to the students who engage in street behavior at school, but also to the exaggerated stories they tell others. Street kids often elaborate on these stories to aggrandize their brush with danger. By bringing in street behaviors and stretching the truth, they perpetuate the perception of Hernández High and its students as street kids, and boost their own street reputations at the expense of their student identity. Living up to the stereotype only leads to trouble in school, which often results in their suspension, expulsion, or "voluntary" drop-out.

By contrast, school kids feel uncomfortable with the stigma associated with Hernández High and take people's comments as a personal affront. They are unsure of what others think of them but suspect that their perceptions are not positive. Their suspicions are often confirmed by the questions or comments made by outsiders. Many students face questioning by outsiders who are intrigued by Hernández High and often wonder how they have ended up at such a low-status school. Alma, a stayer, noted: "I ran into some old friends in [another school] and they go, 'Oh, what school do you go to?' 'Hernández,' 'Hernández? But you're too smart for that school.'" As a result, school kids have become very defensive and sensitive to people's comments. Stayers go to great lengths to correct people's perceptions of the school, as they are the most concerned and most determined to set the record straight on Hernández High. They engage in what Suttles (1984) calls "defended typification," a sense of "local patriotism" that leads these students to challenge the stigma and set the record straight, both for the reputation of the school and for their own reputations. They transform the negative reputation of the school by incorporating selective aspects of the school and constructing a more positive image. Often they downplay the stigma by likening Hernández High to other high schools. They argue that the school is just like other schools, with the same problems, nothing out of the ordinary. Lydia, a stayer, even claims that in some aspects Hernández High is better than other schools, especially in racial relations:

> Now they think it's the worst school in the city. And it's not the school, it's the people. The people that makes the school, the students. They choose the kind of behavior. So there are other schools that are worse. They've been having a lot of problems with the Mexicans and the Blacks hating each other. But we don't have that much racial thing here. Everybody is used to living with each other. 'Cause our neighborhood, that's so diverse with so many kinds of people.

Seeking to dispel the negative image, some students insist that rumors and stories, such as the shootings and the tossing of people through windows, are made up by students who want to maintain the school's negative reputation. They point their fingers at their street-oriented peers who use the school's infamous name to enhance their own street reputations. Minor incidents are thus highly exaggerated, other stories are made up, and the rumors are spread by students themselves. Miguel, a stayer, explains:

> The only reason why Hernández has a bad reputation is that people from the school put it down. They lie. They make up lies, they make up stories. Like one little thing that happened they make it into some big deal. Like the shooting that happened, it happened last week. The shooting in front of school and everything, they're gonna make it a real big thing. They're gonna say that it happened in the school or something . . . They [those involved in the shooting] were not students, they were out there, drop-outs or something.

Those students who are sensitive to the stigmatized reputation of the school must constantly be alert, not only to downplay but to openly contradict people's perceptions of the school. They are offended by "putdown" remarks made by people and often answer angrily, especially when it is implied that they are less intelligent or "social misfits" because they attend Hernández High. They contend with the assumption made by people and the media, that any youths involved in fights or shootings in the neighborhood are students at Hernández High. Diana, a returner, recalled an argument she had with her niece who later attended another high school:

> When I was asking her, "Well, what high school are you gonna go to?" and you know, I meant to say a high school and it came out Hernández. I was thinking I come to Hernández so that's why I said Hernández and she goes, "I wouldn't go to Hernández High. Are you kidding? That's a rejects' school. I won't go to a rejects' school." I said, "Hernández is no reject school. You should think again." "Oh, but I won't go there 'cause it's a rejects' school." I mean she rolled her eyes and everything. I said, "Oh, you think you're going to [another school]" and she was like, "Oh, I'll go somewhere but I'm not going to that reject school. That's a bunch of rejects." I mean what kind of attitude is that to say [these things]. She doesn't know what this school is about, she doesn't come here, you know. So she really doesn't know what's going on. So, it's a lot of gang members and our area is low-income, what does she want? Just 'cause she goes to [another high school] it's no better. It's the same thing 'cause they teach

you what they teach you here. And you're getting the same diploma. You know, it says Chicago Public Schools.

While not denying that there are many problems in the school, students like Diana are angered by the quick conclusions reached by those unfamiliar with the school. After all, when it is assumed that Hernández High is a school for rejects, what is being directly implied about them?

Since the image of the school is tied to the image others perceive of them, some students have to prove that the school, and themselves, are not what people assume. They see themselves as pioneers who succeed where so many failed. The fact that the school has a bad reputation makes their success particularly striking. Lydia points out, "I think that the place and the location of the school doesn't make [the school's reputation] up. So when I first started going here, people would say, 'You're risking yourself, you're not going to succeed in that school.' But this far, I guess I've succeeded."

For Lydia as well as other stayers, it is not the school that fails but its students. They insist that Hernández High is a good school and that students can learn if only they are willing to learn. After all, they take themselves as living proof of the success, and they can attest to the school's academic offerings and potential. By standing up for Hernández High, they are really standing up for themselves, disclaiming the stigma extended to them by the mere fact that they attend Hernández High. Their determination to "prove others wrong" increases their commitment to the student identity, making them more likely to graduate from high school.

"CHOOSING" TO ATTEND HERNÁNDEZ HIGH

Implicit in the image of Hernández High School is the notion that good students, or at least those who are not social misfits, can avoid going there. Marisol, a leaver, said, "I wanted to go to Grant [another high school]. I didn't want to go to Hernández High because like they say, it's a lowlife school . . . Everybody thinks that only the people that don't get accepted at the other schools go there. Like it's the place for kids who can't get nowhere." Yet, like Marisol, most Hernández High students do not have a choice as to which school they end up attending.

In a city where place of residence largely determines school assignment, except for the "academically exceptional," who are steered into magnet schools, most students do not have much influence on which high school they will attend. In Chicago, students are "automatically" assigned to their neighborhood school—the local high school that services their area. Most students are simply sent to their neighborhood schools, which do not have selection criteria to weed out "problematic" students. Hernández High is no exception.

Attending other high schools is possible, but this requires either peti-
tions—which can be denied—or meeting certain criteria. Some students in
this study successfully petitioned to be transferred into Hernández High when
they ran into problems with gangs at other neighborhood high schools. Students can also attend magnet schools if they meet the criteria for admission,
such as entrance examinations, standardized test scores, and grades. However,
most students and their parents lack information about these programs. In
reality, it is the elementary school counselors who determine which school
students will attend by assigning them to the neighborhood school or recom-
mending them to a magnet program.

Despite the lack of alternatives, most students are content with attending
Hernández High. Some of them, particularly the high achievers, had a choice,
yet they chose to attend Hernández High. One reason why students chose to
attend Hernández High is the symbolic meaning that it has for Puerto Rican
students. There is an unspoken loyalty to Hernández High School because it
is the Puerto Rican high school and is recognized as such by community members and outsiders. Not only is the school named after a Puerto Rican, but it
is located in the heart of the Puerto Rican community. It espouses a Puerto
Rican atmosphere and fosters pride in Puerto Rican culture. That parents,
siblings, and cousins attended the school reinforces a sense of loyalty to Hernández High. Many students engage in "defended typification" by vehemently
rejecting negative comments about the school because it is an essential part
of their community identity. They take it upon themselves to prove to outsiders, and even to community members who have nothing positive to say about
the school, that their perceptions are wrong. Marta, a stayer, explains: "My
aunt, the first year, she's like, 'Oh, you're going to Hernández, why? Apply to
another school.' I'm like, 'No, I don't want to. I want to be in Hernández.' I
guess one reason why I stayed in this school is to show people [that the school
is not bad]." By defending the school, they defended their community and
themselves from devaluation.

While most students have a sense of loyalty to Hernández High, many of
them also had practical reasons for attending the school. In particular, transportation alternatives impinged on their choice of high school. Students who
choose to attend a school other than their neighborhood school have to take
public transportation, walk miles, or rely on their parents to drive them to
school. One student says that she enrolled at Hernández High because her
brother was already a student there and her mother refused to drive to different schools. Others such as Lydia, whose parents do not drive them to school,
are discouraged from attending other schools because of transportation "has-
sles," especially in the cold winters: "It's closer to where I live and I didn't
have to hassle about taking the bus in the wintertime and all that."

Another practical reason students gave for attending Hernández High
was gang territoriality. Living in a neighborhood or on a particular street im-

plies gang affiliation for students, whether or not they are members of any gang. Few students, especially young men, can venture into schools out of their neighborhoods without being challenged, harassed, or attacked by local gangs. Students are afraid, often with reason, of going into schools dominated by rival gangs. Because of the dangers that attending a particular school pose to some students, Hernández High's staff often agree to transfer in and out students who need to move to another school because of gang problems. One student, Miguel, transferred out of Hernández High because of gang problems, only to return a few months later because gangs were worse at the other school:

> They were picking on me freshman year so I decided to transfer. But in the other school it was worse. There I got beat up by a Black gang. It was worse there because there were racial problems. See, there are few Latinos and many Blacks and gangs are racial.

That the decision to attend Hernández High was usually beyond their control, and that there are symbolic and practical reasons for attending the school, does not mean that the students hate being at the school. On the contrary, most of them, like their parents and older siblings, have grown to have a kind of defensive pride in the school. Hernández High has become an inextricable part of their community and self-identification.

Underlying these reasons, students choose to attend or remain at Hernández High because it says something about themselves. For some, it demonstrates their ability to overcome adversity. That they emerge unscathed marks them as different from the rest, as special. For others, the school's reputation only consolidates their images as "tough" and violent. No matter what their peer group orientation is, all students' reputations were affected somewhat by the stigma of the school.

CONCLUSION

Hernández High bears the stigma of being one of the worst schools in the Chicago Public Schools system. In the collective imagination, Hernández High is a school for "social misfits"—rejects, gang bangers, criminals, and murderers—and it bestows a stigma on its students just because they are students there. Students are constantly confronted with comments from people questioning their choice to attend Hernández High. It is assumed that only those who are not accepted elsewhere go there.

Students react in two ways to this stigma: Many are troubled by the stigma, while others do not mind it. Yet both essentially convey the view that attending Hernández High builds character, although of different natures.

School kids engage in "defended typification" by taking the attitude that their academic and social success at Hernández High will prove others wrong. Whether they attend the school out of convenience or loyalty to their community and family tradition, they are bent on showing others that their views of the school are wrong. They set themselves up as examples of success in the midst of adversity. They become the exception rather than the rule, setting themselves apart from the rest. By contrast, street kids believe that attending Hernández High only adds to their street reputations. Because they subscribe to street culture, they are more concerned with their street reputations and will do anything to boost them. Street behavior in school is part of building and solidifying their street reputations. While the stigma of the school makes more difficult the task of being a student, it is ultimately the peer culture the students subscribe to that determines how they cope with the stigma and the repercussions their actions have on their educational careers.

CHAPTER 5

Peer Cultures and Self-Image

> It was hard to try to go to school and not to worry. It was hard be-
> cause it was scary.
>
> —Marisol, a leaver

At Hernández High School, the school environment consists of two peer cultures, one school-oriented and the other street-oriented. Each peer group
subscribes to a different set of norms and provides students with social approval,
rewards, and prestige. Students at Hernández High experience peer pressure
to subscribe to one or the other peer culture. Although for the most part
remaining separate, these two peer cultures affect each other as they converge
spatially and socially in school. Of the two, it is the street culture that has the
greatest impact on school social life.

The pervasive domain of street culture at Hernández High is problematic
for students seeking to build a dominant student identity. There is more to
being a student than just attending school, doing homework, and passing classes.
Students in inner-city schools, such as Hernández High, must deal with a
hostile social environment that makes being a student much more complicated. The high level of animosity and hostility among students and the presence of students who vow to boost their reputations as street kids by confronting others make it extremely difficult for all students, regardless of orientation,
to navigate their way through school uneventfully. In addition, the overwhelming presence of street culture poses threats to the development of the school-
kid identity because students are exposed to, and can explore, street identities
in school.

Which peer culture students subscribe to directly affects their high school
careers. Those who take on a street-oriented stance may experience role conflict from having contradictory roles and conflicting role obligations brought
by the demands of the student role and the demands of the street-oriented
peer culture. Subscribing to street culture requires constant responses to
challenges by peers that conflict with adequate performance of the student
role. Street-oriented students gain social approval, rewards, and prestige from
their peer group by engaging in street behavior in school. For street-oriented
students, their reputations are built by proving themselves to be fearless,

tough, and confrontational, and getting others to back off. Because they engage in street behaviors at school, such as fighting and breaking of school rules, they usually fail to adequately perform the student role. They are likely to be suspended and expelled from school and eventually end their schooling short of graduation.

School-oriented students experience role strain, but in a different way. For them, it is having to deal with street-oriented peers that affects their student role performance. To successfully overcome street-oriented students' challenges and hostility, students must craft an image that clearly marks them as school kids. They have to learn, sometimes the hard way, how to fend off street-oriented peers. They build their reputations in school-sanctioned ways, obtaining good grades, participating in school life, and staying out of trouble. Becoming school kids eventually shields them from their street-oriented peers who have nothing to gain, reputationally speaking, from confrontations with school kids. For the most part, street kids leave their school-oriented peers alone because a street reputation cannot be boosted by confronting or harassing those who do not respond to challenge in a street-oriented way. Still, it is not easy to become school kids, as challenges to one's identity are persistent at the outset and students must continuously prove themselves to be school kids. Even the most restrained individual is bound to "lose it" at some point, because some challenges must be responded to. In order to avoid trouble, students must practice a large degree of self-control, and refrain from following their impulses to lash out.

The purpose of this chapter is to show how the local school social environment shapes student identity. I start by describing the social environment at Hernández High and the general feeling of "being on edge" articulated by stayers, leavers, and returners alike. I continue with a discussion of how stayers, leavers, and returners have formed distinct self-images that led them to react to and experience the school's social environment differently, and how these self-images had different repercussions on their educational status.

THE REIGN OF STREET CULTURE IN SCHOOL

Previous studies describe a binary school culture constituted by two main peer groups similar to the ones I found at Hernández High. Eckert (1989) classifies these cultures as the jocks and the burnouts, while Coleman (1961) calls them the leading crowd and the rebellious crowd. Regardless of which names are used, these groups represent the dichotomous peer cultures in U.S. high schools, with the former being a school-oriented culture and the latter a street-oriented culture. According to Eckert and Coleman, the jocks or leading crowd are not only athletes but include all students who are "into school" and participate in activities, while the burnouts or rebellious crowd are alienated from school and do not behave in ways approved by the school. They assert that although these two school cultures coexist in schools, the jocks/leading crowd dominates school social relations.

By contrast, at Hernández High it is the street-oriented boys and girls/ burnouts/rebellious crowd who set the tone of peer relations. According to the participants' narratives, the school is full of gang bangers, delinquents, troublemakers, and other students who subscribe to street culture. While not denying that the student climate at Hernández High is charged and intimidating, it is not nearly as chaotic as these accounts would have us believe. After spending a year at Hernández High, I can attest to the exaggerated nature of these remarks, yet when put into context they do not seem so farfetched. The school is not teeming with troublemakers, and street kids are a minority of the student body. However, they create and maintain the hostile environment that pervades the school. As in Bourgois's (1995) study of a New York community, the "law-abiding majority has lost control of public space" (p. 10), which has been appropriated by the "unruly" minority at Hernández High. Furthermore, the achievements of school kids go unnoticed and are overshadowed by the newsworthy street-oriented minority.

Despite the separateness of these school cultures and the limited interaction between the two groups, the two worlds often collide and influence each other. While students tend to remain within the boundaries of their peer group, neither can ignore the existence of the other. The success of street kids in replicating street life at school poses an identity threat to students in general. It disrupts the performance of the student identity because all students must constantly watch their backs instead of devoting all their energies to academic issues. The students say that the atmosphere of the school is "too charged to relax." They are always looking out of the corners of their eyes to anticipate trouble, and feel uneasy and sometimes outright scared. Fear is ever-present because trouble lurks behind every corner, and students have to be prepared to defend themselves. For them, day-to-day school life entails making careful choices to avert trouble, as Diana explains:

> High school is kind of harder. It's a lot harder 'cause you not only have to deal with coming to school and dealing with teachers, then you've got all these people around you. Like here, all gangs and everything. It's hard sometimes to work around them 'cause they're everywhere.

I also sensed the need to be on guard because although it is more threat than substance, the actual occurrence of trouble seems so unpredictable. Fights start suddenly, frequently next to totally uninvolved bystanders, as in this incident Diana witnessed:

[There was a fight] right in front, right outside the door [of the school]. It was right outside the door. It was 9 o'clock in the morning 'cause I had missed my first class. It started right next to me.

The visible presence of gangs contributes more than any other factor to the animosity pervading Hernández High. According to Pablo, "half of school is gang visible [gang-connected]. There is all kinds of different gangs." While gang signs are obvious, only a small fraction of the students are gang members. "Half of school is gang visible" only because the gangs are uniformly marked by signs (colors and body language) and they hang out in the halls. Moreover, gangs have managed to appropriate the halls from other student groups who are afraid to reclaim them. While other peer groups may control a specific space in school, such as a section of the lunchroom, the gang members' control is more spread out and gives the illusion that they are everywhere in the school.

Gangs in school impinge on the daily life of non-gang members. While school-oriented students do their best to stay away from gangs, it is impossible to be a student at Hernández High and not be touched by gang activity. Students say that gangs pose a threat to student safety, especially because there is more than one gang in the school, and the potential for fights is always present. Diana confirms this: "They all be there. There's all kinds of gangs here . . . That's why it's so hard to come to school 'cause you're dealing with so many different kinds of gangs. It's hard." Students fear that one day a "big" gang fight will occur inside the school itself. Yet while I was at Hernández High, there was not a single "big" gang fight but rather several smaller fights involving two students who often were not gang members. Nevertheless, rumors usually portray gangs as the culprits of fights and violent acts in school.

I do not intend, however, to understate the real threat that gangs pose to students. What I want to emphasize is that at Hernández High gangs are seldom active inside the school building. In general, gang members must follow rigid rules of conduct that seek to minimize individual involvement in trouble that can attract unwanted attention to the gang. The last thing gangs want is problems with the police, and gang activities in school will provoke just that. After the 1986 Safe School Zone Act, gang activity in or near schools became more dangerous, with sentences of up to 30 years in prison (Padilla, 1992). Some gang members told me that they prefer to maintain a low profile at school and are not to create unjustified trouble for the gang. However, the problem is that gang members are often unable to refrain from fighting. Gang rules call for the representation and defense of the gang's name at all times. Thus, disrespect and challenges to the gang, not the individual, must be dealt with regardless of the location, even if it is in school. Further, individual gang members want to preserve their street reputation and have short fuses that lead them to respond violently to any personal challenge. Although some gang activities occur in school, most of them, and certainly those that the students told me about, happened outside the school building.

The truly scary and dangerous situations always take place outside the school building, especially when a gang war is going on. Because gangs hang around the periphery of the school waiting for rivals to arrive at school during the morning or to come out at the end of the school day, it is not unusual to find one or more police cars parked in front of the school and others patrolling the area during these periods. I distinctly remember the day after an intense night of gang warfare in the neighborhood. Expecting gang retaliation from a night of inter-gang shooting, the police had squad cars everywhere, and uniformed police officers were in the school lobby and entrance. That day, many students did not come to school, and those who came were encouraged by the school staff to leave early and have their parents pick them up. The school staff and students know that although they are somewhat protected inside the school building, the walk to and from school can be dangerous. Previous incidents, like the following reported by Marisol, a leaver, reinforced the staff's, students', and police's concern:

> One time after school, I was walking with my sister back home and we had to go through this field by the school gym and we had to drop to the grass because of two gangs shooting at each other. We were in the middle of the fire. We waited until the shooting stopped and ran home.

Gang activities also extend to school-related activities that take place outside the school building. Students talked about drive-by shootings on the periphery of the school. Although the athletic field across the school was in such a poor state that it was not in use at the time of the study, Marisol told me about such an incident she witnessed:

> One time I was watching a football game at Hernández's field, and during the game there was a drive-by shooting. I was at the bleachers. My friend, one of the players, got hit in the leg but it wasn't bad because he was wearing all his equipment.

Out-of-school activities, such as parties, are avoided by many students because they draw contesting gang members and fights are a constant threat. Marisol explains:

> You couldn't go to a party because of the gangs. In elementary school, you would go to a party in somebody's home and it would be people from school. But at Hernández, you'd go to a party, and

there were all these gang bangers. You had to be careful. You had to watch out for colors or for the gang in your area.

Although gang violence makes up the lore of the school, it is the general state of animosity, and not specifically the gangs, that keep students on edge. There are just too many factors that are conducive to the development and escalation of animosity. On the one hand, there are 2,600 students at the school. On the other hand, there is a small but significant number of street-oriented students who are not gang members but whose tolerance runs low, and who will initiate a confrontation over petty issues, or make an issue out of anything. As Miguel notes, "It's like you have to be careful 'cause some guy might come and hit you for no reason." A rule widely reported by students, such as Marisol, is that they cannot look one another in the eye without running the risk of provoking a fight: "At Hernández you can't even talk to people and expect them to be nice. If you look at somebody, they'll say, 'What you're looking at?' You can't look at anybody." Everyday situations, even insignificant incidents, have the potential of escalating into a fight, especially when a few students are walking around looking for an excuse to fight.

While students agreed that navigating through the social environment at Hernández High was a challenge, violence and confrontation was not random. Street kids were targeted more often than school kids. How students presented themselves and the identity they had developed in school had much to do with their experiences there. Furthermore, the kind of identity they adopted in school in turn determined their responses and ways of dealing with the dual school cultures. This ultimately had a major effect on their educational careers.

STUDENTS' SELF-IMAGE AND REACTIONS TO THE SOCIAL ENVIRONMENT

Whether students assume a school-oriented or street-oriented identity has repercussions on their educational careers. School-oriented students usually complete high school, while their street-oriented peers tend to drop out. However, it is not always clear-cut if a student is school-oriented or street-oriented. Eckert (1989) adds a third category of students, the in-betweens, who display both jock and burnout behaviors and move between these categories. At Hernández High, some students seem to be stuck in an in-between category, where they drift between a school-oriented identity and a street-oriented identity. Many of these students were initially street-oriented but later moved closer to the school-oriented culture, although they maintained ties with street-oriented peers.

These student categories (school-oriented/jocks, street-oriented/burnouts, in-betweens) match the three self-images (reputation avoiders, self-image promoters, self-image defenders) exhibited by the Mexican American youth Horowitz (1983) studied, and these self-images in turn correspond to the three status groupings in this study (i.e., stayers, leavers, returners). While not all participants in each category display the same self-image, those who take up a particular self-image tend to be from the same status grouping. Most students who present themselves as reputation avoiders, self-image promoters, or self-image defenders are stayers, leavers, or returners, respectively. While the reputation avoiders (school-oriented/jocks) are unconcerned with peer ranking and seek to build their reputations in school-sanctioned ways, the self-image promoters (street-oriented/burnouts) are extremely concerned with establishing precedence within the peer group both outside and inside the school, and the self-image defenders (in-betweens) worry about defending their street-oriented reputation only when necessary.

The Stayers: Reputation Avoiders

> You see the fights. Some of them are pretty nasty, people getting thrown into a wall and windows. But as long as it isn't you or your friends, you have to move on. People start running that way and you go the other way.
>
> —Alma, a stayer

Like Alma, most stayers are reputation avoiders. That is, they stay away from potentially explosive situations by either ignoring challenges or walking away. They have mastered the art of avoiding trouble and go to great lengths to avert any confrontation. They are so successful that they rarely face challenges from peers and are mostly left alone and ignored by others. This is a result of espousing an image of reputation avoiders who do not react to peers' challenges violently. They are simply not concerned with gaining status among their peers by appearing "tough" through the use of violence or intimidation. Instead, they seek to solidify their identity as school kids.

Becoming a reputation avoider is not easy for the stayers, since it demands a conscious effort to control oneself when provoked and to avoid provoking others. Reputation avoiders cannot relax completely because they have to stay alert and on their feet to avoid escalating situations. They have to become what Anderson (1990) calls *streetwise*, that is, they learn to read "safety signals" and negotiate the school space. Although they are not street-oriented, they know the "rules" of the street and thus are able to pick out cues given by others. Because they have learned to read the subtleties of the social environment, they are able to predict and anticipate potential trouble. This ability to read the environment gives them an advantage and the opportunity to steer situations in their favor. These streetwise students used a number of strategies that enabled them to emerge unscathed from potential conflicts.

The most common way to avert trouble used by the stayers is to simply stay away from fights. If they hear about a fight going on, see a fight, or see people crowding around or running in one direction, they walk away in the opposite direction. Stayers worry that fights will escalate and get out of hand, and that spectators will be drawn into them. So by walking away, they minimize their chances of finding themselves in the middle of a fight. While the stayers dread big fights, in reality fights inside the school usually involve two students who claim that one gave the other a "dirty look" or was trying to steal a girlfriend or boyfriend. As Ana said, "Almost all of them, young girls saying, 'I'm gonna jump that girl because she looked at me this way or she called me this.'"

While these fights are relatively easy to avoid, other situations require more sophisticated measures than just walking away. One strategy employed by the stayers is to avoid being alone and defenseless. Students who are alone are more susceptible to the whim of gangs and other street-oriented groups. They are more likely to be picked on, harassed, or beaten up than are students who walk around in pairs or in groups. Miguel describes the dangers of being alone:

> Like in certain areas, like if I see a lot of rowdy guys and so, I don't feel safe. Because you never know, they might come hit you in the back of the head or something. Or something might have gone on. Like when I'm with my friends, then I don't worry. I just walk by.

Students like Miguel have every reason to fear such groups. Getting "jumped" can be serious, and can land you in the hospital. It is especially scary to get "jumped" because students believe that fights will not be fair. Like Ana says, it will not be "one on one. It's twenty-five against one or thirty against one." Many stayers minimize their chances of being caught in these situations by avoiding being alone and in isolated places in school. For this reason, these incidents are rare.

The stayers also avoid sending mixed signals that can be misinterpreted or mistaken by others as a challenge. Looks, gestures, and the way one walks convey messages to others, who react according to the meaning they attach to these actions. Streetwise stayers are particularly wary of behaviors that can be misrepresented by others. Thus, they are careful not to send mixed signals (e.g., stare at others, make "under the breath" comments). However, this is not easily done because even trivialities could be mistaken as challenges. As a result, the stayers, like Ana, are very careful of the way they move, gesticulate, and look around:

I haven't had problems. But you can't look at anybody because immediately they say, "Oh, look at her," you know, "she thinks she's
tough," and I don't like that. Because when I walk around, I don't
look at anybody, and when I look at someone, I look, you know, just
look, and immediately, "What you're looking at?" and I keep walking
because if I stay, there may be two or three to jump me.

The high visibility of gangs at Hernández High requires the use of particular strategies, especially among males. Without exception, male stayers name
the gangs as the major threat to them and talk about having been pressured
to join a gang. They recount their struggles to establish and maintain identity
as a "neutron," or one who is not affiliated with gangs although maintaining
cordial relations with their members. The stayers, such as Miguel, strive to
establish a neutron identity not only because of fear but because they abhor
gang life:

Really because I've seen too many deaths. Too many. It's like they
just act like little kids. They're giving life away. I would turn away
even more 'cause I started reading the Bible a lot and stuff. Then I
was reading about how hell is and this and that and I was like,
"Damn, look at this guys, they're just killing each other." I used to
say that if you're gonna join a gang you're just looking for your
burial, that's it.

As a result, male stayers make a conscious effort to present themselves as
neutrons. Once the neutron status is achieved, this somehow immunizes them
from further gang threats. An indication of having achieved neutron status is
when one becomes "invisible," or uniformly ignored by the gangs, as Miguel
explains: "My first year it was going a little wrong because of the gangs in
here. Then, it got okay. After a while, I started ignoring them and so they
started ignoring me. So that they don't even bother looking at me now."
While young men have different ways to achieve a neutron status, the
male stayers describe three strategies used to deal with gang recruitment and
harassment. One strategy is to maintain cordial relations with gang members
by greeting, talking, and even spending time with them but without becoming
a member. Roberto, for example, said, "I know them and I say hi to them but
nothing else." Stayers often call upon family connections and friendships in
common to fend off gang hostility. This strategy works for some stayers.
Another strategy is to join a gang but maintain a marginal affiliation. This
is more easily done by stayers who have relatives in the gang, usually an older
brother or cousin, or a close friend. Because they came into the gang under
the wing of an active member, they are able to get an "honorary" membership
that differs from regular membership. While being considered members, they

are not required to participate and are often permitted to leave the gang without undergoing a beating. Others have been "honorably discharged" from the gang. For example, Iván, who was a gang member for 6 months, received a "V-out" or violation to get out of the gang. "They were out beating me for about 3 minutes by about six people. You barely noticed 'cause none of my face was touched and there were no bruises on there."

Another creative way of dealing with gangs is the use of religion. Some stayers display outward signs of religiosity that mark them as off-limits to street-oriented peers. Traditionally, wearing rosaries and pendant crosses marked youth as "church" boys and girls, but wearing them has become so common among street kids, particularly gang members, that they are not effective markers anymore. Thus, some streetwise stayers resort to displaying more indisputable signs of religiosity, such as carrying Bibles and making them obvious for all to see. They are usually left alone, since only "church boys" carry around their Bibles. Other stayers counteract gang recruitment by trying to recruit gang members to their church. This strategy is used only by stayers who attend church regularly, especially evangelical churches, and who openly identify themselves as Christians. When gang members approach them, they begin to talk about God, proselytize, and even invite the gang members to church. Roberto uses this strategy:

> The gangs, there are many [students] that are intimidated, they let them [the gangs] intimidate them. That's why so many leave school, never finishing their education. But I don't let them intimidate me. I go on. I talk to them once in a while, I invite them to church and little by little I go on planting the seed.

Surprisingly, this usually works and the gang members back off and leave them alone. Anderson (1990) describes similar streetwise tactics consisting of unexpected answers that catch the "troublemakers" off guard, leaving them perplexed and unable to enact their scheme.

A last-resort strategy used by some stayers consists of transferring to another school when gang recruitment or harassment does not cease or escalates. For instance, two stayers transferred to Hernández High after their first semester in ninth grade in other schools because the gangs were harassing them. Instead of facing gang intimidation, they opted to change schools. One of these stayers, José, had not become streetwise and ran into trouble with gangs who mistook his naivete as an act of disrespect toward them.

> I went to [another school] but I had certain problems . . . At that time I didn't have much capacity, I mean, I had capacity but I didn't know much about gangs. And around that time I was using colors, here the gangs are divided, they are known for colors. And they started ques-

tioning me . . . Well, I knew the colors I was wearing, but I didn't think that it would be that serious. And they started questioning me like I was a criminal, and I answered back and I didn't keep my mouth shut. And then at the end of the period they surrounded me and thank God nothing happened. And I decided that not to cause trouble I decided to leave.

The use of certain strategies among the stayers does not ensure that confrontations with peers will be avoided. Reputation avoiders do everything they can to diminish problems, but this does not mean that they are safe from trouble. They must remain alert to danger, alert to differences, and alert to defend themselves, as Luis recognizes: "One of these days, I'm just scared that some gang member might bump into me and he's gonna take it out on me. In order to defend, I gotta fight." For the stayers, however, the key to avoiding getting mixed up in a fight, or in any kind of trouble, is prevention. By being streetwise, they are more successful in preventing confrontations with street kids. Establishing themselves as reputation-avoiders seems to make them invisible and assures a mostly uneventful passage through high school, and clearly marked them as school kids among their peers and teachers.

The Leavers: Self-Image Promoters

I got in a fight my freshman year, like three fights I had [that year]. But that was because I was new and I would have an attitude. "You can't tell me what to do. I'm the boss of myself." Maybe because I was real bossy. I would rule myself. I wouldn't let nobody tell me what to do, and then teachers would kick me out of my classes and everything.

—Lisa, a leaver

Some leavers are neither street-oriented or school-oriented, but fall somewhere in between. They leave school because they have grown disenchanted, are too far behind to catch up, or have personal problems that need immediate attention. However, a significant number of leavers subscribe to the street culture and become self-image promoters. They are on the offensive, or in "attack mode." That is, they do not wait to be provoked by others, but rather they initiate confrontations or jump into them at the slightest provocation. These leavers, more than the other students, are concerned about their street reputations, which they seek to keep in high standing by appearing fearless and tough individuals to "mess with." They may seek to gain respect by fighting, or by doing daring feats. Their energy is spent in elaborating and carrying out attacks on others to support and further their street reputations. For the leavers, social success is gained by measuring themselves against others. Those who are tougher, daring, and willing to fight are "respected" and climb up in the social hierarchy.

The leavers are overtly preoccupied with establishing their street reputations upon entering high school. Although not all self-image promoters are gang members, gangs provide not only a street reputation, but a peer group that will defend them when needed. This is especially crucial for many freshmen who fear entering Hernández High because they think that gangs will pick on them. As discussed in Chapter 3, the summer prior to high school entrance is a trying time for many leavers because it is when they "prepare" for high school. Worried about their impending entry into high school, many join gangs or intensify their involvement, hoping that membership will provide them with protection and a street reputation.

Gangs also offer an alternative way to achieve in school, especially among youths who are offered little or no opportunity to achieve recognition in ways sanctioned by the school. I found that the structuring of opportunities at Hernández High denies academic and social rewards and recognition to most students (see Chapter 6). Thus, many turn to the peer group for recognition. What makes the gangs singularly important to the leavers, and what makes the leavers especially drawn to gang membership, is that it is the one "extracurricular" activity they can enter and most can excel at. Joining gangs or intensifying involvement in them is the most immediate way to build a reputation in school.

Along with the gang identity comes what students call "crazy things," which help them build or solidify their street reputations. Some leavers say they "act crazy" because they want to solidify their street reputations in school. Thus, they exploit every opportunity to show off by acting defiantly in high school. Like Vitín, they fight, yell at teachers, and walk out of class without excuses. "In freshman year I was messing [up], you know, in the study room. I was telling the teacher, 'Oh, man. Up yours.'"

The obligation of being a gang member includes promoting respect for their gang. Members have to establish their reputations while at the same time protecting and defending the name of the gang. Many try to lay low and "cool down," especially when they have already been suspended for fighting, but inevitably their duty to the gang calls for their involvement in fights to restore the honor of the gang and to "back up" fellow gang members, as César explains: "In school, I laid pretty low of [not] letting people know I was in a gang. That way when we go to war with somebody I can still go to school. But that didn't end up working 'cause I'll see somebody beating up on my friends, and I would jump in." Thus, they become entangled in school fights that have less to do with their own reputations than with their gang's reputation, as in Ernesto's case: "I was in school a year and a half. I would always get into fights in school 'cause like I said I've been a gang banger since '86."

Gang membership has a high cost for many youths. Some, like César, are "jumped" by several rival gang members and risk being physically harmed while at school.

> Because at one time I was the only boy in here. And I was being chased up and down and I still came back to school. They used to try to beat me up all the time. One time I got jumped on the 7th floor by six guys and they scratched me up pretty good on my eye.

They may find themselves involved in serious injuries and in trouble with the law, as in César's case:

> That's when me and a bunch of my friends [got together to fight], 'cause I got jumped inside of Hernández. So I came back after school and I busted somebody's head with a bat and he pressed charges on me.

Staying out of trouble is virtually impossible for gang members, even for those who try not to advertise their gang membership. They constantly face challenges from other street kids, finding that they have to uphold the reputation of their gang and/or help a friend in trouble. It is their adherence to the code of the street and of the gangs that ultimately lands them in trouble at school or with the police. Yet even those street kids who are not involved in gangs find the student culture at Hernández High a constant challenge to their self-images. It pushes them to prove themselves repeatedly and to stay "on edge." As self-image promoters, they take deliberate steps to ensure that their street reputations are maintained, rather than sit and wait for trouble to arrive. Invariably, bringing to school their street-oriented attitudes is what got them in trouble in the first place. Not surprisingly, many end up suspended or expelled, or unable to continue their education because of prison sentences related to their street activities.

The Returners: Self-Image Defenders

> If you stand up to people they won't bother you no more. But if you keep like, "Oh, I'm sorry," and try to avoid things and go away they'll keep picking on you and picking on you. Like now, I have to avoid it 'cause if I fight again I won't get suspended, they'll throw me out of school . . . But, you know, I'll bring it to their attention, "Don't think that I am afraid of you 'cause I am not. You know, I just don't think you're worth it." I don't want to mess up myself 'cause some-

body else wanting to act all brave. I'll tell them, "If you wanna, meet
me outside." It's a whole different story out of school grounds.
—Diana, a returner

Some returners, like Diana, are self-image defenders who wait to be provoked to defend themselves. They quickly assess situations to decide which
ones warrant a confrontation. Unlike the leavers, who take every opportunity
to boost their street reputations, and the stayers, who avoid any confrontation,
the returners seem to occupy an in-between category, where they do not run
away from conflict but try to avert trouble. They are defensive and always
ready to restore their reputations, yet they usually manage to stay in control
of the situation. Like the self-image promoters, some returners feel pressure
to earn respect, but unlike them, they seek respect by showing "heart" and
courage only when necessary.

It is important to notice that some returners were self-image promoters
before dropping out of school. These students, like Jerry, were caught up in
their need to earn respect and establish a reputation in school by street ways.
"I think high school really did it to me. Once you come to high school, you
know, you wanna earn respect. You wanna be known by people. I guess you
only wanna go out and do some crazy stuff so you can get respect and all that."
In fact, many of these returners left school because they were suspended or
expelled due to disciplinary problems. Jerry was expelled from school because
he was involved in a fight in school with a rival gang member who "called him
names."

Yet after re-entering Hernández High, the returners refrain from actually
engaging in fights or other "crazy acts." They do not want to jeopardize their
second opportunity, especially when they left school due to disciplinary problems. They also know that the school staff keeps a close eye on them and that
they will be expelled from school at the first sign of trouble. Diana, who was
suspended early in the year for fighting, takes every precaution to avoid getting mixed up in a fight at school, because that will mean expulsion. It is
important to her to finish high school because she wants to be able to provide
for her son.

Avoiding fights or other trouble is not easy for the returners. Some have
to self-consciously hold themselves back because their instinct is to jump into
a confrontation without giving it a second thought. At times they are successful
and are able to stay out of trouble, but at other times the returners, such as
Diana, cannot contain themselves and end up fighting.

And now, well, next quarter I plan on passing. I mean, 'cause I won't
get suspended 'cause I got suspended for fighting. Which I could
have tried to avoid . . . but my nerves they got to me before anything.

It's like I just seen anger in my head and I just attacked the man and
we were fighting and everything.

The returners work hard, sometimes unsuccessfully, to avoid confrontations, and like the stayers they use a number of the same strategies. In a way,
after re-entering school, the returners begin to resemble and use the strategies
used by the reputation avoiders. Diana explains:

I don't get into no fights. I avoid arguing with people 'cause I just
mind my business. I go from class to class. You know, I talk to my
friends in between but I don't sit there and they'll be, "Oh, there's a
fight." I don't want to see the fight. I'll be like, "That's none of my
business." I stay away from it. If I'm there and they hit me or something 'cause that's what happens. When you're watching a fight, you
gotta watch 'cause you can get hit. So, I'll be like, "No, I avoid it." I
always stay away from the fights or whatever and I just go to my
classes.

However, other streetwise strategies they use are quite different from those
of the stayers. Because they have been self-image promoters in the past, they
are well versed in the code of the street, and can use their street experiences
to anticipate their peers' intentions and manipulate the situation to get out of
trouble. Although they have moved closer to the school-oriented culture upon
returning to school, they never make this change evident to their peers and
continue to display a street-oriented persona. Instead of building a name as
reputation avoiders, the returners rely heavily on their street reputations,
some of which are legendary among their peers. The most valuable asset is
that their street reputations enable them to reassert themselves without having
to actually engage in confrontations.

While their reputations usually keep others at bay, sporadic displays of
street behavior may be required to maintain their reputations. As self-image
defenders, returners do not initiate trouble but do respond violently to street-
oriented peers once in a while. For example, at the beginning of the school
year, Diana consolidated her reputation by fighting a young man and winning.
That she was willing to fight anyone, even a man, got others to back off. Diana
sent a message that while she would not initiate fights, she would beat up
anyone who dared to push her far enough. "You know, 'cause I'm not one that
I would start trouble with anybody. I don't fight to fight with people. If they
want to fight me and they hit me, then they have a fight coming back."

In addition to displaying street behavior intermittently, self-image defenders appeal to family image to back up their own reputations. Having a
family known as troublemakers, gang members, and tough fighters makes it
easier to consolidate a street reputation at school. Many people were afraid of

Diana not only because she has earned a name for fighting, but also because of her family's street reputation.

Close associations with gang members also help some returners maintain a street image. In fact, some are so close to gang members that they are mistaken as gang members even when they insist to me they are not affiliated to any gang. Having siblings, cousins, or friends who are gang members, or talking with, dating, and hanging out with gang members, elicits the assumption of membership. As the Puerto Rican saying goes, *"Díme con quien andas y te dire quien eres"* ["Tell me who you hang out with and I'll tell you who you are"]. For instance, Pablo argues that because his older brother and his friends are gang members, people falsely believe he is one, too. Yet being mistaken for gang members can be an advantage to the self-image defenders so long as they do not provoke trouble themselves.

With their self-image defender stance, the returners take an intermediate position in dealing with the dilemma of earning the respect of peers and staying out of trouble. Their past histories provide them with a street image while they secretly assume a school-oriented stance. This concealment occurs by exploiting their street images and engaging conditionally in street behavior to reinforce it. Maintaining the street reputation they have built before leaving school pays off as long as others hesitate to challenge them.

CONCLUSION

Navigating the school social environment is difficult for Hernández High School students because the street-oriented students, although a minority of the student population, have social and spatial control of the school. Although the street is one of the arenas where street reputations are built, it is in school that street kids come to control the "public space." On the streets themselves, street kids occupy a questionable and very local status. It is in the school that they can become a visible elite who readily display and command deference over a cowed majority. Thus, at Hernández, they set the standards for peer relations, forcing students to define their self-image as school kids or street kids. Which self-image students adopt determines to a large extent how they deal and negotiate with their peers, and ultimately has repercussions in the students' school careers.

To "survive" as school kids at Hernández High, students have to become streetwise, first by learning the street code and then by using this knowledge to avert compromising situations. They go through a trial-and-error period, making mistakes that place them in direct conflict with street-oriented peers. By using a number of streetwise strategies, students eventually achieve a reputation avoider image that excludes and exempts them from the street social hierarchy. These students are free to achieve in ways sanctioned by the school and to behave fully as school kids without eliciting the harassment of street-oriented peers, Ultimately, they usually succeed in school.

Students who subscribe to street culture value the street social hierarchy that exists at Hernández High. They seek to establish a street-kid reputation that requires sustained displays of street behavior. They actively seek to climb up the ladder by engaging in daring feats and acting "crazy." They become self-image promoters who initiate confrontations to boost their reputations. Although some make no direct effort to get in trouble, they end up being expelled from school because street behavior requires the avoidance of shows of deference to school authority and the constant reassertion of their reputations. Invariably, their aggressive attitude and behavior clash with school norms and eventually get them suspended or expelled from school. Even after being expelled from school, much of their time is spent on the school grounds or at its perimeter.

Some self-image promoters return to school and adopt an in-between stance, drifting between the school-oriented and the street-oriented peer cultures. However, they conceal their school orientation, presenting to their peers a street image. They switch from being self-image promoters to self-image defenders, and while still embracing a street image, they do not initiate conflict or engage in aggressive displays of street behavior. While having to behave as street kids occasionally, most self-image defenders rely on their past reputations as self-image promoters and on their family's and close friends' street reputations to reassert their images as street oriented. By pretending to be street-oriented, these returners can still claim a place in the peer social hierarchy without actually having to act on it.

CHAPTER 6

Finding a Safe Niche

Although the social environment of the school is characterized by hostility and animosity, there are many parts of school that provide students with a respite and shelter from the hallways and pervasive street culture. At Hernández High, portions of the physical and social structure allow students to sort themselves out so that they are relatively separate from the remaining student body. These students find a niche, that is, a place and corresponding social position in the school that are appropriate for them. While some niches may be informal, such as students gathering around a teacher in their free time, most are official school programs that cater to particular groups of students. Here I will focus on the four "official" niche categories that I identified at Hernández High: academic, social, athletic, and support services programs.

Finding a niche in school is important because the factors needed to develop a school-kid identity are found in these niches: they provide students with socially appropriate roles (e.g., athlete) at school that engender positive evaluations and rewards, and increase prestige and popularity among school-oriented peers and teachers. The support provided by these niches facilitates student-role performance by providing students with avenues to succeed outside of academics. They also provide students with ways to connect with school, form close relationships with teachers and peers, and develop other identities that are extensions of the student identity (e.g., athlete, club member). As a result, the school identity of many kids who participate in niches becomes dominant, increasing their likelihood of remaining in school and graduating.

Some niches are more successful than others in helping students develop dominant student identities and eventually graduate. Their "success" is due in part to the particular "clientele" they attract. Most deal with students who are highly motivated and are in good academic standing. These students are well on their way to graduation, and the niches just give them an extra push to consolidate their commitment to school. However, the support service programs are less successful in helping students develop dominant student identities because they cater to "at-risk" students, whose commitment to school is already shaky.

Perhaps the most influential factor in the success of school niches is the way these opportunities are structured. At Hernández High, there are many formal and informal constraints that limit student access to and participation in these niches. Unfortunately, many students never find a niche in school. How schools are designed, and how school programs in turn structure opportunities, place constraints on the recruitment, participation, and retention of students in extracurricular activities and school programs. The result is that the school produces and reproduces school kids by affording them opportunities to connect with school that are not accessible to street kids. Furthermore, the school also stratifies the school kids, producing different kinds of school kids according to the niches they fit into. This chapter describes the niches that exist at Hernández High, addresses the importance of niches in the development of strong connections to school, and discusses the structural limitations to widespread extracurricular participation.

NICHES AT HERNÁNDEZ HIGH SCHOOL

One major aspect of niches is that they function as "retreats" where students can segregate themselves from the physical and social world of the school. They are often the only places where students can relax and feel at ease. These niches serve as shelters that insulate, or at least lessen, the negative aspects of schooling. In this section, I describe the four distinct categories of niches at Hernández High: athletics, academics, social, and support services. Each niche produces its own kind of school kid. As a result, athletes, scholars, ROTC members, student aides, club members, and social program recipients become different types of school kids.

Athletic Programs

As a niche, the athletic programs set students physically and socially apart from the rest of the student body. The athletes have "territories" in school that are usually off limits to non-athletes. Coaches' offices and the gym are the athletes' domains, especially after school hours. They also have particular areas they claim, such as a table in the lunchroom where only athletes and a few other students are welcome to sit, the athletes' study hall, the "cage" or baseball batting practice equipment, and a computer laboratory used for study hall. As Miguel says, "The baseball players, when I go to lunch, we're all in one table."

Unlike most students, athletes have alternatives to study hall. They can attend separate study halls for athletes or practice particular skills. Coaches arrange to have their players together in a study hall and use the time to coach them in game strategies. Students in the girls' junior and varsity softball and boys' junior football teams attend a computer center run by their coach instead of study hall. The coach uses the period to require them to work on homework. After finishing their homework, the students can read newspapers or play educational computer games. Some athletes, particularly the baseball players, are required to use their study hall time to practice. Baseball players such as Miguel often use the batting cage in the school gym during study hall.

> Well, during my study time I go to the "cage" 'cause our coach wants us to. 'Cause like in the study rooms here [it] is wild. Nobody does anything. You can't study in there. People are talking all over. So he [coach] tells us, "I want you to come into the cage. I want you to come down here and get your baseball work done." 'Cause that's what's making us, that's what's making the team so good. Constantly practicing, constantly, constantly.

As a result of their distinct territories, the athletes are socially and ethnically segregated and form very close-knit groups according to sport. It is unusual to see athletes interacting even with members of the other teams, with the exception of a core group of athletes. The core are male and female students who participate in the "principal" sports at the school, that is, sports that have a following among the students. The dates and times of their games were broadcast over the loudspeaker, and generated the largest crowds to attend athletic events at the school. The core boys play football or baseball, and often both. The core girls play volleyball, basketball, or softball, or are cheerleaders. These are the most visible of the athletic groups in the school, and they hang out together, rarely allowing outsiders into the group. This core group is composed mostly of Puerto Ricans and other students from the Caribbean, such as Dominicans and Cubans.

There are secondary sports at Hernández High: boys' soccer and boys' basketball. Not coincidentally, these are the sports that are identified with particular ethnic groups, and while they do not appeal to the larger Puerto Rican population, they do have a following among particular ethnic groups who attend their games. The soccer team is made up of bilingual students, usually Mexicans and Central Americans (Guatemalan, Honduran, El Salvadoran). Basketball players are mostly African Americans. In addition, there are small pockets of athletes who participate in "minor" sports at Hernández High, such as swimming and bowling. They have no following among the students, and no one attends their athletic meets.

Social Programs

Many students find their niche in one of the 20 or so student organizations, social clubs, and student government groups. The organizations also have a "territory," a meeting room, usually their teacher-sponsor's classroom when classes are not in session. A few organizations, like the Chess Club, whose members comprise the academic elite of the school, have permanent meeting rooms; however, most organizations are granted exclusive use of unoccupied classrooms for the time of their meetings.

Like the athletes, many students use study hall to carry out their club activities. They hold meetings and organize and staff many club activities, such as bake sales. They also make possible many schoolwide events by doing the groundwork—fundraising and decorating rooms for events, such as the home-coming dance. They could be seen in the halls selling t-shirts, raffle tickets, homecoming dance tickets, and yearbooks. Some clubs serve as public rela-tions representatives, hosts, and school guides for visitors. In addition, many club members run errands for their sponsor during study hall.

Some students find their niche as student aides. These are paid positions that range from clerical workers to teacher's aide. Most student aides work during their study hall at the main office, a computer lab, the library, or art/wood workshop. They are usually selected by the counselors or teachers. Among the participants in this study, two worked in the Book Room (where textbooks are stored and distributed to students), one in a computer lab, one in the gym, and one in the wood shop. While student aides are usually paid for their work, some students become informal student aides who work for their teachers without pay. Except for money, these informal student aides receive the benefits afforded to student aides.

Student aides gain work experience while working closely with adults who usually become their advocates. They often work with other students with whom they develop friendships. Their work gives them access to places in school from which other students are excluded, such as the teachers' offices. For instance, Vanessa, a student aide for a physical education teacher, has access to the teacher's office and telephone. She can make calls without having to go to the pay phone or asking the teacher for permission. Undoubtedly, being a student aide separates students, both socially and physically, from the general student population.

Academic Programs

While academic programs concentrate on intellectual activities, they are also niches that offer students a sense of community. At Hernández High, there are four academic programs that serve as niches for students: the scholars program, the bilingual program, the ROTC, and the Café.

Scholars Program. The honors program at Hernández High School is called the Scholars Program. It is a small group of approximately 35 students per grade level and comprised 11% of the graduating class of 1993. Scholars are recruited for the program because of their outstanding grades and aca-demic potential and must maintain good standing to remain a scholar. According to the *Students and Parents Handbook* (Hernández High School, 1993), "College bound students who are committed to getting a good education and being involved in the Program's activities (i.e. Saturday meetings and summer programs) may join. The classes are honor level." The program provides the scholars with a community, as well as opportunities for extracurricular participation. The program separates the scholars physically and socially from the rest of the school by placing them in honors and Advanced Placement courses in English, social studies, sciences, and mathematics. Although these classes consist mostly of scholars, students in the general education program can take them if they qualify for Advanced Placement in a particular subject. The scholars take physical education and elective courses (such as art and music) with the general education students.

Because they are college-bound, scholars take a heavy class load that focuses on college preparatory courses. Many of their classes, especially English and science, involve field trips to theaters and local museums that are not part of the general education courses. They can also participate in the Saturday College program at a local university. Its goal is to improve the scholars' skills in math and science and to introduce them to careers in these fields. Undoubtedly, this program provides exceptional educational experiences for the scholars that are unavailable to the rest of the students, like the one Lydia described:

> It's like classes [where] every couple of weeks the topic changes. One time we worked on cadavers. We were studying body organs and we went to see them. The smell was so bad that some people couldn't go in. I went in and I was not afraid. The cadavers were already cut opened. They are used by medicine students.

The Scholars Program also involves formal and informal extracurricular activities. The formal activities include the academic and social clubs that require high academic standing or scholar status to become a member. For instance, the Anchor Club was limited to female scholars, while the Key Club was open to all scholars.

As a result of the unique opportunities open to the scholars, they become a tight-knit group separate from the rest of the students. Since they spend so much time together in the classroom and in activities related to the Scholars Program, they also become friends. These friendships often extend outside the school. Some of the scholars told me that they met on Wednesday nights at the local library to study, but somehow I got the impression that their weekly meetings are not entirely about studying. Although an academic program, the small size of the Scholars Program allows it to function like an informal social club, with nonacademic activities. According to Marta, the program "pays off because you get to go to a lot of picnics, everybody is together."

The scholars' social segregation is accompanied by their being considered "smart" by others and their own perception of being "better" than the remaining students. These perceptions perpetuate the differences that separate the scholars from other students. Elizabeth says,

> You could say they [non-scholars] call us nerds because we are in scholars. They separate us. You're [non-scholars] *por cortar* [into cutting], you are like the bad people. You've got the honor students and usually scholars I see hang out with those that have the same aspirations. They associate with other people. Don't get me wrong, but I think that they hang around people that have the same aspirations.

Bilingual Program. Another niche that physically and socially segregates students from the rest of the student population is the bilingual program, which serves the Spanish-speaking and Vietnamese students. Both bilingual programs occupy particular spaces in the school, with the large Spanish bilingual program occupying a whole floor of the school, while the smaller Vietnamese program is housed in one classroom. Bilingual students have virtually no contact with the other students. They are segregated not only because they are physically contained, but because they do not take classes with the rest of the students. With the exception of a few elective courses, the bilingual students generally do not associate with students outside of their program.

The bilingual students are so socially isolated that they seldom participate in extracurricular activities, with the exception of the soccer team, the Spanish Club, and the ASPIRA Club (sponsored by a non-for-profit organization committed to leadership development and education of Puerto Rican and Latino youth). The bilingual students' lack of participation in the extracurricular programs is probably due to the language barrier: Most extracurricular programs are run in English and by English-speaking teachers. During the year I spent at the school, the bilingual students had begun to increase their participation in school activities. An elective class on Fine Arts was developed in the school's cultural center and drew many bilingual students. As a result, they participated in dance performances, plays, and art exhibits in the school.

ROTC Program. Many people, including myself, are surprised to find out that Hernández High has an ROTC program. The ROTC has become a niche for many students who seek spatial, social, and temporal shelter. It has a defined "territory" at Hernández, with offices and classrooms. The territory is marked by posters that display the ROTC logo. Because it has a physical setting, students often retreat there for their study hall.

Members of the ROTC spend a lot of time together, and work closely with their ROTC instructors. They come to school at 6:30 for exercises and then have breakfast together in the lunchroom at 7:40 A.M. They also take the daily ROTC class. Initially, many are attracted to ROTC because they plan to join the military upon graduation or want to avoid physical education. Although many students leave ROTC after a semester or year, those who stay become part of a very tight-knit group. They also become very committed to the ROTC. Several of the students I interviewed participated in the ROTC, at least for a semester.

Hernández High's ROTC is among the top ROTC programs in the city, earning many distinctions and awards in competitions. The students who participate in ROTC, like Alma, gain a great deal of satisfaction from representing the school and doing it well: "Like my sophomore year I went to drill competition, that is like marching and we went to city competition and came out second [out of] thirty schools in the city." Besides the thrill of competition and winning, the ROTC develops leadership among its participants and breaks many gender stereotypes. At Hernández High, the highest-ranking student was a young woman. Also, according to the sergeant, the best "shooters" are women because they have steady and firm hands, and more patience to practice developing their skills.

Many students take ROTC out of curiosity, parental pressure, or as an alternative to physical education. Elizabeth told me that she enrolled in the ROTC because her stepmother insisted she do so. Elizabeth did not mind trying it out, especially because it was a way out of taking physical education. Later, Elizabeth found other benefits to staying in the ROTC. She thinks that it will look good on her college applications, and she also got caught up in the thrill of competition.

> Because I thought that if they look at your transcripts and later they
> see that you moved from ROTC to gym they're gonna say, "She prob-
> ably couldn't hack it." And I was like, "I don't think that looks good."
> So I stayed there. I like going to compete and winning. And different
> activities that we do, parades and all that.

The Café. Another academic niche is the Café, which consists of a small "restaurant" that caters to faculty and staff. It is part of the Food Service program, but it is restricted to advanced students. The Café provides a state-of-the-art kitchen where students are trained in food preparation. It gives the students an opportunity to succeed outside of classroom, and often to earn some money on the side. The Café has a catering business that supplies food, mostly appetizers and desserts, within the school and occasionally to outside activities. The students prepare the food and serve it, for which they get paid. In addition to the catering business, the students, such as Manuel, are placed in jobs in downtown hotels and restaurants.

> I got interested in cooking my second year. And I took all three years
> of food services and I'm working downtown. I work at [a restaurant]

> on Michigan [Avenue] in the 25th floor. It's beautiful. It's like for
> members only. Like big rich people. I work mostly cooking. I get
> $7.50 an hour. That's pretty good.

In addition to his restaurant job, Manuel, who specializes in desserts, has a
side business at home as a result of his learning to bake and decorate cakes
at school.

> I love cooking 'cause I like to work with my hands. I hate to be still
> writing. I'd rather just create 'cause I love decorating. I do cakes. I
> sell them for $35, $40. I do two-floor cakes sometimes. They want
> like more or long ones. They come out nice. I just bake them at
> home and send them to them and they pay me.

Support Service Programs

Support service programs provide assistance to students who have been identified as at-risk. These programs provide a space for students to gather as well
as a sense of community that makes them feel that they have a place in school.
At Hernández High, there are two support service programs: the Teenage
Parents' Program and Youth At-Risk.

Teenage Parents' Program. Few people refer to the Teenage Parents'
Program by its name, preferring to use the name of its coordinator, Teresa.
Teresa is an affectionate and strong woman who wins the hearts and trust of
many girls who have children or find themselves pregnant. Teresa's room
offers more than social services for the girls. In addition to being a place
where students are helped to sign up for public aid and prenatal care, and to
sort out many of their family and personal problems, Teresa's room is a gathering place for the students, who come there during their study and lunch
periods.

In Teresa's room, the girls find a niche that offers them a physical and
social shelter to which they can retreat. It is off limits to students other than
those enrolled in the program, especially boys, who are rarely allowed in the
room. Although boys can sign up for the program if they are prospective
fathers or have children, only two boys have enrolled. One hung out in Teresa's room with his pregnant girlfriend. The other came around only when he
needed Teresa to solve a problem. The girls, then, have the room largely to
themselves. There they are free to talk about "women's things," such as pregnancy, labor, and raising children. They also talk about their relationships with
boys and give advice to each other. Although most of the girls do not know
each other before enrolling in the program, they become friends as they spend
time together talking about intimate issues. Yet their friendships usually

remain within the program, and few interact with each other outside the room.

The girls especially seek refuge in Teresa's room when big fights erupt in school. I observed them rushing in when there was a threat of a fight or fighting had already started. They usually stay there until the trouble settles down, after which Teresa escorts them to their next class, or they use the phone to call parents and boyfriends to come and pick them up. Without a doubt, Teresa's room is a shelter to which these students can retreat, where they feel nurtured and safe.

Youth At-Risk. A social service program that provides group and individual counseling to students, Youth At-Risk serves the special education students and others who are referred there because they are experiencing academic or disciplinary difficulties. Although students can walk in and request services, usually they are referred by teachers or staff members. According to the coordinator, the program provides services to over 1,000 students, but only about 250 receive long-term individual counseling. Of these, 40 students claim it as their niche. For these students, Youth At-Risk has become a socially and physically segregated place where they can go to during study hall. The students congregate in the program's office or in an adjacent room used by the program. There they talk to social workers or to one another. What is important about Youth At-Risk is that the students feel safe there. They often go there when there are gang fights, just to get away from the commotion in the hallways; Youth At-Risk is a "safe haven."

THE SIGNIFICANCE OF EXTRACURRICULAR PARTICIPATION

The extracurricular activities, they help keep some of the kids in school.

—Lydia, a stayer

There is no question that extracurricular participation engenders many benefits for students, and at Hernández High this is no exception. During my field work, I found that most niches have extracurricular components that play a crucial role in shaping the experiences and educational achievement of students at Hernández High. My findings suggest that extracurricular participation and student retention are closely linked. The students who are involved in extracurricular programs have lower drop-out rates than those who do not participate. I found sharp discrepancies in the rates of extracurricular participation among the three categories of students (stayers, leavers, and returners). The stayers disproportionately participate in extracurricular activities throughout their high school years, while the leavers and the returners seldom do. In my sample of 33 individuals, extracurricular participation among the stayers is 85%, in comparison with 20% among the leavers and 40% among the returners. These rates reflect participation since their freshman year, showing that the stayers consistently participate at a higher rate than the other groups.

There are also other differences among these groups. The stayers' participation includes the complete range of activities at the school (e.g., intellectual, athletics, academic clubs, social clubs, professional clubs), while the leavers' and returners' participation is limited to athletics and academic clubs. The only returner who participated in athletics had been cut from the team because of poor grades, whereas the leavers and returners who participate in academic clubs do so only because they are enrolled in a class with an extracurricular component, such as band. Another difference between these status groups rests in the number of activities they participate in. The stayers participate in at least one activity, and most of them participate in three or more activities for more than one school year. In one case, a stayer participated in 13 extracurricular activities in her senior year! By contrast, the leavers and returners often participated in none.

These findings support previous studies that assert that students who participate in extracurricular activities are less likely to drop out of school (Mahoney & Cairns, 1997; McNeal, 1995; Tinto, 1975). Mahoney and Cairns (1997) found that the drop-out rate was lower among at-risk students who had participated in extracurricular activities. McNeal's (1995) research adds that not all extracurricular activities affect student retention to the same extent, with participation in athletics and fine arts programs most likely to reduce the likelihood of dropping out. My findings suggest that it is not participation per se that has a positive effect on student retention at Hernández High, but the many benefits students accrue as a result of participating. These students become attached to school, develop close relationships with adults, are academic and nonacademic achievers, are popular, and enjoy school.

Some studies show that participation in extracurricular programs causes students to take on school norms and expectations, and that students who are involved in these activities exhibit pro-social behavior, value school goals, and comply with school norms (Finn, 1989; Hanks & Eckland, 1976). Although some studies find no relationship between participation and grades (Hanks & Eckland, 1976; Melnick, Sabo, & Vanfossen, 1992), more recent studies suggest that extracurricular participation also has a positive effect on school performance (Gerber, 1996; Phillips & Schafer, 1971; Silliken & Quirk, 1997). At Hernández High, I found that students who participate in extracurricular activities seem to comply more readily with school norms. They have lower absentee and tardiness rates and a lower incidence of trouble with peers and staff than those who do not participate. They also maintain good academic standing. Their cumulative grade point average ranged from 3.77 to 2.62, and all ranked within the top 35% of their graduating class (Flores-González, 1995, 2000).

Perhaps adherence to school norms, goals, and expectations is a consequence of the attachment to school that results from participating in extracurricular programs. Students who participate in these activities come to identify with the school, and its norms and expectations, because they see themselves as part of the school environment and school as part of themselves (Finn, 1989). Furthermore, participation fosters the development of other school-related identities (e.g., athlete) besides the student identity (Snyder & Spreitzer, 1992). This is consistent with what I found at Hernández High, where participants in extracurricular activities exhibit other school-related identities that are an integral part of their student identity. Eventually, the student identity is not only about attending school but also about participating in school activities. For these students, extracurricular participation becomes an essential part of being a student to the extent that it is difficult for them to separate their role as student from that of a participant. For them, it is impossible to draw a line between these two identities, as one is dependent on the other. As pointed out earlier, the extracurricular programs at Hernández High function as mini-societies within the larger school, helping students built a sense of community. They constitute a society that becomes a group of reference. Students gain a social network consisting of peers and often sponsors, teachers or staff who supervise these groups. They foster the growth of school-based friendships among students, making school not only a place of learning but also a place to meet with friends, as Marta explains:

> They're [extracurricular activities] like really helpful in the way that you meet people and you get memories . . . We're like together . . . You're with the same people. Some people say that [school] is boring but not me because I like to learn more about people . . . Knowing people is really good. I used to have friends but not as many as after being in scholars.

In addition, extracurricular activities provide Hernández High's students with individualized or small-group attention from adults. Club or program sponsors and coaches develop close and nurturing relationships with the students. They often encourage students to take school seriously, and offer unsolicited, but constructive, advice to students. Because they have gained the students' trust, sponsors can demand good school performance from the students. Ana, a stayer who has a very close relationship with her softball coach, said,

> She is not interested in sports that much. She wants you to get an education. I love that teacher so much, it's pitiful. She is not interested in

sports, she coaches but she doesn't push it. "You've got to play for
me." If she has to choose between sports and study, she chooses
study. Because you can be the best player, but if you are failing a
class, she makes you quit and take that class. That's what I like about
her. She is not like other coaches in the school that say, "Well, you
have to play for me." No, she is not like that. She knows that you
have a future, and she thinks you have to do your work and she
makes you go. And that's what I like about her.

Dreeben (1968) adds that extracurricular activities provide a break from
the evaluative character of classroom work because they take place outside
the classroom. They also provide an alternative route to achievement for students who are not high academic achievers (Finn, 1989; Murtaugh, 1988). By
having the opportunity to excel outside the classroom, these students develop
a sense of accomplishment and self-esteem (Garbarino, 1980; Murtaugh,
1988). According to Kinney (1993), students who participate in extracurricular
activities develop a more positive personal identity. At Hernández High,
involvement in these programs often brings recognition and reward to the
students. According to Lydia, when participating "you also are recognized.
Like you get a pat in the back and it makes you look forward to more things."
Getting a "pat in the back" is particularly meaningful for students who do not
do well academically and have low self-esteem.

Participation in extracurricular programs also provides social recognition
and prestige to students in the social stratification system of the school
(Hanks & Eckland, 1976; Murtaugh, 1988; Snyder & Spreitzer, 1992). It increases the participants' standing and popularity among peers. Well-known
students are usually those involved in extracurricular activities, especially the
athletes (Goldberg & Chandler, 1989). Because participants are recognized by
others, they enjoy sociopsychological benefits that enhance their self-concept
(Ornstein, 1990). Hernández High is no exception to the rule, as those students who participate in extracurricular activities are also the most popular in
school, as Vanessa points out:

Everyone is like known. Like all the scholars are known. Like I'm in
scholars, they know I'm in scholars. Like my girlfriend she is in all
the athletics. They know who she is because she is in the athletics.
They know the football players because they're in football. It's the
season. If it's the season for football, football is more popular. If it's
the season for basketball, basketball. The most popular people are
the people who are in activities, extracurricular activities. Because if
you are in extracurricular activities you have a bigger chance of people knowing you.

According to the students I interviewed, participation in the extracurricular diminishes the monotony of school life and makes school more interesting and fun. Alma, a stayer who participates in many extracurricular activities and is also a member of the ROTC, said, "If you join clubs and join ROTC, or whatever, you'll have fun. School is not boring if you make it." Even those who temporarily dropped out of school experienced school differently after returning because they joined extracurricular programs. Manuel, a returner, said, "I really left 'cause like the school, it was boring. I wasn't in no sports. There was nothing going on." After returning to school and joining various athletic programs, Manuel's school experience changed significantly.

> I used to be on the tumbling team, the acrobats. They stopped . . . Then the swim team wanted me here but I left them. I don't like swimming for the school. They're slow. I can beat them, and I'm not in the swimming team! I'll race the swimmer, one of the swimmers, and I'll beat him. 'Cause I used to swim for the park when I was a boy. I've got a lot of medals for swimming and tumbling.

Manuel's involvement with the tumbling team was short-lived, but he went on to join the football team and continued to bask in the fact that he was too good for the swimming team.

By contrast, students who do not participate in extracurricular activities expressed to me feelings of alienation from school. Those who do not participate in extracurricular activities also said that they do not like school and feel disconnected from school and peers, and many eventually dropped out. Being temporarily out of school or absent too frequently aggravates these feelings of alienation. As Lourdes, a returner, explains:

> And it's already hard enough for me to fit in here, not just to fit in, it's just sometimes I feel like I don't belong or something like that. It's just that lately I haven't been talking to a lot of friends. It's not that I miss them or anything but it's just there are a lot of people that like to talk to me but sometimes I don't want to talk to them. And sometimes they don't wanna talk to me. And since I've been away from school for so long, I feel like I don't belong.

CONSTRAINTS ON EXTRACURRICULAR PARTICIPATION

With all the benefits of extracurricular participation, it would make sense for schools to encourage widespread participation, especially among students who have marginal attachment to school. As I have pointed out, extracurricular participation can transform the schooling experience by making school much more than a place for academic learning. Its benefits spread to the classroom, helping students develop academic, physical, and social skills. Unfortunately, schools have often structured extracurricular participation in a way that not only discourages, but effectively denies most students the opportunity to participate. According to Davison Aviles, Guerrero, Howarth, and Thomas (1999), Latino students report encountering barriers to participation in school activities and were often discouraged from participating. The four main factors that constrain widespread student participation at Hernández High are limited funds, school size, participation criteria, and limited access to extracurricular activities.

Limited Funding

Hernández High is typical of underfunded inner-city schools. It has many extracurricular programs, but they are not funded adequately. Many sponsors of clubs volunteer their time and are not paid to coordinate the activities, and students have to raise money to fund their activities. Fundraisers are limited to selling small items, such as candy and taffy apples, in the school's hallways. Although all extracurricular programs at Hernández High are generally underfunded, this is more noticeable in the athletic programs. One major problem is the dismal state of the school's football/baseball field. The ground is so uneven that home games cannot be played at the school's field, and students cannot use the field to practice for fear of injury. In addition, funding is so scarce that athletes often have to drive themselves, take a ride, or rely on public transportation to travel to their games because the school does not have the money to pay for a bus. A side effect of the lack of funding is that the general student population does not have the opportunity to participate as spectators for their school teams, even at "home" games.

School Size

In large high schools, those with student populations of over 700, students have fewer opportunities to participate in extracurricular activities. Coladarci and Cobb (1996) report higher rates of extracurricular participation among students in schools with less than 800 students, and lower rates of participation in school with more than 1,600 students. The larger the school, the more negative its effects on student satisfaction, attendance, identification with school, and behavior (Fowler & Walberg, 1991; Ornstein, 1990). According to Ornstein (1990):

> A school is considered too large when a loss of personal or school identity among students occurs; they are unable to fully participate in

social and athletic activities or have difficulty interacting among themselves or feel they do not belong to the student body or school in general. (p. 239)

Although large schools have more extracurricular programs than smaller
schools, they also have more people competing for slots in these programs
(Barker & Gump, 1964; Morgan & Alwin, 1980). In the large schools, average
students, those who are not exceptionally talented, are easily overlooked
(Ornstein, 1990). Because there are fewer students in the smaller schools,
even marginally talented students are needed and encouraged to fill the slots
in the extracurricular programs (Barker & Gump, 1964). As a result, students
in smaller schools participate more often and in a greater variety of extracurricular activities than students in large schools (Barker & Gump, 1964; Pittman & Haughwout, 1987).

Although participating in extracurricular programs fosters connections to
school, only a limited number of students engage in these activities at Hernández High. An examination of extracurricular participation at Hernández High
for 4 academic years yielded similar results (see Flores-González, 1995;
Quiroz, 1993; Quiroz, Flores-González, & Frank, 1996). These studies found
that there are slots in the extracurricular programs for 25% of the student
population. That is, 650 slots are open for a student population of 2,600. However, in 1992–93, only 19% of students, or 494 students, actually participated
in these programs. This disparity is due to students' participation in more than
one extracurricular activity. As a result, 2,106 students did not participate in
extracurricular activities!

I found that at Hernández High the participation rate varies by grade
level. Among those who participated during 1992–93, 19% were freshmen,
25% sophomores, 29% juniors, and 27% seniors. This gives the impression
that participation is spread out rather equally throughout the grade levels. Yet
because each cohort has a different size, due to high rates of drop-out and
grade repetition, participation is not equally distributed throughout the grade
levels. In fact, during 1992–93, there were 714 freshmen, 727 sophomores,
852 juniors, and 298 seniors in the school. Looking at the rate of participation
in each grade level, a disproportionate number of the seniors participate compared to other cohorts: 13% of the freshmen, 17% of the sophomores, 17%
of the juniors, and 44% of the seniors. This is more striking when taking into
consideration that the senior class is only 11.5% of the student population.
The pattern of increasing rates of extracurricular participation throughout the
years suggests that there may be a connection between participating and staying in school. In fact, most of the stayers told me that they had been involved
in extracurricular programs prior to their senior year. Thus, the high participation rate among seniors appears to have more to do with the higher retention
of students who participate in extracurricular programs than to an increase in

participation during the senior year. Although it may seem that the stayers monopolize most openings in the extracurricular programs, it is the way the school structures extracurricular opportunities that limits access of other students to extracurricular programs.

Participation Criteria at Hernández High

Extracurricular programs are viewed as open systems where everyone has an equal chance to participate. In reality, schools place many constraints that curtail widespread student participation. Extracurricular participation is seen as a privilege and not a right. To be eligible for participation, students have to meet certain requirements. At Hernández High, grades, enrollment in classes, and skill level were the "objective" criteria used to admit students to the extracurricular programs.

Grades. At Hernández High, the main criterion for participation is grades. Although some studies find no relationship between extracurricular participation and grades (Hanks & Eckland, 1976; Melnick, Sabo, & Vanfossen, 1992), in most schools grades are used as a prerequisite for participation. Grade requirements, popularly known as the "no pass/no play" rule or the "C-average" policy, normally require students to pass all their classes or maintain a grade point average of 2.0 (Bland, 1990; O'Reilly, 1992). Diana notes, "I wanted to be in the Pom Pons team, but since I had F's, you can't be in no [extracurricular] program unless you have a C average or better. And since I had two F's I couldn't try out. That's the only thing I would be interested in." Not only are students who fail to obtain good grades denied entry into extracurricular programs, but participants are expelled from programs if their grades deteriorate below a C grade point average. Jerry, a returner, said, "I used to play basketball, actually I played for two years. I played baseball but I got cut because [of] my grades. That's about the only two sports I was playing."

Enrollment in Classes/Programs. While some students seek to participate in extracurricular activities, many students end up in them incidentally. This happens while taking classes or enrolling in academic programs that have extracurricular components. Extracurricular activities, such as the physics club, choir, band, and ROTC, are restricted to students enrolled in these particular classes. Students receive credit for taking the classes and at the same time take part in extracurricular programs. Not all students enroll in these courses because they are interested in them. Many enroll to fulfill graduation requirements, or simply to avoid other classes. As I noted earlier, many students enroll in ROTC not because of interest, but as an alternative to physical education. Most students enroll in classes such as band or choir just because they have to complete a number of credits in the various subject areas. Diana, a returner, explained, "I was in band but that's because it was my music credit. Otherwise, I wouldn't have been." While some students come to enjoy these classes because of the extracurricular components, many complain that the diversity of students with different interests and at different skill levels makes these classes slow and boring.

Other extracurricular activities require membership in specific academic programs. For example, members of the Anchor and Key clubs have to be enrolled in the Scholars Program. Some activities heavily recruit from particular academic programs, although participation is not restricted to these programs. For example, although the New Americans and the Spanish clubs are heavily populated by students from the bilingual program, other students could also participate but often do not.

Skills. Some extracurricular programs require a minimum skill level for admission. These are more notably the sports programs, for which students have to compete with other students for the limited slots on the teams. One would assume that in a school like Hernández High, with 2,600 students, competition would be fierce. Yet few students actually go to the tryouts, and none of the students I interviewed said they had been rejected because of competition. Rejection is usually the result of not having the required grade point average. In other programs, such as advanced band and advanced choir, skill level is not always strictly enforced. Because students at different skill levels are bunched together in these classes, those with advanced skills eventually lose interest because the class becomes too elementary for them. For instance, Ana, a stayer who has played the clarinet since elementary school, eventually became utterly bored with band because she was required to play simple pieces that her less skilled peers could play:

> I like playing, I just don't like the band . . . He [teacher] gives us music for little kids, tutututu. I don't like that. I tell him to pick this and this and this. [He says] "No, it's too hard for all of you." We should be knowing how to play it.

Informal Restrictions

While the structural requirements for participation give the impression that the extracurricular program is fair and that anyone who meets the "objective" criteria (grades, class enrollment, and skills) is eligible, I found that other "informal" factors make competition for extracurricular activities an unfair and unequal system in which most students do not stand a chance. There are subtleties in the extracurricular system of which some students are unaware but that restrict access to extracurricular opportunities. These informal con-

straints include access to information about extracurricular opportunities, recruitment into programs, and the peer group.

Access to information is a valuable yet scarce resource at Hernández
High, where many students do not find out about extracurricular opportunities. Opportunities to join are rarely announced publicly through the school
loudspeaker, newsletters, or fliers. Consequently, most students are not aware
of application deadlines or tryouts. Even when announcements are made over
the loudspeaker system, many students simply cannot hear them because of
malfunctioning loudspeakers in their classrooms. In addition, few teachers
bother to make announcements to their students.

Another vehicle for disseminating information about school activities is
the school newsletter. However, at Hernández High there are several problems with the school newsletter. The schoolwide newsletter is published
sporadically; thus, many events are not announced in it. In addition, its distribution is disorganized. Nobody knows when the next issue will be out, and
not everyone receives a copy. To make matters worse, the newsletter often
announces events that have already happened or with too short notice for
students to be able to make arrangements to attend. Another problem with
the newsletter is that smaller groups within the school have their own newsletters, which only adds to the confusion of where to find and post information.

Flyers are often used to post information about athletic team tryouts
or other extracurricular program deadlines. However, there is no centralized
bulletin board where school announcements can be posted. Thus, fliers are
posted on walls throughout the school, yet few students notice them, and, if
they notice, they do not have the time to read them. In a school with 2,600
students, the halls are packed during class changes, and it is impossible for a
student to stand and read a flyer while other students are pushing and the
hall monitors are telling them to keep moving.

Recruitment into extracurricular programs is not made on an equal opportunity basis because at Hernández High students are selectively recruited
into them. Many students are recruited into extracurricular activities by teachers and the sponsors of the activities. Teachers inform particular students
about opportunities and often ask them to join activities that they sponsor. For
instance, Lydia, a stayer, participated in Future Business Leaders of America
because the teacher asked her to join, since a certain number of students were
necessary to obtain funding.

Students are also recruited into academic programs by teachers and
counselors, especially into the Scholars Program. Many scholars are recruited
by high school counselors while they are still in eighth grade. Selection is
based on their high grades and exam scores. Other scholars are recruited after
their freshman year because of outstanding performance in their classes, as
Marta, a stayer, told me:

My freshman year I was doing real good and my division [home room] teacher was like, "You've got to get into honors classes. That's really good for you." I was like, "No, 'cause I'm gonna mess up." So sophomore year, my other division teacher was like, "You gotta get in, you gotta get in." So when I went to pick my classes for junior year, my counselor was like, "You wanna get in?" I'm like, "Man, everybody is telling me about it, but I don't want to 'cause I'm gonna mess up." And she said, "No, with your brain and your intelligence and your accurateness and everything. You're not gonna mess up if you put your head set on it." So she got me in, and that's how it started.

As Marta's quote conveys, sometimes teachers and counselors are adamant in recruiting students into their extracurricular programs. They continue to insist until they convince the student to join. Of course, recruitment is very selective, since the teachers and counselors encourage only the "good" kids to join these programs. That is, students who are asked to join tend to be good students who do not cause any trouble. Students perceived to be troublemakers are simply not asked to join.

Some students join extracurricular programs because a friend persuades them to participate, or they simply want to be with their friends. For instance, Elizabeth became a scholar because her friends, who are scholars, pressured her to join, and because she asked a counselor to let her in.

Since sophomore year I always took honor classes and I was with them [scholars] always . . . [My scholar friends would say] "Go do it" and I did. Because they were all scholars, only like three of them were not scholars, and I would go to the meetings . . . So I talked to the counselor . . . and she said, "Elizabeth, you have to come to my office. You have to sign these papers." And it was for that. And that's how I got in.

As in the example above, students tend to participate in extracurricular programs where their peers concentrate. Students seldom venture into extracurricular programs on their own.

At Hernández High, the student stratification system usually dictates which extracurricular activities are permissible for each individual. This is most noticeable in the "main sports" at the school. Athletes, particularly those in the main sports like girls' volleyball, girls' softball, boys' football, and boys' baseball, tend to hang out together and are highly visible in school. They constitute an elite clique within the school that monopolizes and seems to control participation in teams. Many participate in more than one sport. For instance, Ana, a stayer, plays volleyball, basketball, and softball. The cliquish nature of the sports culture at Hernández High and such control over the main sports programs may deter other students from participating more than the actual "official" requirements.

The cliquish nature of sports at Hernández High is also evident in the ethnic composition of the athletic programs, especially in the boys' teams. As pointed out earlier, Puerto Ricans and other Caribbeans (Dominicans and Cubans) dominate the "main sports" of football and baseball. African American students, both boys and girls, are usually found on the basketball teams, while students of Mexican and Central American origin (Guatemala, Honduras, El Salvador, and Nicaragua) make up the boys' soccer team.

Because peer groups tend to form among students in the same academic tracks and programs, it is not surprising that students from the same academic track or program tend to concentrate in particular extracurricular activities. According to Quiroz, Flores-González, and Frank (1996), educational tracking lets schools structure the educational experiences of students, and provides them with different opportunities, including extracurricular opportunities.

CONCLUSION

It is easy for students to "get lost" and feel they are not part of the school in large schools like Hernández High. Feelings of isolation are further exacerbated by the hostile social environment they find there and the lack of safe places in school. While there are some niches to which students can retreat, the reality of Hernández High is that far too few students are able to find a niche there. There are many institutional constraints that discourage and even prevent most students from finding one.

Research shows that finding a niche, and specifically participating in extracurricular programs, provides many benefits to students. Among these benefits is the increase in retention found among those who participate. At Hernández High, I found that those who participate in extracurricular activities are more likely to stay in school and graduate because they build dominant student identities, in part due to their participation in the extracurricular programs. The building of dominant student identities is aided by the socially appropriate roles that emerge from participation, and the positive evaluations, rewards, and increased prestige and popularity among school-oriented peers and teachers.

It is commonly believed that interest is the driving force behind extracurricular participation, that is, that students who are interested in extracurricular activities join these programs. Yet, far from being an open system where students match themselves to programs according to interests and skills, extracurricular programs tend to be closed programs that through several mechanisms limit participation to a selected group of students. Thus, participation is not an option for many students, if not the majority of students. Many factors combine to limit opportunities for participation in the extracurricular programs. As Quiroz, Flores-González, and Frank (1996) argue, these opportunities are often structured and determined by the school in its sorting of students into different tracks and programs. Structural factors such as the available slots, grade or skill requirements, access to information, and recruitment strategies deny the majority of students at Hernández High a chance to even be considered for participation.

CHAPTER 7

From School Kids to Graduates

What is crucial to staying in Hernández High and graduating, and what all stayers have in common, is the forging of a school-kid identity that enables them to persist in school. Yet, as I have shown in the preceding chapters, becoming school kids is not easy at Hernández High. The complexities of life among racial and ethnic minorities, particularly among those who are low-income, are such that the conditions necessary for the development of a dominant student identity are often absent. Students at Hernández High have ample opportunities for, and are often driven into, taking on identities that conflict with being a student. The media and community imagine students who attend schools like Hernández High as only street kids bent on raising havoc at school. More directly, some teachers and administrators share these views and treat students accordingly. Yet many students at Hernández High become school kids, students who are into school, cause no trouble, obtain decent grades, and are well integrated into school life. These students persevere against exceptional obstacles, usually completing high school in 4 years and graduating without ever interrupting their education.

Earlier I showed how the stayers begin to construct their school-kid identity in elementary school, how they break away from the stigma of the school by constructing a positive image of themselves, how they take on a reputation-avoider identity in school that enables them to emerge from the social environment unscathed, and how they disproportionately participate in the extracurricular programs. What these chapters do not explain is how and why this particular group of students became school kids while others adopted street identities. Here I argue that these students encounter a combination of factors that build, maintain, and consolidate the high status of their student identities. In short, they reap the benefits of occupying a socially appropriate role and adequately performing the role, which brings about positive evaluations by others, prestige, and rewards, and fosters commitment through intense interaction with an extensive network of supportive people. They also have opportunities to take on identities that support and are often extensions of the student identity (e.g., athlete). School also helps them build positive images of their future. As the student identity becomes more complex and intertwined with other aspects of their lives, it is not surprising that their student identities become more dominant.

School kids, however, are not a homogeneous group but rather encompass a selective group of students who, notwithstanding other differences, share an undisputable commitment to school. This chapter traces the development of their commitment, describing the process by which student identities are developed and reinforced to the point that school kids find genuine satisfaction at Hernández High and overcome any possible threat to the ranking of their student identities. From their interviews, I was able to discern a pattern in the development and maintenance of their student identities. To build and maintain a school-kid identity, the stayers go through three stages, which I call: (1) learning the student role, (2) reinforcing the student identity, and (3) consolidating the student identity. To become school kids, students must first learn the student role and assume its attitudes and behavioral expectations. This process starts in elementary school, when students learn what being a student is about, and continues in high school. As I show in Chapter 3, in the first stage the stayers obtain the rewards, prestige, and connections with teachers that lead to the early formation of a school-kid identity. In this chapter, I describe how school kids are able to maintain this identity throughout high school, and how, in their case, school provides the conditions they need to become school kids: opportunities to engage in a socially appropriate role, social support, prestige and rewards, numerous and close relationships, adequate role performance, the presence of identity-enhancing events, and positive conceptualizations of the future.

REINFORCING THE STUDENT IDENTITY

By the time they reach high school, the stayers have learned to be school kids, and high school reinforces their commitment to the student identity. Being school kids in high school is more than getting along with teachers and obtaining good grades. It means avoiding trouble, and getting involved in school activities and other aspects of schooling. As Chapter 5 shows, the stayers are reputation avoiders, and as such, they seldom get into trouble. This does not mean that they feel at ease at school. They maintain their guard, but are able to fend off trouble. The stayers cultivate school relationships and activities that not only maintain but enlarge their status as school kids. In high school, they become highly recognizable as school kids to teachers because they get along with them, do well in classes, hang around school-oriented peers, participate in the extracurricular programs, and receive awards that mark their social and academic accomplishments. It is their involvement with teachers, school-oriented peers, and activities that in the end help them overcome threats to the student identity. Progressively, the student identity increases in value for the stayers because their experiences at school reinforce and reward being a student.

"Having Fun" vs. "Fooling Around"

I see it [school] like games, that's how I look at it. Everything I do is like a game. I picture it as a game. Like I'm playing a game. And then it is like you're solving a puzzle or something. I like to know about things.

—Miguel

While Miguel is the only stayer who describes school as a game, most stayers concur that school is fun. They enjoy school because they are challenged by learning, their friends are there, and they are involved in school activities. Yet they draw a line between what constitutes "having fun" and what it means to "fool around." To "have fun" in school is to find enjoyment in schooling, including classes, while "fooling around" means having a good time at the expense of learning. Students who "have fun" at school take school seriously, do their homework, are attentive in class, obtain good grades, and participate in school activities. In other words, these are the school kids. By contrast, students who "fool around" do not take schooling seriously. They hang around with friends instead of going to classes, and show off by fighting and showing lack of respect for teachers. These students subscribe to street culture. According to the stayers, fooling around catches up with you, and you end up failing classes, dropping out, or getting expelled from school. The stayers are "having fun," yet they are not "fooling around." Vanessa explains the distinction:

My attitude is you come to school to learn. If you don't want to learn and you wanna be with your friends, go ahead . . . I come to school to learn, not to fool around. I mean, I have my friends, I have fun, but school is school. That's what I tell my mom. I go to school to learn, not to fool around.

Fun Classes, Fun Teachers. One aspect that makes school fun is classes. There is no argument among the stayers with regard to the quality of the education they are receiving. They are satisfied with the variety and content of their courses, and think that generally the school does a good job of educating them, as Roberto, who is in the general education program, comments: "Well, there are a lot of activities here, many classes that help you. It depends on what you want. If it is mechanics, a bit of everything. But academically, I think they are, they teach you well." Yet only the scholars, such as Alma, describe their classes as fun, unconventional, and entertaining:

That was fun. I tell you that [Advanced English] class is fun 'cause we had to present the sixties and the eighties in songs. He videotaped us.

> How embarrassing. We had to make up a song. It was fun. I liked it.
> We dressed up like the sixties. I split my hair. It was fun.

Of course, fun classes are the result of having "fun" teachers. According to the students, it is the teachers who are engaging, challenging, and demanding whom they label good teachers, as opposed to teachers who merely show up and watch them for the class period. The stayers distinguish between two kinds of teachers. According to Miguel,

> The teachers are good. Here in the school [they] are good. They pre-
> pare you for a lot of things but then there's some, there's some, very
> few teachers in this school that they don't know what they're doing
> themselves. They're like lost. They're not preparing you for nothing.
> Or they don't give you homework. Or they just tell you one thing
> right there and just sit back and let the class play around or some-
> thing.

The qualities they attribute to the teachers depend on their personality, the difficulty of the material presented to them, and the amount of homework the students get. In these aspects, the scholars, like Elizabeth, believe they have the best of all three. "Academically, I have the greatest teachers because they look smart and they taught me well. I'm lucky to have good teachers because my brother's teachers are stupid. He never gets homework, he has regular courses so I feel that I have good teachers." Ana, a general education student, agrees that non-scholars do not get homework. "I don't get any homework. Can you believe that? Never. They don't give me anything, I swear."

Opinions about counselors are, more often than not, negative. Stayers talk about having to wait for a long time to see a counselor only to be given a schedule with classes that they do not want or need. Trying to make class changes is frustrating and often impossible because the counselors are inflexible and reluctant to meet the students' wishes. Ana complains:

> They won't let me drop that class and I don't want it. Because we are
> not doing anything, we do the same every day. To try to put the disk
> in the computer, boot it up and log in and like that. And I get tired,
> every day the same thing. And I also do not want it [class] because I
> don't need that, I've got all my credits. They [counselors] don't let
> me drop it.

Although the scholars also complain about the long time it takes to see a counselor, they have two counselors who work closely with them, and provide them with scheduling and with information inaccessible to other students, such as Ana:

See, in this school they give more attention to the scholars. The rest
they pay no attention to. To the scholars they give pre-ACT, they give
them everything. But they don't say anything to us. You know, and
they get scholarships. They give them this they give them that. But to
us that we're doing well and are not in scholars they tell us, "Oh,
well, we can't give you scholarships." And I don't like that.

Regardless of the differences in experiences with teachers and counselors that
result from being enrolled in different academic programs, the stayers maintain
a positive attitude and commitment to school. Furthermore, their overall positive experiences with teachers and counselors result in the development of
intense relationships that foster their increasing commitment to school. As
discussed in Chapter 6, many stayers develop very close, warm, and affectionate relationships with some teachers who encourage and recruit them to participate in the extracurricular activities they sponsor.

The Peer Group. Another factor that contributes to enjoying school by
the stayers is the close-knit relationships they develop with peers. The stayers
not only come to school to learn and obtain their high school diplomas, but
also to be with their friends. The stayers say that their friends are also school-
oriented, as Roberto notes: "I have my friends, I have classes with them, I
hang out with them. But they are not involved in gangs or anything like that.
They're just like me." Because their peers are also school kids, these friendships help reinforce the stayers' commitment to school. School-oriented students at Hernández High sort themselves out into peer groups according to
their interests and aspirations, as Elizabeth, a scholar, explains:

Regular students, you've got the honor students, and usually scholars
I see hang out with those that have the same aspirations as your own.
They associate with other people, don't get me wrong, but I think
that they hang around people that have the same aspirations.

The stayers are thus part of several tightly-knit, school-based peer groups
that transcend school boundaries. These tight-knit groups are usually formed
in or before freshman year. Most stayers say that they have maintained the
same set of friends throughout high school. The groups are made up of peers
who hang out together at school, attend school activities together, socialize
outside of school, and know each other's family. For instance, Lydia, Marta,
and two other girls have been good friends since elementary school. They
spend most of their free time together in school. They also visit each other's
homes and go together to movies and to eat out on weekends. Such relation-

ships foster commitment to school, since students develop intricate and intensive relationships with their peers. Because their peer group remains fairly stable through the high school years, the emotional involvement in these relationships is great.

Extracurricular Activities. As pointed out in Chapter 6, participating in extracurricular activities also makes school more fun. Extracurricular activities provide students with a niche where they feel safe, become part of the school community, find an alternative to academic achievement, and engage in school-sanctioned behavior. Participation in these programs helps students develop other school-related identities that become an inextricable part of their student identity. By participating, they develop commitment and create numerous and intense relationships with sponsors and other participants.

The significance of extracurricular activities for the development of student identities is evident in the overwhelming participation of the stayers in these programs. Eighty-five percent of the stayers participated in extracurricular activities, most in more than one program. While most stayers participate in related extracurricular programs, such as two or more athletic programs, some participate in a wide range of activities. For instance, Vanessa participated in thirteen activities in her senior year! She was a scholar, a class officer, an athlete, a teacher's aide, and participated in several social clubs.

Lack of participation in extracurricular activities does not always mean lack of connections to school, but perhaps lack of time to participate. Those who do not participate are often involved in out-of-school activities that take up most of their after school time. For example, Roberto prefers to participate in activities at church, where he is very active in youth groups: "It [school] has a lot of programs for one to be entertained. Sports. Different social clubs. I like them, but I have never been involved in anything like that. I don't know. Working or things to do at home or in church. Then I'm busy." While Roberto did participate in band for a year, he does not count it as an extracurricular activity because he was taking the class to fulfill a music requirement. Although he could have continued playing with the band, he opted not to do so because other students used profane language that clashed with his Christian training. For Roberto, being a school kid is an extension of being a church boy.

Other stayers also participated in church activities but maintained their extracurricular involvement at school. Some, like Miguel, are involved in Bible reading groups. Others, usually Pentecostals, attend church several times a week. Alma, whose father is a Pentecostal minister, attends church every day but Mondays, is the president of the youth group at her church, and participates in most church activities. Yet she is also involved in the ROTC and several clubs at school. For Alma, participating in church and school activities has made her life extremely structured, as she has to finish her homework before going to the church service at night. Amazingly, Alma is a scholar also.

Awards and Recognition. The school provides certain ways for students to gain recognition for outstanding academic and extracurricular efforts. Since the stayers overwhelmingly participate in the Scholars Program and extracurricular activities, they receive a disproportionate share of the awards and recognition. This in turn strengthens their commitment to school.

Academic awards include making the honor roll and being the top scholar in their class. Any student who obtains a grade point average of A at the end of each marking period makes the honor roll. As a reward for academic efforts, their names are included in the honor roll list displayed on their floor, and occasionally in school newsletters. There are even some material incentives for students to make the honor roll. An assistant principal gave honor roll students free tickets for the seniors' Six Flags Great America trip and raffled two bicycles.

An exceptional experience for the scholars is the annual scholars banquet. The purpose of the banquet is twofold. First, the banquet honors scholars who are graduating seniors. During the banquet, they receive a medal that distinguishes them as scholars during the graduation exercises. Also, their college plans, as well as any scholarships awarded, are publicly announced. Second, the banquet serves to honor individual scholars with the highest grade point averages in each grade level. Thus, the top senior, junior, and sophomore scholars receive trophies. Awards are also given for special effort, such as the one Marta received:

> Last year I got a trophy for keeping up 'cause Ms. Benson was worried about me since I kept saying, "Oh, I know I'm gonna flunk everything." A big trophy in a banquet. It was beautiful. I had so much fun. For keeping up the good work and not letting [down] just because it was honors and high classes.

Some extracurricular programs offer awards and recognition for participants, especially athletics. Every year a banquet is held to honor all school athletes and distribute certificates or trophies for participation. A few athletes receive awards for outstanding athletic and academic performance. The most valuable players are given trophies, as are athletes, like Miguel, who maintain a good academic record. "They gave me a certificate. A paper saying congratulations for being an athlete and having real good grades. They gave it to a lot of athletes. It's like to motivate you." In 1993, for the first time, an athlete received a small monetary scholarship for college. Ana, who participated in three of the "main" sports, was the recipient of the award.

School Behavior

The stayers' school behaviors convey their satisfaction and commitment to the student identity. It also shows that they have mastered the student role and have become "model" students or school kids. The lack of disciplinary and academic problems indicates that they have learned and assimilated the behavioral expectations attached to the student role.

Attendance. While many students cut classes or skip school because they find it boring and have more fun outside of school, the stayers see no need to do this because they enjoy school. Their friends are there, and their involvement in academic and extracurricular program reaps rewards and recognition.

Absences are relatively rare among the stayers; at most 10 days a semester, often much less than that (see Appendix B, Table B.1). Occasionally, some stayers have an unusually high number of absences during a specific semester, yet they are justified by prolonged illnesses (including surgeries), difficult pregnancies, and childbirth. Miguel was absent from school 25 days during the second semester of his freshman year because he had to undergo surgery on his leg. Some, like Isabel, a special education student, show exceptional determination. She came to school up to the day her second child was born and returned less than a week later, even when she could have requested a "home-bound" teacher to visit her at home for a couple of weeks. Isabel came back to school on Baby's Day, when students dress up in baby or child-like costumes. That day I ran into Isabel, who announced to me that her baby had been born a few days earlier. I could not help but smile as I talked to this young mother of two dressed as a baby and carrying a doll and a bottle! Like Isabel, few stayers stay home unless it is necessary.

If absences are rare, so is class cutting. As Lydia put it, "I don't find a reason to cut." The stayers are often tempted by peers who encourage them to "ditch" a class, yet, like Vanessa, they cannot bring themselves to do it: "In fact, my freshman year I never cut, never. And all my friends were like, 'Come on, come, let's go.' I never cut, I was never late for class, I was never tired, I was never absent. And all my friends were saying this . . . And I didn't goof off or anything."

To say that the stayers never miss classes is not completely accurate. Some acknowledge that they cut classes, but not in the conventional way. They usually have a legitimate excuse for not going to class, such as becoming ill or helping a teacher. Alma says,

> I cut 2 weeks ago. I had a headache. I went home. My mom picked me up. Not really cut. If I'm in English and [the teacher] tells me you have to go somewhere. If it takes 7th period, I go tell my teacher, 'I'm doing this.' They go, 'Okay.' So I cut my class.

What is different from other students is that the stayers, and in particular the scholars, have more opportunities to legitimately cut classes because they are often asked by teachers to assist with a special project or task. Opportunities to cut also come through the stayers' participation in extracurricular programs. While students in the Key Club serve as tour guides and escorts for school visitors, other clubs are responsible for selling homecoming dance tickets, t-shirts, yearbooks, and candy for fund raising. Many times I found Marta sitting at a table selling something during times she should have been in class. Stayers often cut their classes, with the approval of teachers, to tend to these responsibilities. Teachers are quick to grant them permission because the stayers are seen as school kids and not as students looking for an opportunity to cut class or to roam the halls. Legitimate cutting of classes is one of the perks of being a school kid and is one of the rewards afforded to good students.

Academic Progress. Academic progress, and grades in particular, are indicators of the stayers' positive attitude toward school and a reflection of their reluctance to cut classes or be absent from school. All but one graduated on time, that is, in 4 years (see Appendix B, Table B.2). Isabel, the special education student who had also given birth to two children during high school, took 5 years to graduate. Some stayers failed a few classes, yet they quickly made up the credits.

The stayers also tend to graduate with more than the required 20 credits, especially the scholars, who graduated with an average of 22.6 credit hours. While general education students fill their programs with art, music, and vocational electives, and often comply with only the minimum core courses required by law, the scholars' excess credits are in academic electives, such as physics and trigonometry. Since the scholars are college-bound, they are required by the program to take additional courses in the sciences and math. While the State of Illinois requires 1 year of science and 2 years of math for high school graduation, the scholars usually take at least 3 years each of science and math to meet college entrance requirements.

Compared to other students, the stayers have higher grade point averages throughout their high school years. Excluding the special education students, the lowest grade point average among the stayers upon graduation was 2.34 and the highest was 3.77 (see Appendix B, Table B.2). Ten had grade-point averages of B or higher, two had C averages, and one special education student graduated with a D average. The stayers' higher academic performance is reflected more clearly in their class ranking (see Appendix B, Table B.2). Except for Isabel and José, the special education students, the remaining 11 stayers ranked within the top half of their graduating class, with eight graduating in the top 25%.

Non-School-Related Identities

While most stayers developed school-related identities as a result of their involvement in academic and extracurricular programs, they are not immune to other identities that place claims upon the students' time and energy. The danger of having multiple identities lies in the conflicts they can create for students. However, very rarely do the stayers get themselves caught in role conflict managing two identities. Non-school-related identities that can potentially conflict with the student identity are avoided. Those non-school-related identities that they take on do not conflict, but on the contrary support, the student identity.

The stayers' avoidance of non-school-related identities shows their commitment to the school-kid identity and their reluctance to take on any identity that can potentially threaten it. Several factors combine to prevent the stayers from adopting competing identities. As noted in Chapter 5, the stayers take the posture of a reputation avoider and, as such, reject the peer ranking promoted by their street-oriented peers. Rather, they exhibit school-sanctioned behaviors and enact a number of strategies to minimize contact and conflict with street-oriented peers. Their low profile makes it possible for them to be selective in their commitments.

Perhaps the most successful strategy for avoiding exposure to non-school-related identities, and street-oriented peers, is involvement in school programs. Stayers have less disposable time to hang out with street-oriented peers, or to be around when trouble arises. Involvement in school programs takes much of their free time in school and often extends after school hours. Social and academic extracurricular programs usually meet during the study hall and lunch periods, thus limiting students' interactions with nonparticipants. Activities that extend after school hours, such as athletics, also limit the amount of time available to spend with non-school-related friends.

On the other hand, extracurricular participation also demands that the students maintain good academic standing. That is, students must not only obtain good grades but also attend their classes and not run into disciplinary problems. Academic or disciplinary probation often leads to a warning, suspension, and even expulsion from extracurricular programs. At Hernández High, as in most schools, extracurricular programs are used as privileges that students can lose due to academic or disciplinary problems. Because the stayers focus their energy on school-sanctioned behaviors, they have little time or even desire to engage in activities that can jeopardize their participation in extracurricular programs. In a way, they are too busy studying, attending their classes, and avoiding trouble to pay attention to competing identities.

It would be misleading to give the impression that the stayers totally avoid non-school related identities. Some stayers try on alternative identities, such as gangs, but their involvement usually lasts for only a short period of time. When the demands of the new identity begin to interfere with performance of the school-kid identity, the stayers drop the competing identity. For example, Iván joined a gang but left it shortly when he realized it was not as much fun. "It [gang] seemed fun at the time, I was sixteen. I got out two years ago. [I was in] for about six months. [I got out] 'cause they would, you know what a violation is, they would give violations for any little reason. That didn't seem fair to me."

However, leaving a non-school-related identity behind is not always easy, or possible, as in the case of young women who become pregnant. For many young women, pregnancy and motherhood mean the end of their education, although not for the stayers. The secret lies in finding a way to manage both identities while minimizing the negative effects of one on the other. Two of the stayers became pregnant and had their babies during the school year, but neither quit school. Margie took a few weeks off from school late in her pregnancy, and after giving birth to her son, she kept up with her school work through a home-bound program for ailing students. Because she also had the support of her boyfriend's mother, with whom she lived, Margie was able to return to school and graduate on time. Isabel had the support of her boyfriend, who took care of their children while she attended school, and the assistance of the school program for teenage mothers. Thus, Isabel was able to balance her obligations as a mother and a student. While supportive partners and relatives are crucial to these young women's uninterrupted education, it is their exceptional determination to graduate "no matter what" that keeps them in school. Their stories show that potentially conflictive identities do not invariably compromise their school-kid identity.

Competing identities that are difficult to shed, such as motherhood, may sometimes strengthen the school-kid identity. These non-school-related identities may unexpectedly add a new dimension or meaning to the student identity. Becoming a mother can motivate a young woman to finish high school for the sake of her child, as with Isabel. It is Isabel's dream to become a mail carrier for the U.S. Postal Service and provide her children with a better future.

At times the student identity becomes an inextricable part of a non-school-related identity. That is, being a school kid is a dimension of another, more complex identity. For example, Roberto defined himself as a Christian, and this identity was very important to him. He frequently mentioned church and his involvement there during interviews. I once found him reading the Bible during study hall. Although he admitted that he did not particularly like school, he was rarely absent. For Roberto, being a "good Christian boy" included being a school kid.

CONSOLIDATING THE STUDENT IDENTITY

It [dropping out] never crossed my mind. 'Cause I always have a goal in my life. I always plan a goal. I wanna make this, I wanna be somebody. 'Cause I would look at some people—examples, look at them out in the streets, suffering. None of that. I don't wanna go through that.

—Miguel

Sometime between their freshman year and their junior year, the stayers consolidate their student identities. Their academic and extracurricular experiences in school provide them with tools to fortify them. So solid have their student identities become that the stayers say they never once thought about dropping out of school. It is just not an option for the stayers, for whom the prospect of dropping out is unthinkable. They, like Marta, simply cannot imagine themselves out of school. "I would feel lost. 'Cause I don't know, I think how can people not go to school. When they feel like they won't get nowhere."

They firmly believe that if they work hard they will achieve the "American dream" of becoming middle-class. They attribute success to individual effort and a strong drive to achieve, ignoring the more complex structural barriers to overcoming poverty. Ironically, their parents, who work hard and have been unable to move the family into middle-class status, provide the motivation to graduate from high school by serving as a negative example of life prospects without a high school diploma. It is their belief in the system and their own simplistic explanations of success that accentuate their own success in school. How the stayers construct possible selves or envision themselves in the future helps consolidate their school-kid identity. They hope to become upwardly mobile, at least middle-class, but foremost they hope to avoid becoming a "lowlife." Their behavior in school as well as their attitudes about the future are a result of their hopes and fears, which motivate them to place much value in a high school diploma and to make plans to attend college.

The Value of the High School Diploma

The high school diploma has much value for the stayers, both practical and symbolic. Most stayers believed that a high school diploma is a requirement for employment. They say that it is very difficult to obtain a good job without a high school education, and "if you don't have a high school diploma, you won't be able to even pick up garbage," says José (my translation). Yet they do not equate a high school diploma with a general equivalency diploma. They put much more value in a high school diploma because, like Elizabeth, they believe that it leads to better job opportunities than a GED:

It helps you in the future. For example, if you take the GED, if you drop out and take the GED and you go for a job, and you tell them, "have a GED" and another person comes with a diploma from a high

school, they are going to chose the one with [a] high school [di-
ploma]. [My translation]

The stayers also believe that education is the key to the middle class, to
happiness and success in the most general sense. They firmly believe in the
American dream that with an education and hard work, they will be able to
own a house and a car, and to provide their families with a comfortable life.
Note that José envisions having a "career," not just a job:

I have stayed in school because I know I need to. I know that I need
to learn . . . I want to get something from my life. I want to do something so that in 10 years from now I'll be satisfied. Like, that I graduated from high, I have a career, a family, a car, a house. I don't want
to be lazy. I want to do something in the future. I want to enjoy my
life.

On the symbolic side, the stayers take much pride in their high school
diploma because they are often the first in their family to have one. Most of
the stayers' parents moved from Puerto Rico to Chicago in search of a better
future for their families. With only a few years of schooling, they work at
unskilled factory jobs, dreaming that their children will not have to work in a
factory or in some menial and low-paying job. Thus, high school graduation is
a major accomplishment and a revitalization of this hope of a better future for
the family. Elizabeth, for example, is the first woman from her mother's side
of the family to graduate from high school. For Elizabeth and her grandmother, that means a lot. "I think that it is that none of my grandmother's
granddaughters, none, none of the daughters of my grandmother has graduated from high school. I am like the only one. And that's what makes me keep
on. That she will be proud of me" (my translation). The stayers are also a
source of pride for their families. As José explains, "To graduate from high
school would be a joy to them [parents] because unfortunately there are many
parents that cannot get to see that because their children drop out or are on
drugs" (my translation).

The stayers recognize their graduation as a collective family accomplishment and credit their parents for their success. According to Elizabeth, people
drop out of school because they do not "have parents that support them like
they support me." The stayers, such as Iván, also say that their parents serve
as a standard to improve on rather than to emulate. "I think I stayed because
I've been determined to achieve more than my parents have achieved. My
father went to college so I want to go further than him."

Fear of Becoming a "Lowlife"

The stayers look down upon some members of their own ethnic group and make marked distinctions in attitudes and behavior between themselves and "others." People who are on welfare, unemployed, in gangs, using drugs, and homeless are called "lowlifes." As Elizabeth explains, "Lowlife, that one who is in the street depending on other people [and] does nothing to rise above all by himself. I call that a lowlife." However, they do not generalize the behavior of the so-called lowlife to include all Puerto Ricans or members of other ethnic groups. Ethnicity never enters the conversation because what they are describing are people who they believe are found in all ethnic groups. According to the stayers, working hard and striving to achieve are necessary if one is to avoid becoming a lowlife. Lack of success is due, Roberto believes, to lack of motivation and drive:

> [I do not want] to follow his [brother's] steps. You learn from other people's experiences. He is kind of lazy, too. He always wanted, since he was in school here, he always wanted to have fun and never wanted to work. That's why he is like he is now. He learned by force. I, you know, the more education I get, the better I think. It would be easier to get a job, to get a career.

For the stayers, the high school diploma is not itself sufficient to raise them above the horror of becoming a lowlife. It is an intermediary accomplishment essential to finding a good job. In the inner city where they live, they see few opportunities without additional years of education. Poverty is something immediately around them and assumed to be very difficult to avoid, as Roberto concludes:

> A high school education helps you more. Well, it's not going to be enough with how the economy is. It will probably help to go to another school, a college, whatever, to study more, to get a career. (My translation)

Most stayers hope to obtain a university degree or further training of some sort. They dread factory work and fear that they may end up working in a factory like their parents. They believe that factory jobs are dead ends where people stagnate and do not improve their lives. Elizabeth believes that only by getting a university education can she avoid factory work. "It's in me, I guess. I don't want to stay in a factory. I have to advance, I don't want to stay in there on the side." In addition, a college degree will ensure that the stayers will not become a lowlife, that they will not end up on the streets, homeless, jobless, and on welfare. For them, as Elizabeth notes, college is the way to avoid a life full of hardships. "All [my friends] feel forced to go [to college]. Like they do not want to be like those on welfare, those that are lowlife. They want to succeed, so they are forced to go to college." Lydia also believes that only by getting a university education can she avoid factory work.

> People have graduated with a diploma of high school and haven't gotten any farther. Like my mom says, "With a high school diploma you can't do anything." You get regular blue-collar jobs. You don't get a good job in an office or something. You get a regular, janitor or something. They even ask for diplomas to clean toilets.

Those not going to college often look into the armed forces. Since the armed forces require a high school diploma or GED for entrance, Roberto says that he stayed in school "to get my diploma. Without a diploma I do not qualify for entrance [into the Marines]." Thus, for the stayers, the high school diploma is a requirement needed for future goals, whether it is getting a good job, entrance to college, or service in the armed forces. Yet the high school diploma is also a sign of their status as school kids, and thus reflects well on them in a community where so few achieve high school graduation.

CONCLUSION

What seems important in becoming school kids is that it requires a firm belief in the "system" and a "willingness" to participate in it. It is not that the stayers strive to succeed more than other students, or are more compliant than other students, but rather that the system works for them, confirming their simplistic notions of success and failure. The three stages into which I have divided the process of becoming school kids shows how this happens.

During the first stage, in elementary school, the stayers learn the expectations of the student role and learn to behave appropriately. From the beginning of these early school days, the stayers are sheltered by teachers who take a liking for them. While the stayers' stories do not tell how or why teachers take an interest in them, they do reveal that they develop close relationships with teachers, who nurture and give them every opportunity to excel. And excel they do. They become "good kids" who obtain good grades and behave properly. They leave elementary school with a well-developed school-kid identity that only becomes stronger in high school.

The second stage begins in high school, where the stayers' commitment to the student identity is reinforced. While the sizable student population and the street culture that seeps into high school make it challenging to sustain the student identity, the stayers find ways of avoiding the chaos brought about by street culture. They become reputation avoiders partly because they find a niche that shelters and nurtures them from the street culture. The relationships they form with others support their commitment to the student identity. They belong to tight-knit, school-oriented peer groups where prestige and positive evaluations are for those who exhibit school-sanctioned behavior (i.e., good attendance, good behavior, good grades). Partly due to their school-mindedness and exemplary behavior, they are "adopted" by teachers who not only look out for their safety and well-being, but also push them into the school culture by encouraging them to participate in school programs. Most stayers become highly visible school kids, earning recognition and awards for participating in extracurricular programs. The stayers' involvement in school programs fosters the adoption of school related identities. The resulting public display of the school-kid identity and its perks lessens the attractiveness of identities that can conflict with school.

The third stage, which is reached by their junior year, consists of the consolidation of the student identity. The stayers reach a point where their student identities are so well cemented that dropping out of school is hardly possible. In this stage, the stayers begin to articulate well-defined ideas about success and failure, attributing failure to lack of effort. According to the stayers, they "work hard" to achieve middle-class status, and according to their ethic and beliefs, they should succeed. They believe that the secret of success lies in the motivation and willingness of people to work hard. Those who fail have only themselves to blame because if they had worked harder, they would have succeeded. These simplistic views of success and failure set them apart from others and hold them as the exception rather than the norm. While they seem convinced of their simplistic explanation of success and failure, they still fear becoming a lowlife. If after all their "hard work" and effort they fail, not only is their reputation at stake, but their very notions of success and hope for a better future.

CHAPTER 8

From Street Kids to Drop-outs

In the public imagination, drop-outs are envisioned as street kids who engage in anything from truancy to hard-core delinquency and who leave school because their street activities are more enjoyable than going to school. According to this view, young men simply run into trouble with the law and end up incarcerated, while young women become pregnant and go on welfare. The problem with these images is that they ignore the complexities that turn off many kids from school and lead them to become street kids. It also ignores the many drop-outs who do not completely fit that street-kid image. These are kids who do not subscribe to street culture per se, but who lose interest in school and adopt non-school-oriented identities. Students who leave school after having a child or to care for an ill relative are not subscribing to street culture, but rather following cultural norms that rank family needs over individual gain. Yet they engage in street-kid behaviors such as underachieving and truancy, which marks them as street kids. Regardless of their reasons for dropping out, both types share a similar story of growing disengagement from school that makes them engage in street-like behaviors and ultimately makes other identities, street-oriented or non-street-oriented, more attractive than the school-kid identity.

This chapter focuses on 10 Hernández High School drop-outs, whom I call the leavers. These are youths who dropped out of Hernández High and had not returned to school by June 1993. Although their reasons for dropping out vary, the leavers share a definite disengagement from school starting in the early grades and escalating in high school. Few were ever school-oriented, and positive feelings toward school were often short-lived, as they increasingly felt inadequate and unaccepted in school. As I discuss in earlier chapters, these are youths whose school-kid identity was too weak to be sustained over time. They were pushed aside by a school system structured to reward a few students, leaving the remainder to create identities or search for them beyond the school grounds. Already disillusioned by their school experience and unable to pursue alternative achievement in school-sanctioned ways, they devise their own system for recognition, often one that clashes with school. Outside of school, or in the street-oriented peer culture, they find the recognition, prestige, rewards, and social support needed to build these non-school-oriented identities.

These students undergo a role-exit process similar to that identified by Ebaugh (1988) and which I describe in Chapter 2. Role exit is a dual process that involves the rejection of the school-kid role and the adoption of another role. It begins with the students' doubting their commitment to the school. After these initial first doubts, they begin seeking alternatives or options, often in street culture, that only increase their questioning and disengagement from school. Unable to form a stable school-kid identity, as their disengagement with school grows, another identity begins to take shape. Eventually, they reach a point where the incongruence between the two identities is such that they cannot be maintained simultaneously. Their inadequate performance of the student role; the lack of rewards, prestige, and social support at school; and the presence of identity-threatening events in their lives tip the scale in favor of the other identity. As they leave school, they create a new identity that contains leftover traces of the student identity. In this chapter, I use Ebaugh's role-exit model to describe how Hernández High students become increasingly disillusioned with school, replace the school-kid identity with street or family identities, and ultimately become dropouts.

FIRST DOUBTS

The process of dropping out of school begins with the questioning of the school-kid role. As experiences associated with being a student become increasingly negative and dissatisfying, doubts as to its importance begin to surface. School experiences take on a negative light, as students reinterpret and redefine what being a student means. Everything that has happened, and everything that happens from then on, is evaluated according to the new reinterpretation of their role as students. As a result, they reminisce about their school experience as negative, omitting and often failing to recall any pleasant experiences. For most, this stage begins in elementary school (see Chapter 3), and by the time they reach high school they are already disconnected from school or have formed such a marginal attachment to school that it does not take long to adopt other identities. Even if they looked forward to high school as a possible new beginning, they are unable to start with a clean slate because their troublemaker reputation from elementary school followed them. When a social worker came looking for him, Vitín learned that

> He heard about me 'cause of my grammar school. 'Cause the principal. Forget it. He already knew who we [gang members] were, how we tagged. He knew everything. Where we were at, if we were in the basement. He already knew where the spot we're gonna be was in.

He really knew everything and he went. Everything we did over there [elementary school], he already had it down.

Since they carried a street-kid reputation, or adopted a street identity as they reached high school, these leavers entered into high school already marked as street kids and treated accordingly. For other leavers, high school marks the beginning of the demise of their school-kid identity. It is in high school that they are exposed to street culture and their street behavior escalates. Yet, regardless of the onset of first doubts, high school taints their school experiences and precipitates their exit from school.

The negative feelings the leavers have during elementary school are usually aggravated in high school. Their disengagement from school accelerates rapidly, and by their sophomore year, many have already left school or are attending so irregularly that they are de facto dropouts. In Chapter 5, I show how attending Hernández High thrusts them into street culture by sustaining a social setting where street culture predominates and becomes an inviting alternative for students who are denied opportunities to achieve in school-sanctioned ways. The treatment students receive from teachers, the quality of their classes, and the structuring of opportunities fosters student truancy and the exploration of identities that are not always compatible with the school-kid identity.

At one point or another, the leavers engage in street-kid behaviors, but the degree of their involvement in street culture and the magnitude of these street-kid behaviors vary. Many are self-image defenders whose truancy escalates over time or participate in fights occasionally. Others adopt a self-image promoter attitude, acting defiantly in school toward peers and teachers.

Dull Classes, Dull Teachers

The leavers are quickly turned off by their teachers and classes at Hernández High. As Marisol says, "I really didn't want to be in class. I wasn't interested at all." Their lack of interest in academics can be traced to several factors. For instance, most leavers see no direct relationship between a high school diploma and subsequent income and believe that diploma in hand or not, they will still end up in low-status and low-paying jobs. Some see the informal economy as a means to make more money than they would ever make as high school graduates. For instance, Ernesto says, "I was making more money in the streets with my drugs." That high school graduation does not pay off makes street culture more enticing.

Another factor affecting their lack of enthusiasm in academics is the dullness that they say permeates most classes. The leavers contend that classes at Hernández High are easy, and as Marisol puts it, "There [Hernández High] you just need to show up [in class] to get a grade, to pass. You don't need to do the work or the homework, just attend." Discipline takes precedence before learning. As long as students abide by the behavioral rules set by each teacher, they will pass their classes, whether they learn or not, according to Eric:

> I didn't like my division [home room] teacher. Nobody liked her. She would make us sit like monks. We were sitting one here, another there, the other over there. And we had to face the front and not look to the side. You talked and she kicked you out of the classroom and marked you absent.

According to the leavers, some teachers have given up on teaching. These teachers sit at their desks, often reading a newspaper, and let the students do as they please as long as they leave them alone. Marisol describes the situation this way:

> A lot of the teachers are old. Some would just sit there, they would give you an assignment and tell you when to turn [it] in. You come in and they give you some handouts and you do them or talk to your friends. Some people play cards, some teachers even play cards with them. It's an easy job. The students walk in and out of class, go to the vending machines. The teachers don't say anything . . . I would go to class and put my head down and sleep.

César says that these teachers "do their little work and sign on the paper and that's it." According to Lisa, these teachers subscribe to an attitude of "You take care of your business, I'll take care of mine." Vitín equates this attitude with indifference; "Some teachers they're like, 'If you wanna do the work, do the work. If not, it's up to you. Whichever you wanna do.'"

Other teachers engage in monologues that do little to engage the students in the classroom. These teachers stand in front of class and lecture for the whole class period, not bothering to making sure that the students are understanding the material. Students have little if any chance to participate in class or ask questions. Ernesto gives his point of view:

> I just found it boring. The teachers were boring, all the teachers were boring. . . . I hate people that talk so much through the whole class and then they give you little time to do your work, you know what I mean. It's like all the teachers would talk for thirty minutes and the ten minutes they had [left], 'cause they used to be forty-minute classes, the ones I used to have, and they used to talk thirty minutes, give you ten minutes to do your work, and if you didn't have your work done, you failed.

As a consequence, students see no sense in engaging in these classes because they are bored, "get nothing out of them," and can get away with doing the minimum work to pass. According to César, "I really didn't like school . . . I think if they're [teachers] gonna teach, they should energize, get you to want to learn. But these people, they just write something on the board and that's it and you just copy it and that's it."

These teachers have not only given up on teaching, but they are detached from their students. The leavers describe them as indifferent, uncaring, and even inhumane. Vitín believes that these teachers are judgmental and quick to label their students as "good" or "troublemaker," and to treat them accordingly.

> What I think is like sometimes . . . sometimes I think when a teacher . . . when I go walk inside a class, the teacher thinks about me like if I was some kind of guy from the street. "That all he comes to do is to disturb the class," and things like that . . . Sometimes a teacher sees that and sees who you are and how you look. "Oh, he's," in their minds, "he's a troublemaker, so I got to make things impossible." So that's when they treat us the way they do.

According to the leavers, even the distribution of grades is based on teachers' perceptions of students. They feel that no matter what they do, their work will be graded as mediocre or poor by these teachers. Vitín concludes:

> When you try your best and you try your hardest, they're like, "Oh, you're not doing this and you're not doing that." Even though you've got proof, they're like, "Oh, you probably didn't and you probably [had] someone else sign it." I'm like, "No, this is the work that you gave me."

Some teachers are so uninterested and distant from their students that they dismiss any story as a weak excuse, even in serious situations, such as Marisol was experiencing:

> Mostly because of the absences, I failed. The teachers didn't care. I would tell them about the problem [that her stepfather was dying] and they didn't care. I wanted somebody to understand but they didn't care. They don't want to become part of the students' lives at all. They don't want to know what's going on. One PE teacher told me, "Well, he's [stepfather] not dead yet, so come down."

Like other leavers, Marisol expected her high school teachers to be nurturing, as were some teachers in elementary school; thus she was taken aback when

Lack
of Teacher
Sympathy.

the teachers did not respond sympathetically to her feelings and problems. Furthermore, the leavers believe that in any confrontation with a teacher they stand to lose because, as Vitín says, at Hernández High "the teachers always win."

Contrary to what one would expect, school counselors do little to help the leavers engage in academics. Quite often they make matters worse. The leavers, like Lisa, report little or no contact with their academic counselors: "To tell you the truth, I barely even knew my counselors. I would like see them at the end of the year to pick my classes for the next year but that was the way you kind of always see them and talk to them." While the leavers report having little contact with their counselors, the contact that they do have usually ends on a negative note. Efforts to make scheduling changes, even when reasonable and beneficial to the students, are often refused by counselors, leaving students, such as Eric, more frustrated and reconfirming their perception of the school staff as uncaring and unresponsive to their needs.

> I had too many studies [study hall], four studies. I would come for class at 7:40 and then have a study at 8:20. Then division, then study, then gym, then study again. I started getting mad because I didn't want the studies, I wanted classes. In study *no se hace na', ahí perdiendo el tiempo* [you don't do anything, just wasting your time]. I went to my counselor, but she wouldn't change my classes and give me more classes. I told her to give me more classes because I wanted to get out of here.

Frustrated by his counselor's refusal to change his schedule, Eric lost his temper and yelled at the counselor. Instead of helping him learn to control his temper, the counselor got Eric suspended from school.

Repeated negative experiences like the ones described above decrease the leavers' commitment to school and push them to find alternative ways of achieving. The lack of support, recognition, positive evaluations or rewards, and relationships with their teachers and counselors pushes the leavers further into the street culture. The leavers continue to spiral downhill as their ventures into street culture create more negative responses from the teachers and counselors.

Extracurricular Activities

In spite of the negative experiences with teachers and counselors, and the disengaging nature of classes, the leavers could find an avenue to school achievement in the extracurricular programs. However, very few participate. Although the leavers say that they simply are not interested in participating in extracurricular activities, many factors converge to make it impossible for them to participate even when willing. In Chapter 6, I explained how formal and informal restrictions obstruct the participation of the leavers. While the number of slots for participation and the skill level required affect their participation, the leavers are most affected by their poor grades, lack of information, and lack of recruitment efforts by teachers. Because they have low grade point averages, they rarely meet the grade requirement for participation. Although the way in which extracurricular opportunities are advertised leaves much to be desired, that the leavers cut classes and are absent so often reduces their chances of finding out about these programs. Since they are labeled as troublemakers, they are not actively recruited by teachers who would rather not bother with "problem" students.

As a result, only 20% of the leavers were ever involved in an extracurricular program, and this includes those who enrolled in music or ROTC classes. More often than not, their participation is motivated by their need to fulfill a course requirement, and after fulfilling it, they do not enroll in the more advanced classes. Some leavers, like David and Aida, enrolled in the ROTC to avoid taking physical education. Others, like Vitín, took it because they planned to join the armed forces upon graduation. "And then I wanted to go to the Marines. I don't know what happened that I was like, 'Let me go to ROTC to see if I like it.'"

Although they may be initially excited about their participation in programs like the ROTC, their excitement soon wanes. They often feel that they are singled out and subjected to a different standard, even when they think they have worked as hard as the next student. Vitín says:

> I was here [ROTC] all the time and then when they were starting giving ranks, they didn't give me rank. They gave me nothing. I mean, they gave all the people rank and all that. I'm like, "What do you mean? I was here and I've been here. We came in second place in the city championship and I ain't gonna get nothing." It was like, "No, you've got to earn it and this and that." I go, "What I did? I come here every morning." And I got mad and I said, "You know what? You all can go to hell" . . . I had [was enrolled in] the class still but I stopped going. I missed it. I let it go because they were lying to me and this and that. I was doing something for myself and for the class, and they're gonna treat me the way they did. Why bother? And there was another freshman there. She just started and she got rank. And she had her ribbon and everything and I didn't get nothing. Forget it.

While students like Vitín think they are subjected to a different standard, their school records do not back up their claim. It may be that Vitín put an extraordinary effort into the ROTC, and felt humiliated by being the only student who was denied a promotion, but he was in ninth grade for 3 years and his highest grade point average ever was .85 on a 4.0 scale (see Appendix B, Table B.3).

Unlike most participants in extracurricular activities, who become attached to school and develop feelings that they belong, the leavers, such as Angie, soon come to see extracurricular classes as a convenient excuse for absences from school and home.

> I would cut class, I would be home late from school. My mom would be wondering where I was at. I was, "Oh, I was in the ROTC." 'Cause since that's the class I was doing the best in, 'cause I was so high there, she would believe me . . . And instead I was with my friends.

This is more prevalent among girls whose parents have strict rules about after-school activities.

Although the leavers rarely participate in extracurricular activities, they are disproportionately enrolled in the social service programs at Hernández High. Participation in these programs can be stigmatizing because they are designed to help "troubled" youths. Ironically, the leavers do not complain of the stigma and speak quite highly about these programs. This is not surprising, given that these programs are staffed with sympathetic adults they can talk to, often the only adults, the leavers say, who listen to them and take them seriously. As Ernesto explains, they feel "cared for" and important enough to be worthy of an adult's time:

> I've been in many jams, and I've been confused many times, and my one way was Janet and Carlos [social workers], you know. I could speak to them. And they are really great people, and they enjoy what they're doing, and I hope they keep doing what they're doing. 'Cause it's nice to see someone cares for a person.

In the social service programs, the leavers, such as Vitín, find the close and personal relationships they are craving and are denied in high school: "He was talking to me and talking to me and then I understood him. And instead of him looking for me, I was looking for him. That's what I needed, someone to talk to. So I would talk to him."

In fact, relationships between students and adults in the social service programs are so "tight," they last well after they leave school. I was able to make initial contact with most leavers with the help of social service staff. While school records classified the leavers as "missing" or "unable to locate," I easily found them with the help of social workers who knew where they lived or hung out and had frequent contact with them. In a way, these students have to "be bad" in order to get attention in school. Only by misbehaving and being truant are they "rewarded" with adult attention.

These programs help many students resolve conflicts and prevent some from dropping out, but for others it just postpones or slows down the process. This is partly due to understaffing and the lack of resources of these programs, but timing of services is perhaps the most crucial factor determining who will remain in school. Often students are referred to these programs when their disengagement from school is too advanced and the undoing of the years of frustration and disappointment is too difficult. For most leavers, these services come too late, and ultimately there is little that the programs can do to stop the process of dropping out.

School Behavior

During the first-doubts stage, the school behavior of the leavers becomes erratic. Their disappointment and increased disengagement from school are manifested in cuing behaviors that signal the erosion in commitment to the student identity. They begin to exhibit truant behavior, such as class cutting and absenteeism. Some show traits associated with street identities, particularly those corresponding to the self-image promoters described in Chapter 5. They fight, act brave, and confront their peers to establish or uphold their street reputations. At this stage, these cuing behaviors are erratic, but they mark a definite shift in attitude toward school. With the exception of a few leavers whose truant behavior is chronic from the first day, these behavioral changes are gradual for most leavers but become more commonplace by the end of their sophomore year.

It is usually those leavers whose first doubts start in elementary school who become chronic truants immediately. These leavers show high absentee rates throughout high school. For instance, David's absences extended from 19 days to 61 days during his 5 semesters at Hernández High (see Appendix B, Table B.3). The most common pattern among the leavers, however, is that of "selective truancy" and the progressive deterioration of attendance and performance in school that usually peaks in their sophomore year. As selective truants, they cut and sneak out of school when opportunity or a whim arises. They come to school with no particular plan to cut a class or leave the premises, but end up doing so impulsively. When they leave the premises it is usually with a particular purpose in mind and not just to sneak out of school. Lisa describes leaving the school for lunch:

> Like we don't have open campus to go out and eat and come back. But we make our open campus. We'll go out, eat, and come back. [And sneak through] the auto shop. Well, you would tell somebody, "Oh, I'm leaving. I'm gonna go eat something. After fifth period,

straight downstairs and open the door. I'm gonna be there." And you already knew when the fifth period was over like at 11:30 so you would be there. While everybody is eating their hamburgers, we're eating at Subway [restaurant]. We always had a car so we would eat something different every day.

Snowball

While they start with a few absences, they gradually increase them over time. Ricardo, for example, was absent only 3 to 5 days a semester during the first two and a half years at Hernández High. During his third year, his absences increased to 19, and reached 83 days in his last semester at Hernández High (see Appendix B, Table B.3).

The leavers say they cut classes and sneak out of school because it is easy and there are few incentives not to do so. According to them, there are seldom any consequences for cutting classes. As Marisol points out, "Even if you get caught, nothing happens. You end up in the lobby until the next class. So it didn't matter." They know that there is not much that the staff can do anyway, and that punishment is usually negligible, according to Lisa: "So they really can't do anything. They would start asking, 'Oh, who were with you? There were three people with you.' You just stay quiet. What are they gonna do, hit me?" The worst that can happen is to be placed in detention. Ernesto says,

> Before if you used to act stupid, they used to give you in-house deten-
> tion. They used to leave you in 711. Room 711, that's what it was.
> I've been in there a couple of times . . . You got to do your home-
> work. They give you homework to do. It's like they suspended you
> from school but they used to put you in in-house. In-house is you
> have to go to school. Starts at 8:00, you don't get out until 3:00 and
> you've got to work all day. And if you never do, like they give you
> worksheets, and if you don't do the worksheets, you're staying there
> until you do it. 'Cause you're not leaving the school, you're not leav-
> ing that class. They stuck me in that place like five times.

Besides detention, students are sometimes assigned to an alternative program for a specified amount of time. This program targets students, such as Lisa, with attendance and behavioral problems.

> They sent me to an alternative [program]. That was a program they
> had here once. And I was there for a while. It was like, you'll be
> there from after division till three. And you'll have to bring your own
> lunch because they wouldn't let you out of the room to get your
> lunch. You couldn't go out of the room. Once you were in there, you
> were in there. And you'll be there like three days, for a week or some-
> thing. It was like a punishment.

Punishment Fails

Although detention and the alternative program are designed both to punish and isolate troublemakers, they seldom achieve these goals. Because students are lumped together in detention and in the alternative program, students end up spending more time with their friends who are also being held in these programs. In addition, they obtain the individualized attention that is missing in the classroom. Lisa explains:

> It was fun. I liked it. Everybody was always in there. You already knew who would always get in trouble. You had to do your work. I felt more comfortable with them. There were two [teachers]. One was a security guard, then a teacher that would explain the things that you had to do. You would get more done in there than in the actual classes.

In addition to the lack of harsh consequences, the leavers say that it is easy to cut classes and violate other rules because the staff "hasn't a clue" of what is going on among the students. Cutting classes and sneaking out of school is described as a game in which the students outsmart the school staff. They gain much satisfaction from fooling the staff. According to Lisa, "they're [staff] slow [to catch on to it]." Ironically, she says that the students, not the staff, are the ones who know what is going on in school.

> For what I've done [here and the] things that I have experienced [in this school] I could do [much] for [the staff] to improve [the school]. I know that they'll stop you from cutting 'cause I know where people go and I know where they hang [out] in the building. Everybody knew where all the drugs was hiding. Or when they start selling. What locker the guns are gonna be in. So the students were the best ones you could talk to. They'll [staff] always neglect you.

Because they think they know the system, the leavers begin to use every trick in the book to cut class or skip school undetected. They take advantage of school regulations that provide reasonable excuses to leave a class or school, although most of the time the leavers cut classes without giving any excuses. They find places where they can hang out with friends without being bothered by the security guards. Side stairways are a favorite hangout because few people use them. They also provide an escape route when security guards are coming. Marisol says: "People hide in the side stairs or the bathrooms to cut classes. When the security came, we would run around and go somewhere else."

They also find "legitimate" ways to cut a class by simply telling the teacher and hall monitors that they have an appointment with a counselor or social worker. Because of their reputations as troublemakers, most teachers readily accept the excuse without question. Vitín explains, "So I used him [a social worker] to cut class. 'I'm gonna go to Youth At-Risk.' And they're [teachers], 'Okay.' I used to cut the class just to go to him and talk and hang around." They would then proceed to the service-oriented program, where they quickly made up a different excuse for not being in class. According to Lisa,

> Like we would try to cut and come here into Youth At-Risk. We would always come over and say to Carlos, "That teacher is not there. They have a substitute." The substitute is not gonna teach you anything. He'll be like, "I'm gonna check." [And we would tell him,] "Yeah, but check later on." Or "She threw me out [of class]."

Sometimes, they do not need to make up an excuse because they *are* expelled from class. Lisa continues:

> We would get thrown out of the class on purpose just to get here [social service program]. We would start talking [in class]. We would sit in the back talking. Slam the books on the floor. And she'll [teacher] look around and finally give up. [We would] let her [teacher] catch us [and] then she'll throw us out. "Go to the office." "Go outside."

Many leavers also just walk out of the school building, either through the front entrance or side doors. One way to do this in a seemingly legitimate way is to say that one is in the work program. Students in the work program leave the school at 1:00 P.M. Lisa says:

> They [security] wouldn't say anything because they had the work program and they would ask you, "Where are you going? Aren't you supposed to be in class?" "No, I have the work program." "Oh, okay." And they would let you go.

Another way to leave "legitimately" is by obtaining an early dismissal. This works for those over 18 because they can sign their own dismissal forms without parental consent, as Lisa explains:

> Once I turned eighteen I used to get early dismissals. If you're eighteen, you got proof of your age, you can sign your own paper and leave. [I would say I had] a doctor's appointment. They wouldn't ask for a doctor's paper or anything. [I would leave] right after division.

However, most leavers do not make it this far, as they have dropped out before turning 18.

SEEKING ALTERNATIVES TO THE STUDENT IDENTITY

Sometime in their sophomore year, most leavers begin to engage in heavy class cutting and prolonged absences from school. Their attendance pattern deteriorates and shifts from selective truancy to indiscriminate truancy. Cutting classes and being absent become routine. With prolonged absences from school, they gain a taste of what awaits them outside of school, and this gives them the time and space to explore other possible identities. As they reach the stage of seeking alternatives, they begin to seriously contemplate dropping out of school, although they do not immediately act on it. For instance, Angie wrestled with the thought of leaving school for some time: "I was always getting in trouble. I was thinking, 'Probably, maybe, I don't belong here. Maybe I should just go work.' But where was I gonna work? I was always cutting and I knew I wasn't doing good so I was like, 'Why am I here if I'm not doing good?'" Although she did not leave school at this time, the idea of dropping out continued to plague her thoughts.

"Testing the Waters"

As their departure from school nears, the leavers begin to test the waters by simulating what it would be like to be a drop-out. This is a period of role rehearsal, when the leavers begin to practice and adopt the attitudes and behaviors associated with being a drop-out. Because of their attitudes and behaviors, their experimentation with the drop-out identity is noticeable in school. Testing the waters is accompanied by an escalation in the cuing behaviors described earlier and a shift in reference groups.

Their increasing discontent with school and their concern with building a reputation outside of school prompts many leavers to change peer groups. The peer group becomes a major force reinforcing their search for something else. They subscribe to a peer culture that is not school-oriented and that encourages behaviors such as cutting, obtaining low grades, and putting minimum effort into school. Lisa tells how her attitude toward studying changed:

> At first, I was getting real good grades. But then afterwards, I was getting by. It was like when I was here there was nobody like, "Oh, I want to set up for a B or an A." Everybody was like, 'Well, if I get a C, I'm fine with that 'cause I'm passing.' Nobody would hit the goal for A. As long as you get a D, you pass the class. I was like that for a

while. Before, I was like, hit the books. Like in elementary school, I never got an F, a C or a D. It was always A's and B's. So I would have that in my conscience. I don't know, I just flipped. And everybody was, "That's true, if you get a D you pass. Why do all the hard work to get an A if they still pass you if you get A, B, C or D?" Just try to get enough. Get your majors [non-elective classes] done.

While their peers push them to become truant, truancy itself becomes a means to gain recognition and prestige among these same peers.

Nearing their departure from school, they increasingly associate with people who abandoned their student identities—the drop-outs. Associating with drop-outs provides the leavers with a reference group that facilitates their assimilation to the dropout identity and provides support. Given the street orientation of their peers, non-school possibilities open up to the leavers. In other drop-outs they find role models to emulate.

The search for alternatives may make the leavers unselective in choosing new friends. Many leavers shift reference groups in high school only to have their new friends introduce them into new identities and accompanying behavior that only lead to additional trouble at school.

Accompanying changes in peer group, there is a radical shift in their attitude toward school. While cutting classes and sneaking out of school may have been a novelty that made school fun and challenging and happened at the spur of the moment, these behaviors later become deliberate and long-term. Having fun outsmarting the staff is replaced by a methodical study of the school's security system and its loopholes. Students piece together bits of information gathered from different sources. According to Lisa, "some of the girls [we knew] worked in the office so we already knew how everything worked."

As chronic truancy sets in, the leavers have time and space to rehearse alternative identities. Being absent from school for prolonged periods gives them a preview of their future life as drop-outs. Their prolonged absences are followed by sporadic returns to school that do not last long. Vitín says, "And I mean, when I was here at Hernández, I used to miss a lot. I used to miss about a month or a month and a half." They continue this in-and-out-of-school pattern for some time, mainly because it is relatively safe to be absent for extended periods, since public schools always "take you back in." Like Vitín says, "I mean, you keep on missing and they suspend you and kick you out, but you're still back." However, as their attendance and grades rapidly deteriorate they begin to realize that despite any efforts they might make, they are hopelessly years behind their cohort and it is too late to catch up. The thrill they previously got from cutting classes and outsmarting the staff is replaced by a realization that they are sinking deeper into trouble, as Eric acknowledges: "That year I failed most of my classes. I only passed two classes. I don't know. Everything changed. It was from one good thing to bad and then worst. *Un año completo de* [a year full of] headaches."

The leavers' school records show high rates of absenteeism, starting in their sophomore year (see Appendix B, Table B.3), which often surpass 50 absences in their last semester. Although attendance generally declines over time, the leavers have intermittent periods in which their attendance improves, only to drop again. Angie's time at school is characterized by episodic attendance: "I would do good for a month or two. Or for a semester then the other semester I would start acting [out]. So it was on and off." Although only attending sporadically, the leavers did not consider themselves drop-outs at the time, nor are they classified as such by the staff. By this time their records usually show that they completed their last semester with a high rate of absence and no credits earned.

Along with high absenteeism are the high rates of class cutting. The leavers often come in late, do not stay in school for the entire day, and cut classes daily. Most leavers, like César, speak of themselves as chronic truants, skipping school and cutting classes often: "I just go outside. Go home. Sometimes with few of my friends or something. There was more to it in cutting than even being in school for me. I felt that way. I knew I was wrong but I got addicted." They generally wait until after division period, when attendance is taken, to slip out through side doors, as Lisa says, "'Cause you have to go to division. They take [attendance] that you're there and they won't call your house. And you just leave after division." The leavers say that the staff did not call or visit their homes when they stopped coming to school, and even if they did, most likely their parents would not be home. However, some, such as Marisol, recall a particular staff member taking some interest in them, but even those staff members eventually ignored them, making it easy to continue in a downward spiral.

> I was absent a lot but nobody inquired. Only one person from attendance kept track of me. She motivated me someway. She'll tell me, "I'm glad you could make it to school." She'll call my mom sometimes, but my mom already knew that I was at home. But when I stopped going to school they didn't call or anything.

Poor attendance results in class failures and failure to earn many credits. The leavers miss or cut so much that they get poor grades for even those classes they pass. Thus, they accumulate few credits each year, making slow progress toward graduation and having few claims for pride in being students. While students need 20 credits to graduate, so that they must earn 2.5 credits a semester or 5 credits a year, most leavers earned less than 2.5 credits each semester (see Appendix B, Table B.3). For instance, Vitín says, "I only had five credits. For three years and a half, only five credits. I only went to the classes that I liked and that's how come they passed me. That's how come I had those credits." Thus by the time they drop out, the leavers are so far behind their cohort in credits that catching up is impossible. For example, David spent five semesters in school but had accumulated only 0.5 credits (see Appendix B, Table B.4). He remained classified as a freshman when his cohort was already in its junior year.

The leavers' grade point averages attest to their high rate of class failure and slow progression toward graduation. In most cases, their semester grade point averages remain well below 1.50 on a 4.0 scale (see Appendix B, Table B.3). Most follow an up-and-down pattern, having fairly "good" semesters followed by "bad" semesters. For example, Ricardo's grades each semester went from 1.22 to 2.75 to 0.64 to 1.18 to 2.27 to .18 and so on. Just before the time they stop attending school, the leavers' grade-point averages drop sharply, ranging from .10 to 1.24 (see Appendix B, Table B.3). With two exceptions, the leavers obtained a grade point average of 0.00 for their last semester at Hernández High. Grade fluctuations, although rare, do also occur within the same semester, with the leavers sometimes obtaining a good grade in a particular subject matter but failing the others. Like Angie says, "So I was getting D's and F's at school, hardly getting any A's and B's. In the ROTC, I always got A's. That was the only thing that kept me from having too little credits." Most leavers tend to receive low marks in all classes.

Over time the leavers' academic record becomes unremittingly bad. The absence of grades good enough to maintain any credible academic standing or identity points to their incompetence in the student role. However, this incompetence does not seem to be the result of lack of intellectual capability to do schoolwork. The instances in which they do well suggest that they can be competent students.

Trying Out Street Identities

In addition to testing the waters, the leavers begin to actively enact alternative identities. Some encounter alternative identities on their own, while others are encouraged to try out other identities by their peers, often at school itself. Most common among these are the street identities of gang banger and drug dealer. However, some also experimented with family identities as caregivers.

The gang identity is perhaps the most accessible street identity to Hernández High's students. For many, their initial involvement with gangs is prompted by friendship, peer pressure, the security they promise to members, or their search to establish a reputation. Gangs are particularly attractive to self-image promoters because they are a sure way to boost their street reputations. Some leavers may not plan to become gang members, but only to gain notoriety by association. They remain "hangers-on" who benefit from their association but are not full-fledged gang members. For others, the gang identity becomes such an integral part of them that they are usually unable to shake it off. These leavers often describe the gang as a pseudo-family or a community. According to César, gangs are like cults for which youths are willing to sacrifice their lives. "It's all because it's all in the heart. You're in this gang and that's your gang. It's like God, you know. Like all Christians. They believe in God and they'll die for him. And it's the gang, the name. But we're doing it for the nation."

Some leavers say that they turn to gangs because of friendship. They have befriended gang members, and the gang becomes a pretext to hang out together. Because of the tight-knit nature of gangs, these friendships become strong and pull them into the gang, as César explains:

> I got in gangs about during my second year in high school. The friends that I had, we used to [hang out with], my partner, he wasn't in the gang but he knew some friends [who were in gangs]. Then I started getting to know them. We're real, to this day, we're still close.

These leavers talked about being allowed to hang around the gang for some time without making any commitment but eventually being pressured to join, as Vitín was:

> And they told me, "What's up? When are you gonna be one of us and this and that." I said, "I don't know." And then one time we got high, and I said, "You know what? Turn me in 'cause I'm always with you guys. I might as well get it over with and turn in."

In addition to peer influence, the leavers say that joining a gang is inevitable. They see gangs as an inextricable part of growing up in their neighborhood, an inner-city rite of passage into adulthood. Gangs are another fact of life in the street culture because, according to César, it is dangerous for a lone person to manage on his own:

> A lot of us are raised to gang bang . . . Basically, the main reason I turned 'cause I don't wanna take nothing [be abused or pushed around] from nobody else no more. Couldn't do it alone. Couldn't against a big posse. Try to make my own little posse. And then I've got a lot of cousins that are boys and all this. So I joined, you know. That's mainly why I started banging. The reason was [I was] chased. One time I got jumped right here by [near] Hernández [while] being a neutron. I got jumped with a bat and everything.

Gangs are also a vehicle for earning respect and status among street-oriented peers, especially for self-image promoters. According to some leavers, gang members enjoy high status and prestige because others have a mixture of fear and admiration for them. Vitín says that he "wanted to follow their footsteps because everybody had respect for them and I've seen that." The reputation gained by gang membership makes self-image promoters feel good about themselves. Gang banging is the thing that they are known for; it makes them popular and respected. It may be also the one thing at which they can succeed both in and out of school.

Drug dealer is another identity tried out by some leavers, often while in school. In spite of the 1986 Safe School Zone Law calling for tougher sentences—up to 30 years in prison—for drug dealers doing their business within 1,000 feet of schools (Padilla, 1992), the leavers say there is still a good deal of drug activity in and around Hernández High. The students know the sellers, where to find them, and the times of drug sales. A few leavers are involved in the consumption and sale of drugs at school or in the streets. Vitín says, "I wasn't dealing in school. I just bring it in and smoke it in the washroom. And then if anybody wants to buy I just said to him, 'Here. Go and don't say where you got it.' It was my own stuff."

Some leavers say they were introduced to the sale of drugs by their gangs. Padilla (1992) found that drug dealing is the main activity of some gangs that have moved away from the typical gang banging to become more businesslike, and this seems to be happening near Hernández High. Selling drugs becomes an attractive and lucrative activity, not only for the gang but for its newer members. The monetary rewards gained by leavers, such as Ernesto, further increase their street reputation, since they are able to buy material goods, such as cars, clothing, and jewelry, far out of the reach of their peers:

> Okay, I dropped out. In my case I was making more money [dealing drugs], and I didn't find school educational for me. And I wanted to be big and bad, you know . . . I had more street knowledge. I could make more money out in the streets—'cause the street knowledge— than what I can make spending four years in a high school. And waiting so long and being broke. I can make $200, $300 in a day if I would like, if I desire.

While it may boost street reputations for self-image promoters, the risks of drug dealing are high. Arrests for drug possession, either for use or sale, are not uncommon among the leavers. Their associations with drug-dealing peers also expose them to the risk of arrest even when they are not actively involved. Vitín recounts his arrest for marijuana possession just outside of school:

> And the last time they found drugs on me. I had another guy's jacket and he was a [gang member]. I was wearing it because I was cold and I didn't have a jacket. The jacket that I had was like a sweater. I told the guy, "Let me borrow your jacket [while] I go out-

side." When I went outside to go to my car, a cop spot me. "Where you going?" "To my house to get something." "What are you gonna get?" "Don't worry about it." He started checking and everything and when he went to the pocket, the inside pocket, he found three bags of marijuana. I was, "That ain't mine, officer." "Who is it? Well, you're going in for it." So they took me up here and they made a student report or something like that and then they took me to the station.

Rarely do arrests for drug possession lead to expulsion from school or time in prison, since those involved are minors caught outside of the school building with small amounts of drugs.

Involvement with street-oriented peers often introduces the leavers to criminal activities in addition to gang banging and drug dealing. Although a few leavers were involved in gangs and the drug subculture—either selling or consuming drugs—only one reported engaging in other criminal activities. César, who was a gang member and a drug seller, was introduced to auto theft by a friend. They would go to the airport and to car lots to steal cars, which they stripped to then sell the parts. After stealing over a dozen cars, they were apprehended by the police.

At first it was a friend from school who started it really [stealing cars]. A friend of mine from school influenced me. We started stealing cars and stuff, and I used to go with him . . . And I ended up getting caught one time with him . . . 'Cause I got caught that time and then I ended up with him again doing something.

Because he was a minor, César served only about 3 months and was later put on intensive probation. Because of his gang involvement, however, he was arrested often for disorderly conduct and once for aggravated battery while still on probation. To make matters worse, after being given a court date, César did not show up because he was afraid that he was going to be tried as an adult and sent away for a long time. He was arrested a month later, and while the aggravated battery charges were dropped, he was still sent to prison for 9 months for his violation of probation. Although not particularly typical of the leavers, César's story illustrates the escalation of criminal activities among some of them.

Trying Out Family Identities

Students who do not feel competent in school and are not street-oriented find at home an alternative to staying in school. While all students have family identities, such as being a daughter and sister, sometimes other family identities are adopted or temporarily assumed by some leavers. These identities can range from permanent to more temporary roles. The former includes parenthood, which drastically and often unexpectedly changes the lives of the leavers. More temporary family roles and identities are often the result of family crises. Two leavers, both females, experienced family identity changes: one after becoming pregnant, and the other as a result of a terminal illness of her stepfather. Both young women said that family responsibilities took precedence over their education. Yet in both cases they had adopted a pattern of increased disengagement from school that made the choice an easy one.

Some students experiment with sex, often with the unexpected consequence of a pregnancy that thrusts them into parenthood at an early age. Becoming a parent can be something positive in these youths' lives, even when they drop out. Having and caring for a child can make some of them feel competent and bring some order into their lives. The responsibility and demands of parenting also may overwhelm other students and conflict with school. Yet despite the public's image of teenage parents, only one leaver, Angie, left school because of motherhood. Other young mothers, however, leave temporarily or remain in school, where they make up a small but supportive peer group (see Chapter 6).

Parenthood, however, is not the only family obligation that can prompt students to leave school. Family crises, especially terminal illnesses, push teenagers to assume adult family roles that interfere with school. Prolonged illnesses, increases in family size, and economic crises can turn their world upside down and disrupt the daily functioning of the household, requiring a rearrangement of duties and obligations among family members. It is impossible for these students to balance school and family responsibilities. Marisol, for example, tried to balance school and take care of her siblings during the prolonged illness and eventual death of her stepfather. "I stayed home to take care of my brothers. I felt I needed to help my mother. I felt it was up to me. And since I am the oldest I felt I should stay home to help her." During that time, she attended school sporadically but failed to make any accommodation with her teachers, whom she describes as unresponsive, as described earlier in the chapter. Finally, she dropped out.

Regardless of the type of identities tried on, the leavers remain in school. For some time they seem to manage these multiple identities well enough to stay in school. However, a time comes when the conflict and the demands from these different identities become unsurmountable, and they are no longer able to maintain both identities.

TURNING POINTS

The leavers' reasons for departing from school are seldom very precise or singular. Most arrive at the decision to drop out of school after a long process of disengagement accompanied by feelings of discontent while searching for other options. However, they do not leave school solely because of negative experiences, following their peers, or the realization that it may be time to leave. They seriously contemplate dropping out and actively try out alternative identities but usually do not leave school until they reach a turning point. This turning point occurs after the leavers have adopted an alternative identity that clashes with the student identity. Since sustaining both identities is not possible, the turning point provides the push for them to decide between the two.

According to Ebaugh (1988), turning points are abrupt and dramatic events that conflict with role enactment and precipitate individuals' departure from the role. Turning points may be new and specific events, the "last straw" in a series of events, or a justifiable "excuse." The leavers feel they are already "pushed to the limit" where they are just not willing to "take it" anymore, and the occurrence of this event is the catalyst that makes their exit possible. Because dropping out of school is socially condemned, having a reasonable justification makes exit easier. These specific events, last straws, or justifiable excuses accelerate the process of exiting, and provide them with a justification for dropping out.

Specific Event

For some leavers, it is the occurrence of a specific "involuntary" event like expulsion, suspension, or incarceration that leads them to drop out of school. While they may have been thinking about dropping out, and may have already adopted an alternative identity, it is this event that forces them out of school. They describe themselves as having no control over their exit because they did not choose to drop out. Although their school behavior is marked with marginal commitment and general disengagement from school, abandoning their student identities can still be seen as involuntary.

Some leavers say they were suspended or expelled from school because of particular behavioral problems, although their records show prolonged disaffection from school and experimentation with street identities in school. David says that he was "kicked out of school" after he and his mother had a heated argument with an assistant principal because of his performance and attendance. David's mother defended him in spite of his dismal attendance and performance record. Eric, another leaver, says:

> I talked back to a counselor, and I think that she told on me and I was suspended until I brought one of my parents. But then my father was in the hospital, and after he came out my mother was hospitalized, she had like an allergic reaction to something. She broke out in a rash. By the time one of them could come to school, I had too

many absences, and I couldn't make up. So I was not accepted back in school.

Others say they were forced out of school because of role conflict, when the alternative identity they adopted made it impossible for them to continue. Some leavers, such as César, are repeatedly sent to prison, or are put on parole or house arrest, making it impossible for them to keep up with school.

> The next year [second year in high school] I was having more problems and then the school couldn't hold me 'cause I kept coming in and out [of jail] . . . I started going back and forth to court for about six months, though. And they sent me in for a while, for about three weeks. And I came back out on a probation program. It was IPS [Intensive Probation]. It was strict though, it was real strict. I've been in there for a year on probation. And you have to do thirty days in there [detention] and you come out home, and after that they give you curfew [house arrest] thirty days and they keep [increasing] it. But I couldn't last on [house arrest]. Then I ended up getting into problems at Hernández.

Last Straw

While some leavers see themselves as being forced to leave school, others seem to reach the last straw or a point where they are unwilling to put up with schooling any longer. These students cannot pinpoint a particular event as the precipitating factor, but, like Vitín, they are convinced that they just ran out of tolerance for schooling. "I was supposed to be a senior. I was supposed to be gone out of here already. I was supposed to be out of here. I wanted to be out of here . . . I said, 'Carlos [a social worker], I can't take it anymore."

The last straw may appear insignificant, and not a reason powerful enough to lead the leavers to drop out. In fact, many leavers cannot recall what event finally pushed them to make the decision to drop out. As Ernesto puts it, "Guess I didn't find fun and nothing, and education wasn't doing nothing for me." While not being able to point out even an insignificant event, the accumulation of disappointment seems to finally tip the scale, and it is just a matter of time until students like Ernesto leave school. For a long time, these leavers have been harboring negative feelings about school and cultivating other identities.

Excuses

More than specific or cumulative events, excuses also provide an excuse or justification for leaving school. Although they have been thinking about dropping out for some time, some drop out only when they find a reasonable excuse to justify their exit. Sometimes it is the realization that they have missed so much school or failed so many tests that there is no way they will be able to pass with their classmates. More often, the excuse is more tangible, and unexpected, such as health problems or increasing family responsibilities.

Some leavers are afflicted with health problems, as was Lisa, which provided her with a reasonable excuse to drop out. "But then I was in a car accident so there was no way I could come to school. I had a cast [in my leg] for six months. I just stopped coming."

Pregnancy and motherhood are less frequent justifications to leave school. Many young women at Hernández High continue to attend school after becoming pregnant and giving birth to their children, but some drop out. Those who drop out often lack their partner's and family's emotional or physical support to care for the child. While the school participates in a governmental program that pays for childcare, some young women are reluctant to leave their children with a stranger. For example, Angie became pregnant in her junior year and struggled to stay in school throughout a complicated pregnancy.

Lack of support

> I didn't think that I was gonna drop out. But I started getting real sick, and I couldn't get up for school. I had morning sickness every single day, and since I am anemic, I was always dizzy. I couldn't get out of my bed . . . So I just said, "I'll just wait until the morning sickness go away and I'll go back to school." It lasted four months. I was like, "Now, I can't go to school. I missed half of the term."

Although she thought that she would return to school after her baby was born, she could not find a suitable babysitting option because of her fears related to the sexual abuse she experienced as a child.

> I never got therapy for it. But every time I see things about incest survivors, I can never forget. It's something that you'll never forget. That's why I don't like to leave the baby with anybody. I don't even trust the family. The only people I trust is [my] grandparents and my aunt and his [her boyfriend's] aunts and uncles. I don't trust nobody . . . I don't trust anybody and it's because of what happened to me.

The health problems of a family member can also justify leaving school, as they did for Marisol. While Marisol does not attribute her decision to leave school solely to her stepfather's illness, it did provide her with a reasonable excuse for finally disengaging herself from school. She acknowledges:

> I also dropped because I didn't want to be there . . . I left school be-
> cause of a couple of reasons. First, I was not doing great in school.
> My grades were not good. I felt depressed and I felt like a lowlife. I
> was always late to school . . . I was upset with myself. I felt like a fail-
> ure. I kind of gave up on myself.

Yet Marisol's stepfather's terminal cancer gave her a reasonable excuse to
leave school.

Like Marisol, others drop out of school when they realize that they are
not going to graduate or pass their classes that semester. Ricardo, for instance,
left school when it became clear that he was not going to graduate. Instead of
wasting his time in a lost cause, he left school with the intention of coming
back the following year.

CREATING THE DROP-OUT IDENTITY

After dropping out of school, the leavers assume the identity of the drop-out.
This new identity contains traces of the student identity left behind. These
role residuals, the vestiges of the student identity, are referred to as a "hold-
over identity" or "continued identity" (Ebaugh, 1988). Role residuals include
values, norms, attitudes, and expectations held while in the student role that
become part of the drop-out identity. The leavers seem to maintain those
parts of the role that help them establish some sense of continuity and consis-
tency in their self-concept and lessen the stigma of dropping out. According
to Ebaugh (1988), "Roles that are highly visible in society and which involve
social support and social acceptability tend to be roles that are very difficult
to exit from in a complete fashion. One reason is that the public keeps remind-
ing the individual of exiting" (p. 175). Because dropping out of school is stigmatizing, the leavers seek to decrease public chastisement by evoking attitudes
associated with the student identity. For instance, they say that their departure
from school is temporary, that they plan to enroll in alternative high schools
and/or GED programs, and even that they want to attend college. Yet when
I talked to them, many had been out of school for 2 or more years, and plans
to return to school or enroll in a GED program had not materialized. Some
had searched for programs, and a few had gone as far as enrolling in and
attending GED programs, but this effort did not last long; soon they dropped
out of these as well.

Despite their failure to enroll in and complete a high school or GED
program, the leavers continue to believe that an education is necessary for
employment. They recognize that even menial jobs require at least a high
school diploma. They know from first-hand experience how difficult it is to

get a job without it. Ernesto faces this problem again and again, every time he applies for employment.

> But I'm not proud of myself 'cause I dropped out of school. 'Cause I mean, education is needed just to wash toilets these days. You know, every place you request [a job asks] if you graduated [from high school] or did you go to college. I can't answer all that 'cause I didn't.

The kinds of jobs that they obtain also attest to the difficulty in securing stable employment. They usually work bagging and stocking items in grocery stores and warehouses, changing oil in cars or other light mechanical jobs, or working at fast food restaurants. Besides the low pay and irregular work hours, these jobs usually offer no benefits. Anyway, the leavers do not keep these jobs for long; they work for a few months and then quit, or they are fired or laid off.

Leavers with criminal records experience even more difficulty obtaining employment. Few employers hire people with a "record," especially inner-city young men. To obtain employment, they must lie on their job applications. After months of looking for work, Ernesto was employed at a hardware store only to be fired later for lying about his criminal record in the job application. Without a job and feeling he does not have a chance, he felt forced to go back to drug dealing:

> The only thing that I went back to is selling my drugs and that's it. And that's because I had to live somehow because if I can't work, then how am I supposed to have an income? If I don't have an income then, how am I supposed to have my things for the future, my plans? I mean if they would give me [a chance], like I told them people from [the hardware store]. I snapped at them. I told them, "If you people would stop treating other people like you do 'cause of their past. You never are gonna get nowhere and they're never gonna get nowhere unless you give them another chance. And they're gonna go back and do the same thing that they were doing."

Ernesto was one of the leavers who expressed interest in obtaining a high school diploma, although his plans never materialize:

> But I've been thinking of going back to school at [local community college] which they have a night program, three nights out of the week and it's Mondays, Wednesdays, and Fridays and it's from 6 to 9:30 and it will help you get your GED.

The leavers' main hindrances to enrolling and competing a program are their unrealistic expectations, high requirements, and unwillingness to make sacrifices. Instead of committing to any program (high school, alternative school, GED), they are highly selective, wanting to find a program that fits their needs with minimal sacrifice on their part. Since nothing is convenient enough, they end up not enrolling or dropping out quickly.

Some leavers see training programs offered at educational institutes as an option to GED programs because they come out of them with marketable skills. For instance, César is thinking about enrolling in a security guard training program while he works on his GED. He believes that being a security guard beats his present job at a grocery store.

> I figured at least I can go to school for two days a week and try to get something out of it. I look at a lot of opportunities . . . they take you to school to be trained to be a security officer. And I've been thinking about that recently, about going for that. But you've got to get a loan and stuff. But I hear they give you loans out for that. And since I'm going [for a] GED, my GED might get me a loan for that. I'm gonna see what they can do. And then that's only three months of my time and I can finish that up and I'll be able to be a security guard anywhere I want. I'm looking to get a good job.

Obviously, it has not occurred to César that he will never be able to become a security guard given his criminal record. He has been in prison for car theft. Vitín, who also has a criminal record, has unrealistic expectations that include attending college and becoming a police officer.

> And for me, I wanna be a cop . . . All you need is a diploma, but I'm gonna take two years of college there and study law enforcement and then go to the academy. Because if I go to the academy now, then I won't know nothing about law. So I rather take two years of law and then sign up for the academy and take the tests. If I already know everything, then the more you know the more higher ranking you get.

While some may be unrealistic about their possibilities, others, like Lisa, have a clearer idea of what they need to obtain their diploma.

> Well, now I was gonna go to a YMCA and get my GED. But since I already got 14 and a half credits I could graduate in night school with 16 credits. So I'm supposed to talk to Alberto [assistant principal] to see what are the two majors that I need that I can take in night school so I can start in January and graduate in June.

However, acting on those ideas is another matter altogether, a step that most never take or follow through. After assessing the programs available to them comes the harder part of the process: enrolling and completing the program. Some find reasons to keep postponing their enrollment. For example, Angie could not find a suitable babysitting arrangement for her child and decided to wait a few years before pursuing her high school diploma. Others manage to enroll and begin attending programs but leave before completing them. César, for instance, was attending a GED program the first time I talked to him. A year later, he had left that program, tried another and quit it, and was looking for yet another GED program. Similarly, Vitín dropped out from a GED and training program after several months.

The last avenue for many youths in the community and for some leavers is to join the armed forces. They believe that they can learn a trade in the armed forces and find employment later. For instance, César signed up with the Marines. In case he does not get accepted there, he plans to join the reserves through a local college.

> Last week, I had a call. I signed up for selective service 'cause I said, "Man, I can't stay here. I can't [stay] in the streets" . . . So I'm gonna call and see what they got for me. They can finish my GED in there, I think, in the Marines. So I might just end up with two months and stuff. And then I heard about [a community college], they got the academy I think it is. They got a thing for Reserves, people that want to be in the Marines or whatever, the Force. They give you schooling there, too, and they give you a little check while you're going to school but if you mess up that's it. They kick you out. So it's a challenge. So I was thinking about that too. If I can't make for the Marines, then I'm just gonna go there [Reserves]. 'Cause it'll be better in a way.

Although the armed forces may be a viable avenue, those contemplating joining usually back out of it. Like their plans for attending a GED program, joining the armed forces never materializes because they either do not sign up, or are discouraged by recruiting officers because they lack a high school diploma or have criminal records.

Deepening of Commitment to an Alternative Identity

The overwhelming majority of the leavers do not return to school but become more entrenched with the alternative identity. Having more time to dedicate to this identity, they often intensify their commitment to it. While getting more involved with the alternative identity that facilitated leaving school, they still continue to hold onto an identity that has some vestiges of the student identity. This lessens the stigma of being a drop-out, and maintains the possibility, even if very remote, that one day they will return to school.

However, a year after the study, all but one of the leavers remained out of school. The exception was Marisol, who after visiting her aunt and uncle out of state decided to stay with them. She enrolled in high school and graduated a year later. Marisol liked the attention she received in the new school, which was substantially smaller than Hernández High. Her senior class had only 200 students. After graduating, she returned to Chicago and was looking forward to enrolling in college.

Of the remaining leavers, none could be found in the Chicago Public Schools computerized records, meaning that none were back in any CPS program. Through word of mouth, I also learned that for many, returning to school is improbable because their lives have become more complicated since the last time I contacted them. For instance, Lisa, who left school after a car accident, went to live with her father and began taking care of her half-siblings. Angie not only had a second child, but had separated from her husband. She remained at home taking care of her two sons. Ernesto continued to sell drugs and participate in gang activities. César's girlfriend had a child, and soon after he was incarcerated for participating in a gang shooting.

CONCLUSION

The stories told by the leavers show how the school-kid identity progressively becomes less attractive, while non-school identities become more alluring and ultimately replace it. The student-kid identity's lack of appeal is a result of the cumulative disappointments with school experienced by the leavers. Their experiences in elementary school and especially in high school inspire efforts to distance themselves from the student role that translate into problematic school behavior. The structuring of opportunities adds to their disappointment, since they are denied participation in extracurricular programs and the perks that come with it. Also, there is the ever-present hostile and sometimes dangerous street culture that prevails in the school, which poses an alternative to students who are disconnected from school. Although street culture is more pronounced in high school, even elementary schools are not entirely exempt from it.

Because the leavers lack the opportunities to achieve socially and academically, they search for other means of achievement. For many leavers, the street culture becomes the only available social world in which to build some sense of achievement. Increasingly in the high school years, the leavers begin to explore these options and to adopt non-school identities. Their increasing truancy affords them the time and space to explore these options.

While initially some leavers may be able to manage dual school and street identities, over time they come into conflict. Because these identities cannot be supported simultaneously, as one affects the other, the leavers have to choose. Sometimes the decision is easy, but more often the leavers agonize over the decision. It is clear that they do not like school and would rather be somewhere else, but the stigma attached to dropping out of school and being a street kid keeps them from making a hasty decision and prolongs their stay in school. At the end, they reach a point at which either they are made to choose or the decision is made for them.

Still, after dropping out, the leavers maintain some vestiges of the school identity in their expressed desire to return to school. This lessens the stigma of having dropped out and eases their transition into other identities. Over time, however, the leavers get farther away from their expressed intention of returning to school as they become more and more engaged in other identities.

CHAPTER 9

(In) Between School Kids and Street Kids

Dropping out of school is generally taken as an irreversible process by which people leave school "for good." The previous chapter attests to the frequent irreversibility of dropping out of school, or rather the unlikelihood of returning to school after leaving, even when the high school diploma is desired. Yet a significant number of dropouts return to school and manage to obtain their high school diplomas. Many dropouts leave school briefly, sometimes more than once, only to return the following semester or subsequent year. This chapter describes the experiences of 10 temporary dropouts whom I call the returners.

While it might be assumed that the returners are just like the leavers, I found that they differ enough to warrant a separate category. The returners can be best described as "in-betweens" because they display behaviors associated with stayers and leavers at different points in their educational careers. Furthermore, some returners behave like school kids, while others are street kids. Those who resemble the stayers do so up to the time, or just before, they drop out of school. They are school kids who, although not enthusiastic about school, perform relatively well before dropping out. Like the stayers, these returners are reputation avoiders who stay out of trouble after returning to school. Unlike the stayers, they are not involved in extracurricular programs, nor do they receive any of the perks, incentives, and rewards typically afforded to school kids. These returners' departure from school was sudden and unexpected, and nothing in their records would have predicted it. Their education is disrupted by unexpected family crisis or personal problems. As these problems are resolved, they promptly return to school and assume their school-kid identities. These returners are "in-betweens" in another sense. Since they do not excel socially or academically and are not problematic, they become invisible to the teachers and staff, and go unnoticed both before dropping out and after returning to school.

Most returners, however, resemble the leavers. They subscribe to the street culture that they find in school, and show marginal commitment to school, both in grades and attitudes. As pointed out in Chapter 5, they are self-image promoters who subscribe to street culture. It is in the street culture that they satisfy their need to become somebody and where they find the rewards, prestige, and positive evaluations from others that they do not get in school. They develop strong relationships with street-oriented peers, and try on street identities that conflict with being a student. Because their school performance is poor, they are habitual truants and have often been in trouble in school; their exit from school is foreseeable. Despite their pre-exit profile, these returners begin to resemble the stayers more upon returning to school. Although their commitment to school continues to be marginal, the restoration of their student identities changes many of the leaver-like street behaviors they engaged in before dropping out. They return to school with a renewed resolution to make it through and graduate. They become self-image defenders, maintaining a street reputation but keeping out of trouble in school. They calculate their steps so as not to mess up their chance to finish school. Many are aware that this is their last chance, and they set out to "make it" this time around. Their change of attitude, however, does not alter the image they project in school and how they are evaluated and treated by teachers and staff. Despite their efforts to make it this time around, they remain marked and treated as street kids.

This chapter describes the travails of this group of students, who dropped out of school but returned soon afterwards. Their experiences outline a more complex process than that undergone by the leavers (see Chapter 8). While the initial three stages (first doubts, seeking alternatives, and reaching a turning point) of the returners are similar to the leavers', I identified two additional stages that account for their return to school: resolution of conflict and the reestablishment of the school-boy and -girl identity. Since their stories up to the time they dropped out are similar to those of the leavers, in this chapter I focus on what prompted them to return and how they fared upon returning to school.

THE "RENAISSANCE": RESOLUTION OF CONFLICT

Regardless of the reasons that prompted their exit from school, being a dropout becomes a burden for the returners, who promptly seek to go back to school. Being a drop-out is made difficult by the stigma attached to it. Not only do the returners have to contend with public, and their own, stigmatizing views about drop-outs, but they quickly realize that being a drop-out is not what they imagined. Suddenly, staying at home; working in low-paying, dead-end jobs; or the responsibilities that come with alternative identities, such as parenthood, are not as attractive as they once seemed. Reality comes crashing down, shattering any argument they used to justify and talk themselves into dropping out. As they contemplate their lives from the other side, they begin to acknowledge that dropping out was perhaps a mistake. Adding to this realization is the fact that the circumstances surrounding their exit from school change. What some of them once viewed as insurmountable problems that impeded them from continuing in school are resolved.

The returners' experiences while out of school convince them that what they are doing is not what they want. Some had glamorized the life of the drop-out, envisioning it like a big party. They thought that they would be free to do whatever they wanted, whenever they wanted to. Manuel explains his reasoning about dropping out:

> I left the second semester [of freshman year]. I left early [freshman year]. I though it was easy out there without school and then just stay home. Let your parents take care of you. They worked for me. Staying at home. Sleeping all day and messing around . . .

Initially, dropping out may live up to their expectations, but not for long. Eventually the fun wears out, and they realize that most drop-outs do not lead lives of adventure. Many returners, such as Jenny, say they became bored and had nothing to do but to sit at home. "After a while you get sick of being home and I was like, 'Man, what am I gonna do with myself. I can't always be at home.'"

As disillusion sets in, many of the events that triggered the returners' exit from school become resolved. Problems that seemed insurmountable before are reevaluated and do not seem that big after all. They come to the realization that whatever triggered their exit from school is manageable now. As crises wane, their lives become more stable, and a sense of normalcy is restored. For example, Lourdes left school when she and mother became homeless after her parents' divorce.

> My freshman year everything was like predictable for me. I knew what I was gonna do tomorrow. I knew what time I was gonna come to school, what time I had to be out. My father always woke us up and made breakfast for us since he worked second shift. He was like the house father in the mornings and then my mother would come home and she would cook . . . I left school when my parents had started to split up. I was, I couldn't make it to school because there wasn't any [energy] in me anymore . . . [Then my mother and I] couldn't afford rent anymore and we were about to move into a shelter because the rent was getting real real bad.

Moving around from one relative to another, they finally were able to find separate but more permanent accommodations, and Lourdes began to attend school again.

Interestingly, it is sometimes the same events that prompted them to leave school that propel them to return; that is, provide a justification for leaving as well as for returning to school. For instance, Diana said that she left school to care for her son, yet she returned to school "to make a good future for my son."

Sometimes their lives turn around after another drastic event. Fearing that they will spend the rest of their lives with regrets, the returners reconsider their decision to drop out of school. For them, it is a matter of now or never. For example, Angel, who dropped out of school when his girlfriend became pregnant "'cause you think that is the right thing to do," returned to school after the baby died of Sudden Infant Death Syndrome.

> I just pushed it a long year working at Cubs Foods. $4.55 an hour. And after my daughter died, I told myself, "If I don't do something now, I'm gonna be suffering for the rest of my life." I don't know. I just decided that school is it. That's the only way, that's the only ticket.

As problems disappear or are reassessed, the returners reexamine their lives more objectively. Feeling free of the pressures that led them to drop out, they can think clearly about their situation. As Angel puts it,

> My junior year, that's my rebirth. That's like my renaissance. My new year was junior. My daughter died, I was off drugs. My mind was clear, and I was ready to make the push. I didn't want to fail again. That's when I really started pushing myself. That's what changed everything. So in my junior year that's when I knew. It was my daughter's death. It was just a shock. It's one of those things. I just took control. I set on my own. My parents, they didn't help nothing. Everything I've done is on my own so I took control of myself.

ON BECOMING SCHOOL KIDS: REESTABLISHING THE STUDENT IDENTITY

Having resolved their conflicting role identities, the returners become convinced that it was a mistake to drop out, and take steps to enroll in school. Getting back in school is relatively easy. Most of the returners just walk into school and are reinstated as students. They usually wait to re-enroll until a new academic year starts. Regardless of the timing of their return, they go back to school with a firm commitment to make it through this time. For them, getting to graduation day is all that matters, and they are resolved not to let anything stand in their way. Sylvia expresses this determination:

> If one really wants to make a difference in one's own life and wants to go to classes and wants to succeed, gangs and everything is not

gonna stop you. It's not gonna stop you. Because one has the goal that "I want to graduate. I am going to get out of this school."

Returning to school is fairly simple, but remaining there proves to be a challenge for the returners. Not only do they have to deal with the stigma of having been a drop-out and being left behind their cohort, they must contend with the school reputations they had built previously. Many returners were street kids before dropping out, but because this identity conflicts with being a student, the returners have to reach some kind of resolution. As I explain in Chapter 5, many returners take on a reputation-defender stance, by which they capitalize on their street-kid image without having to engage in street behaviors that clash with being a student.

Because of their past truancy and poor grades, and the time spent out of school, they are still far from graduation (see Appendix B, Table B.5). Although some manage to graduate only one year behind their cohort, most take 2 or more years to graduate (see Appendix B, Table B.6). Overall, most spend 5 years in high school, without counting the time they were out. To some, like Diana, it seems they have "been here a lifetime. It's like six years is a lot for high school." Angel adds, "I've been here like forever. It is a long time. You get tired of it."

The Value of a High School Diploma

For the returners, school takes on a new meaning. Although graduating from high school has practical value, the returners stress its symbolic value. This may be due to their uneasiness with the image of the drop-out and their reluctance to concede the practical disadvantages that go with it. The returners' discomfort with the drop-out identity is expressed in the value they place on the high school diploma over the GED, and their fear of becoming a "lowlife." Jenny says that she "didn't want that [GED]. What I wanted was my high school diploma. You know, to me [it] is more valuable." Like the stayers, they place more value on a high school diploma than a GED, particularly because they will be the first in the family to graduate and it will prove to others that they can "make it." Like most Hernández High students, the returners usually come from families where parents and siblings have not completed high school. It is their parents' dream to see them graduate, as Manuel explains:

My brothers dropped out sophomore year, freshman year. None of them made it, and I'm the first out of six of my brothers, I'm the first one I'm gonna graduate. I'm the second youngest. My little brother, he comes here, he's a freshman . . . I'll be the first one to graduate this year. My mom is happy. It's the first graduation she is gonna see in high school.

For some returners who come from families where parents and siblings have graduated, however, their fear is that they will be the only ones who do not graduate. Lourdes returned to school "to get my diploma. In a way I just think because my sister got one I wanna get one." Parents and siblings who graduated from high school often serve as role models for the returners. Angel was inspired by his father's completion of a college degree despite drug addiction and being HIV-positive. He says that "my father's achievements is what made me come back to school. Made me go to college, and it's made me do all this stuff." Most returners say that their parents and siblings encourage them, or "push" them, to finish high school. Jerry describes his situation:

> I've got to [graduate]. I just got to. I have to do it for my dad. When I had that fight and was kicked out of school, they told my father that I was a gang member. He didn't know. I've been banging for three years and my parents had no clue. My friends covered up for me. When my dad found out, he was disappointed. He even started crying right in school. He made me promise to leave the gang and to graduate from high school.

Family example or encouragement to return to school and graduate seems to be a pattern among the returners.

For the returners, one main difference between the high school diploma and the GED is the graduation ceremony. The returners talk about the graduation ceremony as a major event in their lives. They look forward to graduation and begin making plans in advance. Because graduation means so much to them, having their families attend the ceremony is very important. Diana expresses her feelings:

> I want all my sisters and brothers and my mother there. 'Cause we get like seven tickets, and it's six of them I need for my sisters and my brothers and my mother mandatory. Whoever else don't come that's not my problem as long as I have them there . . . I've been crying, crying for the past week, I don't understand. My mother is leaving me [to return to live in Puerto Rico] . . . And I was just crying. "Mom, how can you say this to me. Don't you wanna watch it that I worked so hard in high school and finally gonna make it and you're not gonna be there? You know, you made it to all the other girls' graduations, you can't make it to mine?" She's like, "Diana, I'm sorry, I don't know what to do." But I'm hoping she'll change her mind and come back 'cause I really want her in my graduation.

Possibly linked to their families' encouragement is the returners' near obsession with obtaining a high school diploma as a way of proving to themselves and to others that they can do it. Their concern with how others perceive them drives their motivation. While they may have made what they consider to be "bad" decisions, finishing high school is a shot at redemption. For Manuel, high school is a way to show others, as well as himself, that he can do it: "That's why I don't really care. I laugh at them, they'll be saying, 'No, you're not gonna graduate.' Look, I only got two months to go and I'll be on stage. I don't worry about them."

Perhaps the most compelling reason to regret leaving school is their feelings of shame and embarrassment for dropping out. Of particular concern is what they believe people think of them. They know what the drop-out label connotes, and they do not want to be associated with it. Some, such as Angel, are wary because in addition to dropping out, they had assumed socially undesirable identities:

> When I was in school, I showed that I was [in a satanic cult]. Everybody knew . . . They don't really know me. They know me as the guy, the devil worshiper that came to school. That's all they know about me . . . [They ask] "Was that you?" I go, "No, it wasn't me." I don't admit it because I don't want that person. That's old me.

More than avoidance of the dropout label, the returners express fear of becoming a "lowlife." They, like the stayers in Chapter 7, use this term to refer to people who are unable to support themselves through socially approved means. Among those included among the lowlifes are the unemployed, welfare recipients, gang members, drug dealers, drug addicts, alcoholics, and homeless. The returners are afraid that the drop-out identity may become a self-fulfilling prophecy, and they will end up becoming lowlifes. Some returners talk constantly about the "need to get a life" as the only way to prevent becoming a lowlife. Diana believes that the only way to "get a life" is through school. Her boyfriend epitomizes what she fears becoming. "He dropped out his sophomore year. He needs to get a GED. He needs to get a life if you ask me. He's twenty. He just bums around 'cause there's nothing else to do when he should just get a job. I always tell him."

Academic Performance

Because graduating is their priority, the returners discipline themselves so that they are not diverted from their goal. Because they are older than most of their classmates and feel "more mature," they know that this may be their last chance to earn a traditional high school diploma. They are aware that the school does not have an obligation to readmit them after they have reached

16 years of age, the legal age for leaving. They also know that the administration keeps a close eye on their progress and, in some cases, may be looking for pretexts to expel them. The sense of this as their last chance makes them careful about what they do in school. Nonetheless, they find themselves with little margin for failure.

In light of their motivation to graduate, one would expect them to improve their academic performance. Yet most barely make it through school after re-enrolling. Not only do they hardly pass their classes, their attendance is poor in comparison to the stayers (see Appendix B, Table B.5). This is more noticeable among those who are farther from graduation. Wanting to ensure that they will graduate this time around, the returners become more deliberate and careful about their behavior. However, this is not a reflection of a change in attitudes toward school, but rather a more serious commitment to the student identity despite their dislike for school. When the prospect of graduation draws near, the returners are much more careful because missing school and failing classes can cost them another year in school. Since the degree is within their grasp, they curb their class cutting and absences, like Jenny:

> [Now it is] a lot different 'cause now they're [friends] like, "Let's cut," and I'm like, "No, I'm not going nowhere." If I cut, I cut on my own, and that's just if I have to do something that I have to do then. But other than that, it can wait. 'Cause I really wanna get out of here. The experience that I went through last year it's like I don't want it. I wanna finish school. I really do wanna finish school.

Returners who are still far from graduating are less careful about absences, cuts, and grades. Their attendance continues to be sporadic and their grades poor, and they do not seem to be improving. For example, Jerry earned only 1.50 credits (0.50 the first semester and 1.00 the second semester), and his grade point averages were .18 and .89 respectively in 1992–93. He was absent an average of 22.5 days a semester that year (see Appendix B, Table B.5). At the end of his fourth year in school, Jerry had only 12.50 credits and a cumulative grade point average of 1.07 (see Appendix B, Table B.6).

These returners are aware of their truant behavior and try to talk themselves into becoming more responsible in school. For instance, they say that they make resolutions to improve their attendance, but, like Lourdes, do not fulfill them.

> It's just I don't go to my classes. I just go to the easy ones. Not the easy ones, because all my classes are easy . . . I just sit down in the hallways and read. The teachers are right there, but they do not say

anything. Most of the time that they don't notice that I'm cutting. I just go to Youth At-Risk.

These returners fall into a "I'll start tomorrow" routine, but never keep their promise. They switch from "tomorrow" to "next week" to "next semester," and soon the semester or the academic year is over and they did not improve their attendance. Lourdes acknowledges:

> I know, I'll go to classes next semester. It's cause I keep on telling my-self I'm gonna do better and I'm gonna start going to all my classes next week. But then it's like, "Okay, I'm missing this one, they won't count." It's not that I don't want to 'cause in a way I do. But then I al-ways have a choice.

What makes it difficult to discipline themselves in school is the peer *old peer pressure* group. Their old friends may put too much pressure on them to cut classes and revert to their old street-like behavior patterns. Those returners who are close to graduating usually replace their old friends with school-oriented friends. As Diana says, "I haven't seem them hardly [the wild crowd]. That way I could be more into school." It is not too difficult to avoid old friends because many have continued to advance and are not in the same grade level. Their old friends themselves have usually replaced them with new friends. Thus, many returners are forced to carve their space again in the students' social structure, and they are more selective the second time around. Since many returners are more careful when selecting friends, their friends can be a positive influence. For example, Diana found that when she attended school mainly to hang out with her new friends, their school-kid orientation contributed to her improved academic performance:

> I had my friends and they would encourage me. 'Cause they're so into school, they would encourage me. People would call me when I wouldn't come. But just to hang out with them, and I'll be, "All right, I'll come to school today." I passed my classes last year. 'Cause when I first came in I had straight F's for the first 10 weeks. And for the last 10 weeks when I started hanging with [the nerdy crowd], I only got one F.

School is still a meeting place where the returners visit with old friends, but they tend to restrict their time with friends to the periods when they have no classes. They are less likely than before to skip classes just to be with a friend. They stress the fact that they have returned to school because they want to graduate. Diana stays focused on her goal "[be]cause I really wanna get out of here. The experience that I went through last year it's like I don't want it. I wanna finish school. I really do wanna finish school."

Finding a Niche

Besides rectifying their behavior and selecting peers carefully, some returners also become more involved in school programs. One returner joined several extracurricular programs right after returning to school, and remained active in at least one sport until he graduated. Manuel says that "when I came back we started with the tumbling team. I joined the football team, swim team. Then it got fun." Jenny participated in her senior year: "And I've joined the flag team. We come out in parades dancing with flags."

Those returners who do not participate in programs after returning to school tend to say that they fear that participation would only aggravate their academic problems. According to those such as Jerry, participating will distract them from schoolwork, and they may end up failing their classes and not graduate:

> I don't wanna play no more sports [so that I can] get out of school. 'Cause I know myself, and I know if I join basketball again, I'm gonna forget all about school, and I'm gonna start failing again just to be in basketball, and I ain't gonna graduate next year. That's why. So I better stay this way.

Being aware that they are likely to get in trouble in school, many returners seek assistance from the social service programs at Hernández High School. The returners are overrepresented among those in the service-oriented programs, with 60% of them receiving some kind of assistance. It does not seem to bother them that these programs are often stigmatizing. The stigma is apparently a low price to pay for what they get out of these programs, as Lourdes explains:

> My sister was with Youth At-Risk because she was having like, she was all mixed up, right. And so I was all mixed up and then I just asked for a counselor. Irma is good to talk to. It's like when you need somebody to talk to and she's around, you talk to her. She helps you out most of the time.

In the social service programs, the returners also find other students who are having similar difficulties. The mere knowledge that others are undergoing similar situations helps the returners cope with their problems. They can also get practical advice from peers. For instance, young women participating in the Teenage Parents program exchange stories about pregnancy and childbirth as well as information about doctors. Lourdes, who became pregnant after returning to school, tells how she values her contact with her friend Sara:

> Lately, we've been talking a lot. I known her since my freshman year, but lately we've been talking a lot. She got me a doctor. I feel more safe talking to somebody that has gone through that 'cause I'm scared right now. If I feel a couple of pains and she is like, "Oh, yeah. I used to have that before." And I feel like, "Oh, okay, it's normal." It's like, when I go inside the room and talk to like mothers already, I'm always asking them questions. Sometimes I'm thinking I didn't know anything, but I don't care, I just ask them a lot of questions. I'm confused because some people say, "No, it's just the contractions that really hurt," but I'm scared to have it natural 'cause I'm scared that it's really gonna hurt me.

Social service programs like Teenage Parents and Youth At-Risk are as much places for students to talk to one another as to receive professional counseling.

Others find a niche in a particular class or school program. They may like the teacher or, like Jenny, find the class challenging and interesting.

> 'Cause I was in the Law program . . . You know, we would go to courtrooms and take mock trials. I passed it with an A. And I like that class a lot. I took it this year [again] but I needed another English that would count as a History and I couldn't take it. So I had to drop it. And I really liked that class. I find it very interesting.

Other returners like classes in which they excel because of their talents. For instance, Pablo enjoys physical education because he is good in sports. Yet others enjoy classes that are hands-on and provide them with practical skills, like Food Services.

Graduating or Dropping Out Again

Returning to school does not mean that a student will graduate. Most returners continue to struggle with their feelings and debate whether they should remain in school. Some leave school again, only to return again. When they leave school a second time, it is because they have reached another turning point in their lives, another disruption that affects their schooling. Most are able to reach a resolution to their problem, return to school, and graduate. Some returners eventually become drop-outs, never returning to school. Only one of the returners in my sample dropped out of school, although not officially, before the study ended, Lourdes. She had been living with her boyfriend's family, but her father-in-law's sexual advances after the birth of her daughter forced her to leave. She began again to move from place to place, this time with her newborn daughter, and stopped coming to school. A year after the study, people told me that she was still out of school and using drugs.

The one thing the returners share is their desire to graduate. For most, school is merely a burden they have to put up with, but hopefully not for long. Their antipathy to school stems from their feelings of alienation and their previous school experiences. Many, like Lourdes, feel that they do not belong in school.

> I was thinking about for this year transferring to another school. But then I'm like too into the school. I feel like if I go to, I was planning on going to Cyril or Limpscomb, I feel like I wouldn't fit in. And it's already hard enough for me to fit in here, not just to fit in, it's just sometimes I feel like I don't belong or something like that.

Others did not feel as alienated as Lourdes, but Jerry went as far as to compare school to prison, and equated staying in school as serving time.

> Teachers, everything, the security. They harass you too much. Like this is jail for real. They start pushing you and stuff. Yeah, they push you, "Get out of here." Harassing too much . . . A lot of people feel like that [school is like jail]. [They don't complain] 'cause ain't nobody gonna do nothing. Nobody gonna do nothing.

Yet most of the returners put up with school because they see the "light at the end of the tunnel." A year after the end of the study, 7 of the 10 returners had reached their goal of graduation, Jerry and Pablo were still in school, and Lourdes had become a drop-out again.

CONCLUSION

As a group, the returners present an enigma because they switch status so often. They are street kids to the extent that they exhibit street-like behaviors that lead them to drop out of school, sometimes more than once. Yet they are also school kids because they return to school and often graduate. Perhaps better than the school kids or the street kids, they exemplify how students deal with multiple identities and the role conflicts that emerge from contradictory role obligations. With the street kids they share a story of increasing disappointment with school. Lacking opportunities to develop school-related identities, they search outside of school for viable identities. Over time, their experiments with alternative identities conflict with their claims to the school-kid identity. Given their lack of enthusiasm for school, it is usually easier to give up their student identities.

However, leaving school is not an easy decision for the returners. Many hang on to school for a very long time, but ultimately they cannot sustain their school identity. They drop out of school with feelings of guilt that do not let them remain out of school for long. They feel shame for dropping out and fear becoming a lowlife. This fear, accompanied by their discontent with being a drop-out and the reduction of role conflict after leaving school, led them to rethink their decision. Although role conflict drove them out of school, after dropping out they are able to resolve the conflict or reach a balance that allows them to reactivate their student identities.

Upon returning to school, the returners become committed to school and move closer to being school kids. Although they are determined to graduate this time around, their commitment to school is conditional, and they put minimum effort into it, just enough to make it through. Many still engage in street-like behaviors but are careful not to push it too far. Finding themselves in between the school kids and the street kids, most ultimately succeed in barely graduating from high school.

CHAPTER 10

Creating School Kids
and Effective Schools

The previous chapters show how students become school kids or street kids
and describe the kind of school experiences that shape each identity. I found
that schools provide students with different kinds of experiences, and as a result,
schools produce two types of students—school kids and street kids. What type
of identity students take on has implications for school completion. In simple
words, students who develop a school-kid identity tend to graduate from high
school, while those who become street kids are more likely to drop out. In
this chapter, I reiterate what I learned from the participants' narratives about
how kids become school kids, and suggest what schools can do to help create
more school kids. I begin the chapter by identifying the seven conditions that
are crucial in the development of school-kid identities. In the second part of
the chapter, I pose that to effectively transform the school experiences of kids
and help students develop school-kid identities, systemwide school reform is
necessary. School-based changes, such as the ones happening at Hernández
High at the time of the study, are not enough to effect meaningful educational
experiences for all students. What I learned from Hernández High's efforts is
that school-based reform has limited success when the structural features of
the school system remain untouched.

THE CHALLENGE OF CREATING SCHOOL KIDS

My research explores the sociopsychological dimensions involved in the development of student identities and the effect that school practices have on them.
Developing and maintaining these identities is contingent on the presence and
configuration of seven factors I identified using the role-identity literature:

1. School kids have opportunities to take on the socially appropriate role
   of students.
2. They can count on the support of their teachers and peers.
3. They get recognition and rewards.

4. They develop close and warm relationships with teachers and other school kids.
5. They receive constant positive feedback for their adequate performance as students.
6. They are given opportunities to explore and incorporate into their school-kid identity various other school-related identities.
7. They are encouraged to explore possibilities for their future and to aspire—and expect—to become socially mobile.

In all schools, at least some students have these experiences, but in many schools, particularly in inner-city schools such as Hernández High, the proportion of students who do not is very high. It is then imperative that the school staff think long and hard about how they structure school experiences. Schools should strive to provide all students with opportunities to become school kids. I offer six recommendations of what schools can do to help students become school kids.

First, schools should set clear and consistent standards, rules, and expectations—both academic and disciplinary—of what it means to be a student, and must apply these to all students regardless of ability, race/ethnicity, class, gender, or language skills. At the same time students are subjected to high standards, they should be exposed to a challenging curriculum that prepares them to compete in college or the job market. At a minimum, the curriculum should meet the entrance requirements of 4-year colleges—in many schools they do not—so that all students can exercise the option of attending college upon graduation. Besides being challenging, the curriculum should be meaningful to the students. Students find the curriculum meaningful when they can relate to the lessons because they speak to their reality. The curriculum should comprehensively incorporate multicultural perspectives that reflect the cultures of the students in the school.

Second, schools should make each student "count," and make them feel like they are "somebody" and not "invisible." The current size of schools facilitates the invisibility and anonymity of most students. When attendance is taken by calling out identification numbers—as I observed at Hernández High—or when teachers cannot name their students, students feel like they do not matter and that if they leave nobody will notice. In sum, students should be treated with respect and dignity.

Third, schools should help kids develop numerous and deep relationships with their teachers and peers. Teachers can provide social support by listening to students, being understanding of their needs, and encouraging them to develop their skills to their fullest potential. These relationships should be characterized by caring, respect, and dignity. Students should have opportunities to interact with teachers outside the classroom, and to get involved with their peers in academic and social activities at school.

Fourth, schools should redefine achievement by minimizing the promotion of competition—for grades, for spots in extracurricular programs, for teacher attention—and by providing alternative avenues for achievement. The current emphasis on individualization and competition means that some kids win while most must lose. Schools should offer students diverse opportunities to engage in school that are based on interests and not on competition. Furthermore, students should be rewarded, or at least acknowledged, for their efforts regardless of their performance.

Five, schools should help students develop multiple identities connected to school. Students generally assume school-related identities through participation in the extracurricular programs, but these opportunities are limited to about 20% of the students, who must meet grade or skill-level requirements. No matter the size of high schools, there is the usual array of extracurricular programs, and specific numbers of students may participate in each. Therefore, the larger a school is, the larger the number of students excluded from the extracurricular programs. In addition to the logistics of space, there are recruitment practices and requirements set up to screen out students who want to participate. Regulations that restrict participation in the traditional extracurricular programs (sports teams) should be modified to accommodate more kids. Schools should create additional extracurricular options (such as intramural sports), nontraditional extracurricular activities (such as a poetry writing group), and after-school programs that do not require that students meet criteria such as grades or skill level. Furthermore, current recruitment practices whereby program sponsors handpick participants should be abolished. These recruitment practices favor students who have connections to teachers, and end up excluding those kids who most need to build these relationships.

Finally, schools should help students construct ambitious yet realistic conceptualizations of themselves in the future, and should help them concretize and reach their goals. Promises of success through hard work and good behavior are hollow unless these are accompanied by a truthful discussion of the structural barriers (such as discrimination) that students will face outside of school. Schools should prepare students to deal with real life by telling them "how it is" and giving them concrete and practical advice. Schools can move students closer to accomplishing their dream of becoming middle class by helping them to set a goal, make a plan to reach it, and take concrete steps to realize it, that is, by giving them the tools they need to stand on their own two feet.

SCHOOL REFORM FOR LATINO SUCCESS

To help students become school kids, schools must provide the kind of meaningful experiences that are part of what researchers delineate as the characteristics of effective schools (Garbarino, Dubrow, Kostelny, & Pardo, 1992;

Hetherington, Cox, & Cox, 1982; Lucas, Henze, & Donato, 1990; Nieto, 1999; Romo & Falbo, 1996; Valenzuela, 1999; Werner, 1990). These schools have clear and consistent standards, rules, and expectations—both academic and disciplinary. They put an emphasis on high academic achievement. Furthermore, they closely monitor student progress to prevent failure. In these schools, teachers are warm and caring, and hold a positive attitude toward students. The school leadership embraces unconventional and innovative practices, recruits good teachers who share a similar educational vision, and invests resources in whatever can help teachers reach their goals. They also involve parents, teachers, and students in the educational process. These schools build the students' self-esteem by providing students with opportunities to excel academically and/or socially and rewarding the students' efforts. More important, these schools have a multicultural curriculum and programs that celebrate the diversity of cultures, and that particularly focus on integrating the students' cultures into the schooling process.

Recent studies argue that making schools effective for Latino students involves systemic school reform that addresses the needs of the students (Nieto 1999; Romo & Falbo, 1996; Valenzuela, 1999). These studies posit that the "damage control" or "putting out fires" approach currently undertaken by schools does little to significantly and permanently transform the educational experiences of Latino students. According to Valenzuela, problems were ignored at Seguín High School until they exploded, although the staff could see the storm coming. Thus, they were caught in a cycle of perennial damage control that prevented a genuine transformation of the school experience for the Latino students. The only way to create meaningful school experiences for Latinos is through major restructuring—"the entire educational system must be overhauled so that schools can meet the needs of all students" (Romo & Falbo, 1996, p. 218). To be successful, school reform must be culturally relevant and guided by what Nieto (1999) calls a multicultural perspective, and Valenzuela (1999) describes as an authentic caring pedagogy that fosters the cultural integrity of the students.

Although we know the characteristics of effective schools, we understand what it takes to become a school kid, and we are aware of what schools can do to foster the development of school-kid identities, producing more school kids is easier said than done. It is hard enough for the school itself to make modifications, but added to this is the burden of having to deal with a school system whose policies are not always in tune with the school's needs and efforts. As a result, it is very difficult for schools to effect meaningful and lasting change when they have to comply with, and are subjected to, systemwide policies. Furthermore, systemwide policies address the common denominator, neglecting the needs of many kids. It is improbable that schools can undertake a successful educational reform as long as they remain responsive to, accountable to, and constricted by systemwide policies that do little to transform schooling. For changes to be meaningful and lasting, they must happen systemwide. The case of Hernández High is a good illustration of what happens to reform efforts when they are school-based and not part of systemwide reform.

Halfway There: School Reform at Hernández High

In 1989, Hernández High began a series of reform efforts stemming from the Chicago School Reform. The 1988 Chicago School Reform decentralized school control by giving local schools discretionary power over curriculum, staff, and budget as long as they complied with state and federal laws, Board of Education rules and policies, and union contracts (Bryk et al., 1998; Hess, 1995). Schools were responsible for drafting and implementing a school improvement plan, making marked improvements in student achievement, and reporting the results of their reform efforts to the central office annually (Bryk et al., 1998; Hess, 1995). The reform also set parameters and sanctions for schools that did not show substantial improvement. Hernández High is an example of a school where school-based educational reform has resulted in innovative changes, yet efforts to show substantial improvements remain limited because systemwide policies still dictated the structuring of schools—large size, run-down facilities, scant resources, inadequately trained staff—and the reform initiative is subject to the push and pulls of local politics. Below I show how Hernández High steered reform efforts and implemented innovative policies to deal with what was handed down to them by the system. I conclude with a discussion of why reform efforts at Hernández High were thwarted several years later, highlighting the need for systemwide reform.

School leaders at Hernández High envisioned a truly community-based school and committed themselves to accepting all students who came to its doors, regardless of their educational records. It is this vision that allowed students like Diana, a two-time drop-out who returned to school, to graduate on her "third try" at age 21. This vision was accompanied by innovative programs based on a multicultural perspective that sought to integrate the students' cultures into the schooling process. These programs also addressed concerns with the large school size and safety, and sought to transform the depersonalizing nature of schooling, the irrelevance of curriculum and ineffective teaching practices, and the lack of meaningful relationships between students and teachers. The underlying goal of the reform efforts at Hernández High was the creation of leadership among its teachers, students, and parents. These reform efforts were concretized in five programs that included the development of schools within a school, a multicultural curriculum, multicultural programs, staff development, and parental participation in school.

Schools Within a School. Hernández High's large size, both structurally and in student population, forced it to come up with an ingenious way to deal with that size by symbolically "decreasing" it. In 1991, Hernández High began to slowly implement a "house" or schools-within-schools system. This called for the division of the school into five smaller units coexisting within the same structure. Each house had one "floor" of the school. Each student cohort (freshman, sophomore, junior, senior, and the bilingual program) was assigned to a particular house, where they had to remain together for their four years in school. The house system was adopted to alleviate the problems created by the large student population, to make students feel they belonged, and to foster closer relationships between students and teachers.

While schools within a school can be highly effective, the potential benefits of this system remain unrealized at Hernández High. First, grouping the students into smaller units did not change the fact that the school still had over 2,500 students entering and leaving the building at the same time as well as converging on the halls and escalators during class changes. Second, house affiliation had no real appeal to the students. They did not have "themes," and membership was assigned based on grade level. The bilingual program is not a "theme" because students are automatically assigned to it if they have limited English proficiency. As Powell, Farrar, and Cohen (1985) notice, houses are more effective if students "choose—and are chosen by—schools or sub-schools than if they are simply assigned to them" (p. 316). Third, the distribution of staff into the various houses did not mean a lower staff-pupil ratio. No more teachers and counselors were hired. Instead, teachers and counselors were still handling the same number of students, but the only difference was that they were housed with the same group of students for 4 years. Although the staff-pupil ratio remained quite high, at least the staff worked with the same students year after year, and hopefully got to know them.

Multicultural Curriculum. Hernández High was making curricular changes that revolved around multicultural awareness, and in particular around Puerto Rican culture. The school leaders sought to incorporate a comprehensive multicultural curriculum that included all grade levels and all substantive courses. Specific history courses that emphasized Puerto Rican, Mexican, and African American culture and history were developed, along with inclusion of these groups' experiences in other courses. For instance, in addition to reading the canon, students would also read Latino and African American authors in their literature courses. In addition, students could get credit for participating in mini-courses hosted by the cultural center. Curricular changes at Hernández High were slowly but systematically planned and implemented. Although curricular changes were still in the works, students said to me that they were glad that the school was finally teaching them about Puerto Rican and other Latino cultures.

Multicultural Programs. In addition to the traditional student activities
(e.g., band, athletic teams, social clubs), Hernández High instituted a number
of cultural programs that centered on the learning and promotion of Latin
American and other cultures. School leaders believed that lack of achievement
was partially due to students' lack of cultural knowledge, particularly of their
own cultures. Many of the students were Puerto Rican or Mexican but had
little understanding of their cultures and knew even less about their groups'
history. To help students learn who they are, Hernández High brought in
guest speakers, developed a student leadership program, and established a
cultural center. Invited guests varied from poets to motivational speakers to
dance troups that performed for large audiences at the school's auditorium.
Many of these guest speakers also participated in programs sponsored by the
school's cultural center, which carried out workshops for smaller groups of
students. The cultural center also offered workshops on crafts and other activities that were linked to the student leadership program. The student leadership program's purpose was to train students to become student leaders. Their
cultural activities included the painting of murals throughout the school and
a salsa band. Students readily participated in these activities, and many valued
being able to learn about their cultures and being encouraged to freely express
it in school.

Staff Development. Besides curricular changes, other policies implemented at Hernández High were hiring Latino teachers and leadership staff,
providing staff development for teachers and staff, and providing incentives
and opportunities for advanced degrees for the staff. One of the main priori-
ties at Hernández High has been to have a staff that is representative of the
racial and ethnic composition of the student body (83% Latino, 12% African
American, 3% Asian, and 2% White). However, this is difficult to attain because of regulations that stipulate the credentials needed to fill positions or to
be promoted, and few Latinos and African Americans have them. As a result,
the school leaders have sought to create its own educational leaders from
among its staff. The school provided workshops and seminars on multicultural
education, and assisted teachers in developing and implementing a multicultural curriculum. The school also entered into an agreement with a local university so that Hernández High teachers could pursue graduate degrees in
education, and thus obtain the certification needed for promotion.

Parental Participation. The leadership at Hernández High strongly believed that in order to effect real change for their students, they had to reach
out beyond the school walls, to incorporate families and the surrounding community into their educational efforts. Dupper and Poertner (1997) espouse the
concept of "school-linked family resource centers," service-oriented programs
designed to assist students and their parents find solutions for their individual

and community problems. At Hernández High, the incorporation of parents took the form of the Family Center, but it offered more than assistance to parents, it sought to develop leadership among parents. The Family Center served as a link between school and parents and became a welcoming place for parents who had any kind of business at school. Family Center parent-volunteers served as guides, translators, and "mentors" who helped others navigate the school bureaucracy. It also allowed the presence and participation of parents in daily school life instead of on special occasions. Parental participation took on different forms—from adult educational programs to teacher aides to hall monitoring. Since the office where I carried out interviews was next to the Family Center's room, I was able to see parents participate in "social hours," conduct craft workshops for students, and engage in critical discussions of personal and community issues. In its different facets, the Family Center provided an invaluable service to the school, parents, and the community.

The Need for Systemwide Reform: Hernández High School Today

At the time I finished my study, the reform efforts were well under way, but there was still much to be done at Hernández High. However, I left with the feeling that the school was moving—although slowly—in the right direction. I expected these reform efforts to pay off in a few years, especially because they addressed the issues that had been raised in the literature on effective schools for Latinos. I was particularly impressed by the respect, dignity, and compassion with which students were being treated. However, 4 years after I left Hernández High, all of the reform programs—and others not mentioned above, such as the bilingual program—were dismantled and replaced with more traditional approaches to schooling by the new school leadership. A new principal and newly elected members of the local school council brought with them a more conservative view on schooling. They succeeded in drastically altering the path and speed of the reform at the school, even though these reform programs were in accord with what the literature identifies as characteristics of effective schools for Latinos. The reasoning behind the dismantling of reform efforts was the lack of substantial improvement in standardized test scores. Ultimately, the dismantling was possible because of the provisions stipulated in the reform initiative.

Under the Chicago School Reform, schools had a 5-year "grace period" at the end of which they had to show improvement (usually in the form of increasing standardized test scores). Schools that fail to show substantial improvement could be put on probation or even reconstituted (schools could be closed or the whole staff replaced). Hernández High was one of the schools placed on academic and financial probation, and thus under the direct supervision of the school board. As a result, school programs came under scrutiny, and their educational value was questioned. Added to the school's probationary status was the school board's imposition of a new principal for the school and the election of new members to the school council who did not share the vision of creating a multicultural and community-based school.

Essentially, the problem at Hernández High lies in the limited scope of the Chicago School Reform, which calls for school-based changes that are not followed by systemwide policy changes in the ways kids are schooled. Each school is then responsible for coming up with and implementing its own improvement plan but is subjected to the intervention of the school board if improvement is not deemed sufficient. What constitutes "sufficient" is too vague and thus subject to the sometimes arbitrary interpretation of the school board. Although educators, parents, and students welcomed the reform, many felt that the expectations set for the schools were unrealistic and that the 5-year grace period was not enough to get schools on track. They thought that the reform was a ploy to shift blame from the school board to local schools, and that at the end of the 5 years, the school board could exonerate themselves by pointing to the schools as the culprits of the educational chaos.

In addition, schools are forced to make do with limited authority and have no real power to change the structural problems that besiege them. For example, despite consistent findings that delineate the negative impact of large school size in effectiveness, and the increasing public acknowledgment of this problem, school buildings remain large. It is systemwide policies like this that make local school reform more difficult. To be effective, school systems need to change the way they do business, and that may mean that current high schools must be replaced by more and smaller schools. To do otherwise is to just pay lip service to the concept of reform.

ONE FINAL COMMENT

Although reform efforts are constrained by the school system, schools can still do much to help students become school kids. As the experiences of the kids presented in this book shows, schools are accomplices in a system that thrives on producing inequality. Why would schools provide such disparate opportunities to students? My research points to macro-level mandates that imposed equal standards and rigid measures of success on schools with different social realities. Those who believe that there is a magic formula that will work wonders on all schools are probably not familiar with the diversity of our public schools. To produce effective change, we need first to tune in to the students' needs, leave behind prejudices and stereotypes that confine students to narrow roles, and truly open opportunities to all students regardless of our personal likes and dislikes.

What I hope to accomplish with this book is to make teachers and staff think about their own students and schools. My goal is to help teachers, staff members, and policymakers consider how their own teaching practices and prejudices and the structure of the school system keep so many students from becoming school kids. Most of all, we need to transform the educational system to be inclusive of the realities and experiences of all children.

Appendix A

Conducting the Study

SELECTING THE PARTICIPANTS

I used two sampling strategies to select the participants: random sampling and snowball sampling. I randomly selected from school records 15 possible stayers. I intended to make a list of all students who fit the criteria and then select randomly from that list. However, the school registrar only allowed me to pick students' cards randomly until I found 15 who fitted the criteria. Students' cards included information such as address, phone number, name of parent or legal guardian, place of birth, and elementary and high schools attended. To determine if a student was Puerto Rican, I relied on place of birth and sometimes on names and/or last names that are common among Puerto Ricans. After contacting the students, I narrowed the sample down to 10, eliminating students who were not Puerto Rican or did not wish to participate in the study: two were not Puerto Rican, one refused to participate, and two others failed to secure consent from their parents. I later added three additional stayers to diversify the sample because seven of the 10 initially selected were in the honors/accelerated program. This was a "convenience" sample of students whom I met during the first few weeks of fieldwork and were willing to participate. It included two special education students and one bilingual student.

I then identified 10 leavers and 10 returners through snowball sampling. Some I met at the school when they came to be reinstated, "officially" dropped, or just to visit. But most I found through staff members, particularly the social workers. Because of difficulty accessing school records at the beginning of the school year, and the unreliability of addresses and phone numbers (due to frequent residential mobility) listed in the students' records, snowball sampling provided a better way of recruiting participants. By asking people at the school if they knew someone who had dropped out or returned to school, I was able to identify potential participants. Furthermore, those suggesting the names often volunteered to contact or recruit them for my study. This technique proved tremendously fruitful because prospective participants were approached first by someone they knew and trusted. As a result, almost all agreed to participate in the study.

In the course of the academic year, I got to know many of the participants very well. Most generously shared details about their everyday lives at school and home and in the neighborhood. While at times it was painful to recall past events, they graciously shared them with me.

GATHERING DATA

To gather the data, I used three methodological techniques. First, I carried out ethnographic observation to assess the climate of the school and the participants' daily life there. In addition to observing daily life at school, I attended local school council meetings and many activities held at the school. These activities included speakers, student assemblies, the pep rally, homecoming games, talent shows, performers, sports events, parties at the gym, annual banquets, graduation, and open houses, among other activities.

Second, I conducted unstructured in-depth interviews with each participant to gather his or her life history. Most interviews were spread out through the school year; thus I ended up with an average of three or four interviews per participant. The number of interviews varied from two to over 10 in some cases. Most interviews took place in a small room at the school. Sometimes more informal interviews took place in restaurants, in the lunchroom, or in the hallways. Most interviews were tape recorded, but informal conversations were not recorded. Five participants were not tape recorded at their request.

Third, I used school records, students' transcripts, school reports, yearbooks, the 1993 *Students and Parents Handbook*, newsletters, and other school documents. These documents provided invaluable data to complement the observations and interviews.

AN AFTERTHOUGHT: THE ROLE OF THE RESEARCHER

Mr. Harris had a look of urgency as he hurriedly walked toward me. He said, "We have a situation with a student and her mother. I need your help." Like Mr. Harris, most teachers thought that I was a social worker or a psychologist. The security staff often mistook me for a student and asked me for my pass or rapidly began to chastise me for not wearing my student ID, which students were required to wear hanging around their necks. Most students thought I was a staff member; some wondered if I was a music teacher, since I carried a case to store cassettes that looked to them like a flute case. Even those I was interviewing viewed me as a psychologist or, as Jerry proudly announced to his friends as I walked by and greeted him, "This is my psychiatrist, my shrink." Since there is no role for a sociologist in a school, in most people's minds I remained the psychologist or social worker regardless of my explanations. I do not doubt that the participants' notion of me as some sort of therapist, regardless of my explanations of what a sociologist is, helped them open up and reveal intimate details about their lives.

Over the course of the year, I became aware of my role as a researcher and how it meant something different to each individual I encountered. Although I had to formally petition the local school council for access to the school and secure the support of the principal, I still had difficulties gaining access to various spheres in the school, either because people did not trust an outsider prying into their school or resented the extra workload I created for them. For instance, I had to deal with an uncooperative registrar whenever I needed information about students. Others were sympathetic to my research efforts, extending their assistance beyond the call of duty. They offered unsolicited information and became great informants during my research. With time, I learned that I could obtain information about the students from the assistant principal or at the attendance or programs office, instead of relying on the disgruntled registrar.

Having a "sponsor" in the school helped much. Initially, I relied on a fellow graduate student doing her Ph.D. dissertation research at Hernández High to tell me about the politics at the school, and to introduce me to key people in the school, among them two assistant principals. They, in turn, introduced me to others and legitimated my presence there. That the focus of my investigation was the students and not the school and its staff assuaged their fears of being put in the spotlight. Yet trust was not automatic, and although some people were cooperative, they were cautious and it took them a long time to trust me. I will never forget the afternoon in late January when a Puerto Rican administrator with whom I had been working closely with for the past five months asked me to walk the halls with him. He proceeded to question me about what I thought of the politics in the school. Shortly after I began to respond, he interrupted me and proceeded to set me straight on "what is going on here." He then justified his intervention because, as he explained, "Because you are Puerto Rican, the White staff will not trust you." From that day on, he talked to me extensively about the history of the school and its politics.

Being Puerto Rican was definitely an asset in my relationship with the students. It gave us a common ground regardless of age, socioeconomic, and educational differences. My actually having being born and raised in *la Isla* and speaking "beautiful" Spanish added to this bond. The students felt free to speak in English, Spanish, or Spanglish (a mix of anglicized Spanish, "spanglicized" English, and code switching), and they often used different languages during the same conversation. Although some participants did not seem at ease, most seemed comfortable talking with me. Most students were cordial and amicable, but some maintained their distance or set some form of boundaries. One participant, upon entering the small room I used for the interviews, commented that it resembled the questioning rooms at the police station. To this day I am not sure if he sought to intimidate me, if this was part of his presentation of self as a tough guy who has had run-ins with the police, or if it was truly a spontaneous reaction. Cases like this were the exception. Most participants looked forward to our meetings and often invited me to school events in which they would be participating.

APPENDIX B

Student Data

Table B.1. Stayers: Summary of Attendance, Credits Earned, and Grade Point Average by Grade and Academic Semester

Student	Grade Level	Semester Ending	Days Absent	Credits Earned	G.P.A.
Alma	09	1/90	04	2.75	3.09
	09	6/90	00	2.75	3.27
	10	1/91	01	3.25	3.23
	10	6/91	00	3.25	2.92
	11	1/92	00	3.25	3.84
	11	6/92	00	3.25	3.69
	12	1/93	01	2.50	3.60
	12	6/93	02	2.75	3.73
Ana	09	1/90	03	2.50	3.20
	09	6/90	00	2.50	3.00
	10	1/91	00	3.00	3.16
	10	6/91	00	3.00	2.83
	11	1/92	02	2.50	3.00
	11	6/92	01	2.50	3.20
	12	1/93	01	2.50	3.50
	12	6/93	03	2.50	3.40
Elizabeth	09	1/90	04	2.75	2.96
	09	6/90	08	2.75	3.00
	10	1/91	12	2.75	2.27
	10	6/91	12	2.75	2.45
	11	1/92	06	3.25	3.15
	11	6/92	08	3.25	3.07
	12	1/93	11	2.75	2.63
	12	6/93	15	2.25	3.22

(Continued)

169

Table B.1. Continued

Student	Grade Level	Semester Ending	Days Absent	Credits Earned	G.P.A.
Isabel	09	1/89	05	1.75	2.00
	09	6/89	29	0.50	0.22
	10	1/90	07	1.50	1.45
	10	6/90	13	2.00	1.27
	10	1/91	38	0.25	0.07
	10	6/91	19	3.00	1.86
	11	8/91	*	1.50	2.50
	11	1/92	07	2.75	2.94
	11	6/92	18	2.25	2.18
	12	1/93	26	1.50	2.00
	12	6/93	22	3.00	3.16
Iván	09	1/90	00	2.75	3.36
	09	6/90	01	2.75	2.73
	10	1/91	04	3.25	2.62
	10	6/91	03	3.25	3.38
	11	1/92	08	2.75	3.09
	11	6/92	07	2.75	3.82
	12	1/93	05	2.75	2.45
	12	6/93	09	2.75	2.63
José	SE[†]	1/90	12	1.25	0.46
	SE	6/90	22	0.50	0.36
	SE	8/90	*	1.00	2.33
	SE	1/91	17	2.50	1.60
	SE	6/91	11	3.50	1.73
	SE	1/92	13	2.50	1.27
	SE	6/92	12	2.75	2.09
	SE	8/92	*	0.50	2.00
	SE	8/92	*	0.50	2.50
	SE	1/93	08	2.75	1.36
	SE	6/93	03	2.50	3.11
Luis	09	1/90	02	2.75	2.90
	09	6/90	04	2.75	2.63
	10	1/91	02	3.00	2.50
	10	6/91	03	3.00	2.25
	11	1/92	06	2.50	2.40
	11	6/92	01	2.50	3.20
	12	1/93	04	2.25	2.77
	12	6/93	07	2.25	2.33

Table B.1. Continued

Student	Grade Level	Semester Ending	Days Absent	Credits Earned	G.P.A.
Lydia	09	1/90	01	2.75	4.00
	09	6/90	05	2.75	4.00
	10	1/91	06	2.75	2.77
	10	6/91	02	3.25	3.38
	11	1/92	06	2.75	3.36
	11	6/92	00	2.75	4.00
	12	1/93	04	2.75	2.91
	12	6/93	08	2.25	3.55
Margie	09	1/90	00	1.25	0.82
	09	6/90	07	2.75	2.00
	10	8/90	*	0.50	3.00
	10	1/91	00	3.25	2.31
	10	6/91	00	3.25	2.23
	11	1/92	03	2.75	3.18
	11	6/92	01	2.75	3.73
	12	1/93	09	2.25	2.55
	12	6/93	30	2.25	2.33
Marta	09	1/90	04	2.75	3.18
	09	6/90	01	2.75	4.00
	10	1/91	01	3.25	2.69
	10	6/91	06	3.25	3.77
	11	1/92	00	3.00	4.00
	11	6/92	01	3.00	4.00
	12	1/93	03	2.25	3.44
	12	6/93	09	2.50	2.90
Miguel	09	1/90	04	2.75	2.63
	09	6/90	25	2.50	1.64
	10	1/91	17	2.75	1.36
	10	6/91	12	2.75	2.45
	11	1/92	05	2.50	3.60
	11	6/92	02	2.50	3.20
	12	1/93	03	2.75	3.82
	12	6/93	03	3.25	2.80

(Continued)

Table B.1. Continued

Student	Grade Level	Semester Ending	Days Absent	Credits Earned	G.P.A.
Roberto	09	1/90	04	2.75	2.45
	09	6/90	12	2.50	2.00
	10	1/91	04	3.00	2.75
	10	6/91	06	3.00	2.66
	11	1/92	08	2.75	3.36
	11	6/92	07	2.75	3.54
	12	1/93	05	2.25	3.66
	12	6/93	13	2.50	3.60
Vanessa	09	1/90	00	2.75	3.09
	09	6/90	00	2.75	3.27
	10	1/91	00	3.00	3.50
	10	6/91	05	3.00	2.91
	11	1/92	00	3.00	3.41
	11	6/92	03	3.00	3.58
	12	1/93	04	2.25	2.89
	12	6/93	05	2.25	3.44

* Not shown in transcript.

† Special Education.

Table B.2. Stayers: Age, Cumulative Credits, Cumulative Grade Point Average, Class Rank, and Total Number of Years in High School

Student	Age	Cumulative Credits	Cumulative G.P.A. (4.0)	Class Rank (N=318)	Total Years in School
Alma	17	23.75	3.42	19	4
Ana	18	21.00	3.15	41	4
Elizabeth	17	22.50	2.90	70	4
Isabel	19	20.00	1.69	265	5
Iván	18	23.00	2.89	71	4
José	18	20.25	1.10	N/A	4
Luis	18	21.00	2.62	109	4
Lydia	17	22.00	3.32	25	4
Margie	18	21.00	2.34	150	4
Marta	17	22.75	3.77	9	4
Miguel	18	21.75	2.68	98	4
Roberto	17	21.50	2.97	60	4
Vanessa	18	22.00	3.20	34	4

Table B.3. Leavers: Summary of Attendance, Credits Earned, and Grade
Point Average by Grade and Academic Semester

Student	Grade Level	Semester Ending	Days Absent	Credits Earned	G.P.A.
Aida	09	1/89	11	1.75	1.09
	09	6/89	13	2.25	1.18
	10	1/90	15	2.50	1.40
	10	6/90	14	2.25	1.10
	10	8/90	*	0.00	0.00
	10	1/91	08	2.25	1.00
	10	6/91	21	1.25	0.45
	11	8/91	*	0.75	2.00
	11	1/92	27	0.50	0.18
	11	8/92	*	0.50	3.00
	11	1/93	11	1.25	0.64
	11	6/93	67	0.00	0.00
Angie	09	1/90	04	2.25	2.00
	09	6/90	07	2.25	1.55
	10	1/91	06	0.75	0.78
	10	6/91	15	0.25	0.29
	10	8/91	*	1.00	1.00
	10	1/92	64	0.00	0.00
	10	6/92	06	0.00	0.00
César	09	1/90	10	1.00	0.30
	09	6/90	16	1.00	0.36
	09	1/91	27	0.00	0.00
David	09	1/90	44	0.00	0.00
	09	6/90	19	0.00	0.00
	09	1/91	36	0.50	0.46
	09	6/91	61	0.00	0.00
	09	1/92	42	0.00	0.00
Eric	09	1/88	07	2.25	1.66
	09	6/88	10	1.75	2.11
	10	1/89	23	1.25	0.63
	10	6/89	37	1.25	0.63
	10	8/89	*	1.00	1.50
	10	1/90	59	1.50	1.66
	10	6/90	12	1.50	0.92
	11	1/91	45	1.00	0.66
	11	6/91	69	0.50	0.22

Table B.3. Continued

Student	Grade Level	Semester Ending	Days Absent	Credit Ear	
Lisa	09	1/89	13	1.50	
	09	6/89	33	0.50	
	10	1/90	04	3.25	
	10	6/90	19	3.25	
	10	1/91	14	1.50	
	10	6/91	23	1.75	
	11	1/92	14	2.75	
	11	6/92	32	0.50	
	12	1/93	53	0.00	
Ricardo	09	1/89	04	1.75	1.22
	09	6/89	05	2.75	2.75
	10	1/90	05	1.25	0.64
	10	6/90	05	1.75	1.18
	10	1/91	03	2.75	2.27
	10	8/91	*	0.50	2.00
	10	6/91	19	2.75	1.77
	11	1/92	19	2.75	1.54
	11	6/92	54	0.50	0.18
	12	1/93	44	0.50	0.18
	11	6/93	83	0.75	0.45
	12	1/94	*	0.00	0.00
Vitín	09	1/90	22	0.25	0.09
	09	6/90	23	2.25	0.85
	09	1/91	17	0.85	0.27
	09	6/91	39	0.00	0.00
	09	8/91	*	0.50	0.25
	09	1/92	35	1.00	0.36
	09	6/92	28	0.00	0.00
	11	1/93	28	0.25	0.09

* Not shown in transcript.

Note: Data for Ernesto and Marisol are not available.

ble B.4. Leavers: Age, Cumulative Credits, Cumulative Grade Point Average, and Total Number of Years in High School

Student	Age	Cumulative Credits	Cumulative G.P.A. (4.0)	Total Years in School
Aida	18	15.25	0.79	5
Angie	18	6.50	0.77	3
César	17	2.00	0.24	1.5
David	17	0.50	0.10	2.5
Eric	18	12.00	0.93	4
Lisa	18	15.00	1.16	4.5
Ricardo	19	18.00	1.24	5.5
Vitín	18	5.00	0.25	3.5

Note: Data for Ernesto and Marisol are not available.

Table B.5. Returners: Summary of Attendance, Credits Earned, and Grade Point Average by Grade and Academic Semester

Student	Grade Level	Semester Ending	Days Ending	Credits Earned	G.P.A.
Angel[*]	09	1/88	17	1.25	0.75
	09	6/88	32	0.50	0.36
	09	1/89	25	1.75	0.64
	09	6/89	15	3.25	2.00
	10	1/90	21	0.50	0.18
	10	6/90	16	2.25	1.00
	11[†]	1/91	63	0.00	0.00
	11[‡]	6/91	§	§	§
	11	1/92	§	1.00	1.00
	11	6/92	13	2.75	1.91
	11	6/92	§	1.00	1.00
	11	1/93	16	2.75	2.27
	12	6/93	19	3.00	2.17
Diana[*]	09	1/88	41	0.50	0.31
	09	6/88	31	0.00	0.00
	09	1/89	17	2.50	0.17
	09	6/89	28	2.50	1.51
	10	1/90	26	3.00	1.85
	10	6/90	35	2.00	1.45
	11	1/91	36	1.50	0.55
	11[‡]	6/91	§	§	§
	11	1/92	§	1.00	Passed
	11	6/92	25	2.25	2.30
	12	8/92	§	1.00	2.50
	12	8/92	§	0.50	2.50
	12	1/93	16	2.50	2.90
	12	6/93	24	2.50	2.30
Elena	09	1/90	05	2.75	2.82
	09	6/90	09	2.75	2.73
	10[‡]	1/91	§	§	§
	10[‡]	6/91	§	§	§
	10	1/92	04	3.25	3.00
	10	6/92	18	3.25	2.85
	11	1/93	12	2.75	2.55
	11	6/93	19	3.50	2.71

(Continued)

Table B.5. Continued

Student	Grade Level	Semester Ending	Days Ending	Credits Earned	G.P.A.
Jenny[*]	09	1/89	09	1.00	0.36
	09	6/89	07	1.25	0.82
	10	1/90	19	1.00	0.55
	10	6/90	13	3.75	1.65
	10	6/90	§	2.00	Passed
	10	8/90	§	0.50	3.00
	10	1/91	17	3.00	2.27
	10	6/91	15	1.75	0.86
	11	1/92	28	1.00	0.50
	11[†]	6/92	39	0.00	0.00
	12	1/93	16	2.00	1.33
	12	1/93	§	1.00	2.00
	12	6/93	24	2.50	2.00
Jerry	09	1/90	05	2.25	1.15
	09	6/90	04	2.25	1.23
	10	1/91	02	2.75	1.43
	10	6/91	02	2.75	1.34
	11	1/92	11	1.00	0.55
	11[‡]	6/92	§	§	§
	11	1/93	25	0.50	0.18
	11	6/93	20	1.00	0.89
Julio[*]	09	1/89	§	2.50	1.80
	09	6/89	§	2.50	1.60
	10	1/90	05	2.75	1.64
	10	6/90	10	2.75	1.73
	11[‡]	1/91	§	§	§
	11[‡]	6/91	§	§	§
	11	1/92	10	2.25	2.64
	11	6/92	20	3.75	2.47
	11	6/92	§	1.00	3.50
	12	8/92	§	0.00	0.00
	12	1/93	21	2.25	1.36
	12	6/93	29	2.50	1.70

Table B.5. Continued

Student	Grade Level	Semester Ending	Days Ending	Credits Earned	G.P.A.
Lourdes	09	1/90	01	2.75	2.72
	09	6/90	03	1.50	1.33
	10	1/91	07	2.75	2.18
	10	6/91	19	1.75	1.00
	10	1/92	26	1.00	0.36
	10[†]	6/92	52	0.00	0.00
	11	1/93	46	0.50	0.31
	11[†]	6/93	52	0.00	0.00
Manuel[*]	09	1/89	17	2.00	1.56
	09[†]	6/89	57	0.00	0.00
	10	1/90	18	0.50	0.36
	10	6/90	08	1.75	1.00
	10	8/90	§	1.00	1.00
	10	1/91	11	2.50	2.55
	10	6/91	09	2.25	2.44
	11	1/92	14	0.75	0.82
	11	6/92	18	1.25	0.85
	11	8/92	§	1.00	3.00
	11	1/93	11	3.00	2.36
	11	1/93	§	1.00	1.00
	12	6/93	07	3.00	3.18
Pablo	09	8/88	§	1.00	2.00
	09[†]	1/89	§	0.00	0.00
	09[†]	6/89	§	0.00	0.00
	09	1/90	§	2.50	2.20
	09	6/90	§	2.50	2.20
	10	1/91	08	2.25	1.82
	10	6/91	14	1.75	1.27
	11	1/92	11	2.75	2.09
	11	6/92	07	1.75	1.18
	12	1/93	11	1.50	1.13
	12	6/93	11	1.75	1.00

(*Continued*)

Table B.5. Continued

Student	Grade Level	Semester Ending	Days Ending	Credits Earned	G.P.A.
Sylvia	09	1/89	22	1.25	0.55
	09[†]	6/89	34	0.00	0.00
	10[†]	8/89	§	0.00	0.00
	10[†]	1/90	39	0.00	0.00
	10[†]	6/90	79	0.00	0.00
	10	1/91	08	2.50	2.91
	10	6/91	24	2.75	2.83
	10	1/92	17	2.25	1.55
	10	6/92	26	1.75	1.55
	11	1/93	37	2.50	2.40
	11[†]	6/93	78	0.00	0.00

[*] Graduating senior.

[†] Year in which student dropped out.

[‡] Did not enroll in school that year.

[§] Not shown in transcript.

Table B.6. Returners: Age, Cumulative Credits, Cumulative Grade Point Average, and Total Number of Years in High School

Student	Age	Cumulative Credits	Cumulative Grade Point Average	Class Rank	Total Years in School
Angel*	20	20.00	1.13	311 of 318	6
Diana*	21	21.75	1.49	281 of 318	6
Elena	19	18.25	2.73	79 of 604	4
Jenny*	20	20.75	1.15	310 of 318	5
Jerry	17	12.50	1.07	438 of 604	4
Julio*	18	22.25	1.93	228 of 318	5
Lourdes	17	10.25	0.91	491 of 604	4
Manuel*	19	20.00	1.47	283 of 318	5
Pablo	19	17.75	1.28	377 of 604	5
Sylvia	19	13.00	1.15	418 of 604	5

*Graduating seniors

References

Anderson, E. (1990). *Streetwise: Race, class, and change in an urban community.* Chicago: University of Chicago Press.

Barker, R., & Gump, V. (1964). *Big school, small school: High school size and student behavior.* Stanford, CA: Stanford University Press.

Barreto, J., et al. (1986). *Puerto Ricans: Growing problems for a growing population.* Washington, DC: Full Employment Action Council.

Barrington, B. L., & Hendricks, B. (1989). Differentiating characteristics of high school graduates, dropouts, and nongraduates. *The Journal of Educational Research, 82*(6), 309–319.

Beck, L., & Muia, J. A. (1980). A portrait of a tragedy: research findings on the dropout. *The High School Journal, 64*(2), 65–72.

Bland, J. (1990). Implementation of the C-average policy. (ERIC Document Reproduction Service No. ED 331 032)

Bourdieu, P. (1973). Cultural reproduction and social reproduction. In R. Brown (Ed.), *Knowledge, education and cultural change* (pp. 71–112). London: Tavistock.

Bourgois, P. (1995). *In search of respect: Selling crack in El Barrio.* New York: Cambridge University Press.

Bowles, S., & Gintis, H. (1976). *Schooling in capitalist America.* New York: Basic Books.

Brantlinger, E. A. (1993). *The politics of social class in secondary school: Views of affluent and impoverished youth.* New York: Teachers College Press.

Bryk, A. S., Sebring, P.B., Kerbow, D., Rollow, S., & Easton, J. Q. (1998). *Charting Chicago school reform.* Boulder, CO: Westview.

Burke, P. J., & Reitzes, D. C. (1981). The link between identity and role performance. *Social Psychology Quarterly, 44,* 83–92.

Calitri, R. (1983). *Racial and ethnic high school dropout rates in New York City: A summary report/1983.* New York: Aspira Inc. of New York.

Callero, P. L. (1985). Role-identity salience. *Social Psychology Quarterly, 48*(3), 203–215.

Caplan, N., Choy, M. H., & Whitmore, J. K. (1991). *Children of the boat: A study of educational success.* Ann Arbor: University of Michigan Press.

Clark, R. M. (1983). *Family life and school achievement: Why poor Black children succeed or fail.* Chicago: University of Chicago Press.

Coladarci, T., & Cobb, C. D. (1996). Extracurricular participation, school size, achievement, and self-esteem among high school students: A national look. *Journal of Research in Rural Education, 12*(2), 92–202.

Coleman, J. (1961). *Adolescent society.* New York: The Free Press of Glencoe.

Davidson, A. L. (1996). *Making and molding identity in schools: Student narratives on race, gender, and academic achievement.* Albany, NY: SUNY Press.

Davison Aviles, R. M., Guerrero, M. P., Howarth, H. B., & Thomas, G. (1999). Perceptions of Chicano/Latino students who have dropped out of school. *Journal of Counseling & Development, 77,* 465–473.

Delgado-Gaitan, C. (1988). The value of conformity: Learning to stay in school. *Anthropology & Education Quarterly, 19*(4), 354–381.

Dreeben, R. (1968). *On what is learned in school.* Reading, MA: Addison-Wesley Publishing.

Dupper, D. R., & Poerter, J. (1997). Public schools and the revitalization of impoverished communities: School-linked, family resource centers. *Social Work, 42*(5), 415–422.

Ebaugh, H. R. F. (1988). *Becoming an ex: The process of role exit.* Chicago: University of Chicago Press.

Eckert, P. (1989). *Jocks and burnouts: Social categories and identity in the high school.* New York: Teachers College Press.

Felice, L. G. (1981). Black student dropout behavior. *The Journal of Negro Education, 50*(4), 415–424.

Fernandez, R. R., & Shu, G. (1983). School dropouts: New approaches to an enduring problem. *Education and Urban Society, 20*(4), 363–386.

Fine, M. (1991). *Framing dropouts: Notes on the politics of an urban public high school.* Albany, NY: State University of New York Press.

Finn, J. D. (1972). Expectations and the educational environment. *Review of Educational Research, 42*(3), 387–410.

Finn, J. D. (1989). Withdrawing from school. *Review of Educational Research, 59*(2), 117–142.

Fligstein, N., & Fernandez R. (1985). Educational transitions of whites and Mexican-Americans. In G. Borjas & M. Tienda (Eds.), *Hispanics in the United States economy.* Orlando, FL: Academic Press.

Flores-González, N. M. (1990). *The alternative school as an educational sink.* Unpublished master's thesis, University of Chicago, Chicago, Illinois.

Flores-González, N. M. (1995). *Diverging educational paths: Sustenance, exit and re-entry into the student role.* Unpublished doctoral dissertation, University of Chicago.

Flores-González, N. M. (1999). Puerto Rican high achievers: An example of ethnic and academic identity compatibility. *Anthropology & Education Quarterly, 30*(3), 343–362.

Flores-González, N. (2000). The structuring of extracurricular opportunities and Latino student retention. *Journal of Poverty, 4*(1/2), 85–108.

Foley, D. E. (1991). Reconsidering anthropological explanations of ethnic school failure. *Anthropology & Education Quarterly, 22*(1), 60–94.

Fordham, S. (1988). Racelessness as a factor in black students' school success: Pragmatic strategy or pyrrhic victory. *Harvard Educational Review, 58*(1), 54–84.

Fordham, S., & Ogbu, J. U. (1986). Black students' school success: Coping with the burden of acting white. *The Urban Review, 18*(3), 176–206.

Fowler, W. J., & Walberg, H. J. (1991). School size, characteristics, and outcomes. *Educational Evaluation and Policy Analysis, 13*(2), 189–202.

Gándara, P. (1995). *Over the ivy walls: The educational mobility of low-income Chicanos*. Albany, NY: SUNY Press.

Garbarino, J. (1980). Some thoughts on school size and its effects on adolescent development. *Journal of Youth and Adolescence, 9*(1), 19–31.

Garbarino, J., Dubrow, N., Kostelny, K., & Pardo, C. (1992). *Children in danger: Coping with the consequences of community violence*. San Francisco: Jossey-Bass.

Gerber, S. D. (1996). Extracurricular activities and academic achievement. *Journal of Research and Development in Education, 30*(1), 42–50.

Gibson, M. A. (1988). *Accommodation without assimilation*. Ithaca: Cornell University Press.

Goffman, E. (1963). *Stigma: Notes on the management of spoiled identity*. New York: Touchstone Books.

Goldberg, A. D., & Chandler, T. J. L. (1989). The role of athletics: The social world of high school adolescents. *Youth & Society, 21*(2), 238–250.

Goode, W. (1960). A theory of role strain. *American Sociological Review, 25*, 483–496.

Gregory, T. B., & Smith, G. R. (1987). *High schools as communities: The small school reconsidered*. Bloomington, IN: Phi Delta Kappa Educational Foundation.

Hanks, M. P., & Eckland, B. K. (1976). Athletics and social participation in the educational attainment process. *Sociology of Education, 49*, 271–294.

Hemmings, A. (1996). Conflicting images? Being Black and a model high school student. *Anthropology & Education Quarterly, 27*(1), 20–50.

Hernández High School. (1991). *Racial and Ethnic Survey*. Chicago: Author.

Hernández High School. (1993). *Students and Parents Handbook*. Chicago: Author.

Hess, G. A. (1995). *Restructuring urban schools: A Chicago perspective*. New York: Teachers College Press.

Hetherington, E. M., Cox, M., & Cox, R. (1982). Effects of divorce on parents and children. In M. Lamb (Ed.), *Non-traditional families*. Hillsdale, NJ: Erlbaum.

Hogg, M. A., Terry, D. J., & White, K. M. (1995). A tale of two theories: A critical comparison of identity theory with social identity theory. *Social Psychology Quarterly, 58*(4), 255–269.

Horowitz, R. (1983). *Honor and American dream: Culture and identity in a Chicano community*. Chicago: University of Chicago Press.

Illinois State Board of Education. (1992). *Illinois school report card*. Author.

Illinois State Board of Education. (2000). *Illinois school report card*.

Kielcolt, K. J. (1994). Stress and the decision to change oneself: A theoretical model. *Social Psychology Quarterly, 57*(1), 49–63.

Kinney, D. (1993). From nerds to normals: The recovery of identity among adolescents from middle school to high school. *Sociology of Education, 66*, 21–40.

Kronick, R. F., Peterson, L., Morton, J., & Smith, G. (1989). Dealing with dropouts: A review of the literature and preliminary findings. *Education, 110*(1), 123–129.

Kyle, C. (1984). *Los preciosos: The magnitude of and the reasons for the Hispanic drop out problem: A case study of two Chicago public schools*. Chicago: Aspira, Inc. of Illinois.

Kyle, C., & Kantowicz, E. D. (1991). *Kids first—primero los niños: Chicago school reform in the 1980s*. Springfield, IL: Sangamon State University.

Labov, W. (1982). Competing value school systems in the inner-city schools. In P.

Gilmore & A. Glatthorn (Eds.), *Children in and out of school* (pp. 148–171). Washington, D.C.: Center for Applied Linguistics.

Laosa, Luis M. (1979). Inequality in the classroom: Observational research on teacher-student interactions. *Aztlan 8*, 51–67.

Lucas, I. (1971). *Puerto Rican dropouts in Chicago: Numbers and motivation.* Chicago: Council on Urban Education.

Lucas, T., Henze, R., & Donato, R. (1990). Promoting the success of Latino language-minority students: An exploratory study of six high schools. *Harvard Educational Review, 60*(3), 315–339.

MacLeod, J. (1987). *Ain't no makin' it: Aspirations and attainment in a low-income neighborhood.* Boulder, CO: Westview Press.

Mahoney, J., & Cairns, R. B. (1997). Do extracurricular activities protect against early school dropout? *Developmental Psychology, 33*, 241–253.

Marks, S. R. (1977). Multiple roles and role strain: Some notes on human energy, time and commitment. *American Sociological Review, 42*, 921–936.

Marks, S. R., & MacDermid, S. M. (1996). Multiple roles and the self: A theory of role balance. *Journal of Marriage and the Family, 58*, 417–432.

Markus, H., & Nurius, P. (1987). Possible selves: The interface between motivation and the self-concept. In K. Yardley & T. Honess (Eds.), *Self and identity: Psychosocial perspectives* (pp. 157–172). Chichester, NY: John Wiley & Sons.

Matute-Bianchi, M. E. (1986). Ethnic identities and patterns of school success and failure among Mexican-descent and Japanese-American students in a California high school: An ethnographic analysis. *American Journal of Education, 95*(1), 233–255.

McCall, G. J., & Simmons, J. L. (1978). *Identities and interactions: An examination of human associations in everyday life.* New York: The Free Press.

McLaren, P. L. (1994). *Life in schools.* New York: Longman.

McNeal, R. B. (1995). Extracurricular activities and high school dropouts. *Sociology of Education, 68*, 62–81.

Mehan, H., Hubbard, L., & Villanueva, I. (1994). Forming academic identities: Accommodation without assimilation among involuntary minorities. *Anthropology & Education Quarterly, 25*(2), 91–117.

Melnick, M. J., Sabo, D. F., & Vanfossen, B. (1992). Educational effects of interscholastic athletic participation on African-American and Hispanic youth. *Adolescence, 27*(106), 295–308.

Merton, R. (1957). The role-set: Problems in sociological theory. *British Journal of Sociology, 8*, 106–120.

Metz, M. H. (1978). *Classroom and corridors: The crisis of authority in desegregated secondary schools.* Berkeley: University of California Press.

Mickelson, R. A. (1981). Social stratification processes in secondary schools: A comparison of Beverly Hills High School and Morningside High School. *Journal of Education, 162*(4), 83–112.

Morgan, D. L., & Alwin, D. F. (1980). When less is more: School size and student social participation. *Social Psychology Quarterly, 43*(2), 241–252.

Murtaugh, M. (1988). Achievement outside the classroom: The role of nonacademic activities in the lives of high school students. *Anthropology & Education Quarterly, 19*, 382–395.

National Center for Educational Statistics. (2000). *The condition of education* (Report No. 2000-062). Washington, DC: U.S. Department of Education.

National Center for Educational Statistics. (2001). *The condition of education* (Report No. 2001-072). Washington, DC: U.S. Department of Education.

Newmann, F. H., Wehlage, G. G., & Lamborn, S. D. (1992). The significance and sources of student engagement. In F. H. Newmann (Ed.), *Student engagement and achievement in secondary schools* (pp. 11–39). New York: Teachers College Press.

Nieto, S. (1999). *The light in their eyes.* New York: Teachers College Press.

Oakes, J. (1985). *Keeping track: How schools structure inequality.* New Haven, CT: Yale University Press.

O'Reilly, J. M. (1992). *Did the kids win or lose? The impact of "no-pass/no-play" rule on student achievement.* (ERIC Document reproduction Service No. ED 357 410)

Ornstein, A. C. (1990). School size and effectiveness: Policy implications. *The Urban Review, 22*(3), 239–245.

Padilla, F. M. (1992). *The gang as an American enterprise.* New Brunswick, NJ: Rutgers University Press.

Phelan, P., Davidson, A. L., & Yu, C. H. (1998). *Adolescents' worlds: Negotiating family, peers and school.* New York: Teachers College Press.

Phillips, J. C., & Schafer, W. E. (1971). Consequences of participation in interscholastic sports: A review and prospects. *Pacific Sociological Review, 14*(3), 328–338.

Pittman, R. B., & Haughwout, P. (1987). Influence of high school size on dropout rate. *Educational Evaluation and Policy Analysis, 9*(4), 337–343.

Powell, A. G., Farrar, E., & Cohen, D. K. (1985). *The shopping mall high school.* Boston: Houghton Mifflin Company.

Quiroz, P. A. (1993). *A study of decision-making in the educational process of Latino high school students.* Unpublished doctoral dissertation, University of Chicago.

Quiroz, P. A., Flores-González, N., & Frank, K. A. (1996). Carving a niche in the high school social structure: Formal and informal constraints on participation in the extra curriculum. *Research in Sociology of Education and Socialization, 11*, 93–120.

Richardson, R. L., & Gerlach, S. C. (1980). Black dropouts: A study of significant factors contributing to a black student's decision. *Urban Education, 14*(4), 489–494.

Rist, R. (1970). Social class and teacher expectations. *Harvard Educational Review, 40*, 411–451.

Romo, H., & Falbo, T. (1996). *Latino high school graduation.* Austin: University of Texas Press.

Rosenholtz, S. J. (1985). Effective schools: Interpreting the evidence. *American Journal of Education, 93*(3), 352–388.

Schmid, T. J., & Jones, R. S. (1991). Suspended identity: Identity transformation in a maximum security prison. *Symbolic Interaction, 14*(4), 415–432.

Sieber, S. (1974). Toward a theory of role accumulation. *American Sociological Review, 39*, 467–478.

Silliken, S. A., & Quirk, J. T. (1997). The effect of extracurricular activity participation on the academic performance of male and female high school students. *The School Counselor, 44*, 288–293.

Snyder, E. E., & Spreitzer, E. (1992). Social psychological components of adolescents' role identities as scholars and athletes: A longitudinal analysis. *Youth & Society, 23*(4), 507–522.

Steinberg, L., Dornbusch, S., & Brown, B. (1992). Ethnic differences in adolescent achievement: An ecological perspective. *American Psychologist, 47,* 723–729.

Streeter, C. L., & Franklin, C. (1991). Psychological and family differences between middle class and low income dropouts: A discriminant analysis. *The High School Journal, 74*(4), 211–219.

Stryker, S. (1968). Identity salience and role performance: The relevance of symbolic interaction theory for family research. *Journal of Marriage and the Family, 30*(3), 558–564.

Suttles, G. (1984). The cumulative texture of local urban culture. *American Journal of Sociology, 90*(2), 283–304.

Thoits, P. (1987). Negotiating roles. In F. J. Crosby (Ed.), *Spouse, parent, worker: On gender and multiple roles.* New Haven: Yale University Press.

Thoits, P. (1991). On merging identity theory and stress research. *Social Psychology Quarterly, 54*(2), 101–112.

Tinto, V. (1975). Dropouts from higher education: A theoretical synthesis of recent research. *Review of Educational Research, 45,* 89–125.

Valdés, G. (1996). *Con respeto: Bridging the distances between culturally diverse families and schools.* New York: Teachers College Press.

Valenzuela, A. (1999). *Substractive schooling: U.S.–Mexican youth and the politics of caring.* Albany, NY: SUNY Press.

Vigil, J. D. (1982). Chicano high schoolers: Educational performance and acculturation. *The Educational Forum, Fall,* 59–73.

Villegas, A. M. (1988). School failure and cultural mismatch: Another view. *The Urban Review 20*(4), 243–265.

Werner, E. E. (1990). Protective factors and individual resilience. In S. J. Meisels & J. P. Shonkoff (Eds.), *Handbook of early childhood intervention* (pp. 115–132). Cambridge, England: Cambridge University Press.

Willis, P. (1977). *Learning to labor.* New York: Columbia University Press.

Index

About the Author

Nilda Flores-González (Ph.D., University of Chicago, 1995) is an Assistant Professor with a joint appointment in the Department of Sociology and the Latin American and Latino Studies Program at the University of Illinois at Chicago. She studies race, ethnicity, and identity among U.S. Latinos. Previous works have been published in *Anthropology & Education Quarterly, Journal of Poverty, Latino Studies Journal,* and *Research in Sociology of Education and Socialization.* At the University of Illinois she has been a faculty fellow both of the Great Cities Program and the Institute for Research on Race and Public Policy.